Politics

Felicity Matthews

PRACTICAL LESSONS FROM POLICY THEORIES

Edited by Christopher M. Weible and Paul Cairney

First published in Great Britain in 2021 by

Policy Press, an imprint of
Bristol University Press
University of Bristol
1–9 Old Park Hill
Bristol
BS2 8BB
UK
t: +44 (0)117 954 5940
e: bup-info@bristol.ac.uk

Details of international sales and distribution partners are available at
policy.bristoluniversitypress.co.uk

British Library Cataloguing in Publication Data
A catalogue record for this book is available from the British Library

ISBN 978-1-4473-5982-1 hardcover
ISBN 978-1-4473-5983-8 ePub
ISBN 978-1-4473-5985-2 epdf

Cover design by Policy Press
Front cover image: Asif Akbar

Bristol University Press and Policy Press use environmentally responsible print partners.

Printed and bound in Great Britain by CPI Group (UK) Ltd, Croydon, CR0 4YY

FSC
www.fsc.org
MIX
Paper from responsible sources
FSC® C013604

Contents

List of figures and tables

Figures

Tables

Notes on contributors

Krister P. Andersson is Professor of Political Science at the Institute of Behavioral Science at the University of Colorado Boulder. His research focuses on the challenges of environmental governance in the developing world. He directs the Center for the Governance of Natural Resources, which brings together scholars committed to collaborative and problem-driven research that can inform decision making about shared natural resources.

Paul Cairney is Professor of Politics and Public Policy, University of Stirling, UK (@Cairneypaul). His research interests are in comparative public policy, policy analysis, and policy theories, applied to UK and devolved government policy, and the use of evidence. His website summarises these themes: https://paulcairney.wordpress.com/1000-words/.

Deserai A. Crow is Associate Professor in the School of Public Affairs at the University of Colorado Denver. Her research focuses on policy processes related to environmental policy and disasters or crises. Her work includes National Science Foundation funded studies of community-level flood recovery processes, COVID-19 state policy promulgation, and environmental justice concerns related to stakeholder participation in oil and gas development.

Claire A. Dunlop is a Professor of Politics at the University of Exeter. She researches, teaches and writes on science and politics, regulation, policy processes and EU public policy. She is editor of *Public Policy and Administration*, and from 2021 *Policy & Politics*. From 2020 to 2023, Claire is Vice Chair of the UK Political Studies Association (PSA).

Tanya Heikkila is a Professor and Associate Dean in the School of Public Affairs at the University of Colorado Denver, where she co-directs the Workshop on Policy Process Research. Her research explores collaboration and conflict in the context of natural resource governance.

Karin Ingold is a Professor of Environmental Policy Analysis and Governance at the Oeschger Center for Climate Change Research of the University of Bern, Switzerland. She is the Director of the Institute of Political Science at the University of Bern, and leads a research group at the Environmental Social Science Department of Eawag, the Water Research Institute of the ETH Zurich Domain. In her research she combines the application of the Advocacy Coalition as well as the Social Ecological Systems Framework with Social Network Analysis and focuses mainly on Climate Change, Water Pollution and Energy Policy.

Michael D. Jones is an Associate Professor at the University of Tennessee, Knoxville and a faculty fellow at the Howard H. Baker Jr. Center for Public Policy. He is the editor-in-chief of the *Policy Studies Journal* and his primary research interest is policy theory, where he has devoted most of his attention to developing the Narrative Policy Framework.

Seo Young (Serena) Kim is a Scholar in Residence in the School of Public Affairs at the University of Colorado Denver. Her research focuses on collective action and energy policy.

Chris Koski is Associate Professor of Political Science and Environmental Studies at Reed College in Portland, Oregon. His research focuses on applications of policy process theory to environmental policy, food policy, energy policy, and state budgets. He is chair of the Science, Technology, and Environmental Policy section of the American Political Science Association.

Claudio Radaelli is Professor of Comparative Public Policy at the School of Transnational Governance (EUI, Florence, Italy), on long leave of absence from the School of Public Policy, University College London. He is the chief editor of the *International Review of Public Policy*.

Richard Simmons is Senior Lecturer in Public and Social Policy and Co-Director of the Mutuality Research Programme at the University of Stirling. His research focuses on the governance and delivery of public services, user voice, and the role of mutuality and co-operation in public policy.

William L. Swann is Assistant Professor at the School of Public Affairs at the University of Colorado Denver. His research focuses on local government, public management and collaborative governance in health policy and sustainable development contexts.

Christopher M. Weible is Professor in the School of Public Affairs at the University of Colorado Denver. His research focuses on policy conflicts in environmental and natural resource issues. He is the editor of the *Theories of the Policy Process*, Co-Editor of *Policy & Politics*, and Co-Director of the Workshop on Policy Process Research.

Samuel Workman is Associate Professor in the Department of Political Science at the University of Oklahoma. He is also a faculty member in the Center for Risk and Crisis Management. His research focuses on agenda setting in institutions and organisations. He is the author of *The Dynamics of Bureaucracy in the U.S. Government* (Cambridge University Press).

CHAPTER ONE

Purposes and paths in drawing practical lessons from policy theories

Christopher M Weible and Paul Cairney

Introduction

We challenge policy theory scholars to change the way we produce and communicate research: translate our findings to a wider audience to gauge the clarity and quality of our findings. Policy theories have generated widespread knowledge of the policy process, but the field is vast and uncoordinated, and too many scholars hide behind a veil of jargon and obfuscation. Some of the most visible outcomes – such as limited relevance to practitioners, and anxiety and confusion among students or early career researchers with a limited grasp of a complex field – reflects a less visible but more worrying academic problem: we often assume, rather than demonstrate, that policy process research contains insights that add cumulative and comparable knowledge to the field.

Yet, if we do not take the time to check if we understand the state of the art, and can share a common understanding with our peers, how can we state that we are accumulating knowledge collectively rather than producing work of limited relevance beyond our own narrow individual concerns? Is there genuinely a cohesive, advancing, field of policy theories or are we each producing our own theories and assuming they are useful to others? We need to ask these searching questions more often and place them front and centre of academic debate.

Some thematic reviews already try to compare insights across many theories (Heikkila and Cairney, 2017) but they only scratch the surface and provide limited assurance about a coherent policy process research agenda. We need more work from theory-specific experts to explain their theories and empirical knowledge clearly enough to help others gauge progress and compare it to progress among other approaches. To add clarity and communication across the entire field of public policy theory, we need theoretical specialists to explain state of the art knowledge to their peers. To do so, we should explore better ways to communicate its lexicon. If we succeed, we can proceed with confidence. If not, we should ask ourselves uncomfortable questions about the state of our field or, at least, key approaches.

In this new context, a process of 'translation' no longer has a single purpose, to describe the value of scholarship to a wider audience (Flinders, 2013). Rather, a fundamentally important additional purpose, and the focus of the book, is to help policy scholars communicate clearly with each other to improve their knowledge and insights. Sometimes, we need to lift our heads up from the detail, take stock and explain our project to a wider audience and our academic peers to see if the conceptual logic still holds and the empirical analysis is rewarding (Ayres and Marsh, 2013). Such efforts are an effective way to be clear enough to invite critical analysis, rather than relying on jargon which can obfuscate as much as explain. Our aim is to show leadership by first subjecting ourselves to this challenge. We present eight ways to synthesise and communicate state of the art knowledge from intellectually distinct fields, each with their own reference points and key foundational texts.

We argue that this new agenda requires new ways to write academic chapters. The format should be flexible, to allow authors to experiment with different ways to communicate. The judgement of a theoretical contribution should change, from the need to provide new empirical material in each chapter (the traditional judgement) to the value of demonstrating why we should think a particular way about a theory or approach. The latter is too easy to dismiss as a review essay, in which we have heard the arguments before. Yet, almost no scholar can make this claim with confidence, because the field is too vast, and there are too many approaches in play, to understand more than a few in sufficient depth. Consequently, scholars with the ability to synthesise knowledge make the largest contribution to our field.

How to communicate, compare and combine insights? For practitioners, the contexts and choices in policy processes are too complex to provide recommendations that apply to all situations (Cairney and Weible, 2017). However, for scholars, we can produce frameworks, theoretical insights and a conceptual language that helps structure the analysis of all such situations. For example, this book identifies lessons from policy theories for persuasion and learning, political participation and collective action, and structuring governments and designing public policies.

To that end, we first explain why it has taken so long for many policy theorists to embrace the agenda we have described. Then, we plot a path for this new agenda, identifying what we know from the collection and what we still need to know from the field of public policy research.

The principal audience for this book are new and experienced policy scholars interested in theoretical clarity, knowledge synthesis, and the practical meaning of the theories that populate the field. Further, since we argue that theoretical clarity comes from explaining concepts to a wider audience, we hope that the issue will appeal to many practitioners. Of course, no single collection can bridge the gap between theory and practice, but it can serve as a landmark in bringing attention to this important issue, initiating the process of translation, and serving as a guide for similar scholarship in the future.

Policy process research has mostly continued in its theory-focused tradition

Policy process research can be defined as the study of the patterns of interactions surrounding public policy over time, often focusing the nature of political systems, policy subsystems within larger political systems, and authoritative decision-making venues (Weible 2017). To make sense of the complexity of policy contexts and human choices, scholars have developed theories to help specify the scope of research and establish common vocabularies via abstract concepts and foundational assumptions about causal relationships. For policy scholars, theories serve as the medium within which knowledge is built, stored and advanced. However, in their quest for better theories, policy scholars have often treated their peers as their sole audience, with little incentive to think about their usefulness to wider audiences or practical implications. We have theories deep in knowledge but we are unclear about how to communicate or use it.

Most of the strains between theoretical and practical orientations are in the past

Since the founding of the field (Lasswell, 1951, 1956), policy process research has featured rifts between the value of doing theory-based research versus applied research (Ranney, 1968; Sabatier, 1992). Some of these discussions continue, with some scholars criticising the lack of discussion of more democratic and normative ideals into policy process theories (deLeon, 1997; Ingram et al, 2016). Yet, the field is shifting, with a number of scholars bringing practical relevance to the field of policy processes (Weible et al, 2012; Cairney, 2015; 2016; Shipan and Volden, 2012). Compared to the past, most contemporary policy scholars recognise the value of doing applied and theory-based research, even if they choose to do one or the other (Cairney and Weible, 2017). Of course, some tensions and dilemmas remain. For example, some policy scholars struggle to strike the right balance under an incentive structure in their academic units that rewards basic over applied science in promotion or tenure decisions. Nonetheless, there are fewer calls to maintain a theory and practice divide, particularly in countries – like the UK – in which there are now more incentives to demonstrate wider audience 'impact' (Cairney and Oliver, 2020).

Our ability to describe practical relevance from policy process theories remains elusive

Given the theoretical tradition of the field, policy process scholars have struggled to develop strategies for translating their science into practice. This is not from a lack of effort (deLeon and Weible, 2010). For example, some strategies have been oversubscribed, including writing policy implications in the conclusions of articles published in academic journals. Some scholars also participate directly in the policy process and/or develop normative theories that combine descriptive and prescriptive analysis. Social Construction and Policy Design is a key example, in which it identifies 'degenerative politics' and describes how it undermines a democratic governing system (Schneider and Ingram, 1997). In contrast, the Advocacy Coalition Framework (ACF) is more of an empirical-based theory because it does not explicitly make claims that a certain type of politics is good or bad for a governing system (Sabatier and Jenkins-Smith, 1993). Each of these strategies can be useful but face limitations. For instance, most articles in academic journals are unavailable to policy actors, normative-based theories are often just as inaccessible as empirical-based theories to people outside the field, and direct advocacy is not for everyone. For example, it is debatable whether Social Construction and Policy Design with a normative orientation is more or less accessible to new students than the Multiple Streams Framework without a normative orientation. Less debatable are the benefits that students (without long-term academic aspirations) could receive and use in the real world if practical insights were gleaned from both.

Other strategies for bridging the theory-practice divide are undervalued, overlooked, or misguided. For example, policy process scholars often imagine their research affecting the thoughts and actions of current policymakers when in fact their largest audience is not just 'policymakers' but rather a broader set of policy actors involved in the policy process (Cairney and Weible, 2017). Moreover, the argument that our work as published in academic journals actually reach this broader set of policy actors has not been substantiated, and we would not make journal articles accessible simply by removing the paywall (deLeon and Weible, 2010).

Our argument is not that policy recommendations found in the conclusions of journal articles are ineffectual, but that we should not rely upon them as our main strategy for outreach.

Additionally, many scholars often expect their research to produce precise prescriptions about how to improve specific instances of policymaking. However, relatively abstract policy theories will rarely provide concrete advice of how to act and what to do in all given contexts. There are too many variables in play to make this happen. The complexity of policy processes, its continuously changing nature, and its diversity across contexts, prevent precise prediction for policy actors seeking influence or policy change. Further, policy actors pursue different goals. Some might be motivated to produce change or to stop change. Each of these policy actors need a different set of strategies to increase the likelihood of being effective. Our role may be to help them make sense of policy theories so that they think more critically about how they make their choices and how they make sense of their complex context (Cairney and Weible, 2017).

Summarising the contributions

Even if policy process research embraces more applied science today than in the past, scholars still struggle to make theoretical work relevant. Effective translation requires full chapter length treatment. Translation into practical lessons, such as for policy analysis and engagement in the policy process, should not be tacked on to published research. Rather, to do it justice we need to incorporate practical lessons into state of the art research. Therefore, to take this agenda forward, this book consists of eight chapters that each focus on making scholarly and practical sense of a different theoretical terrain:

Three habits of successful policy entrepreneurs

Cairney (2021) argues that we need one coherent story of the Multiple Streams Analysis (MSA, often described as the Multiple Streams Framework, MSF) to bring together a vibrant and diverse but uncoordinated field. At the heart of this story are the policy entrepreneurs who understand how to be effective in policymaking: influence how people understand policy problems, prepare a technically and politically feasible solution, and pounce on the temporary motivation and ability of policymakers to select it. State of the art MSA research suggests that, although we still describe this process in the same way, the role of the entrepreneur has changed markedly since Kingdon's (1984) foundational study.

MSA informs current debates on 'evidence-based policymaking' in which too many commentators strive for 'rational' policymaking, which privileges scientific evidence, in a process akin to a policy cycle. Yet, policymakers are more likely to be driven by 'irrationality' in a far messier policy process. The key messages for policy actors are simple: focus on exercising power to reduce ambiguity, rather than bombarding policymakers with evidence to reduce uncertainty, and exploit 'windows of opportunity' to act, rather than expecting one stage of policymaking to lead inevitably to another.

Narratives as tools for influencing policy change

Crow and Jones (2021) synthesise insights from the Narrative Policy Framework (NPF). They show how policy actors influence the ways in which policymakers understand and seek to solve policy problems. Again, this process is not driven primarily by a universal acceptance of the evidence (the 'knowledge fallacy'). Nor can actors rely on a universal form of human empathy in which all people care about the same things (the 'empathy fallacy'). Rather, policy influence through persuasion comes from telling an effective story built on acknowledging the storyteller's biases and exploiting the audience's biases. Crow and Jones (2021) argue that other interpretive scholars analyse narrative without drawing practical lessons; they do not tell us which stories work. In contrast, by using scientific methods to analyse the relative success of persuasion strategies, the NPF provides a template for understanding, analysing, and writing effective narratives. Put most simply, a good story requires four elements: the setting, hero and villain characters, a plot outlining their motives, and a clear moral, which represents the policy solution.

Using cultural theory to navigate the policy process

Simmons (2021) focuses on how policymakers develop effective policymaking strategies when they are so limited by bounded rationality. They use cognitive shortcuts to act quickly and make adequate decisions despite high uncertainty. One can criticise their reliance on 'cognitive frailties', and perhaps design institutions to limit their autonomous powers, or praise their remarkable ability to develop heuristics, and work with them to refine such techniques. Simmons synthesises key insights from cultural theory (CT), and presents one of many possible CT stories, to identify the value of a policymaker's 'internal compass' (based on a valuable combination of cognitive processes) combined with a 'map' of the 'policymaking terrain' (the organisations, rules, and other sources of sources of direction and learning in a policymaking system). In doing so, Simmons helps bring much needed clarity to the study of CT, which has produced a diverse and potentially unwieldy literature, and identifies ways to help policymakers think about and ask the right questions as they navigate their policymaking environment.

The lessons of policy learning

Dunlop and Radaelli (2021) provide the same service for scholars of policy learning. Learning has been a staple of policy scholarships for decades, but remains one of the most elusive concepts in the study of policy processes. Too many scholars have responded by generating taxonomies, concepts, and methods, which describe how to organise analysis without showing the intellectual and practical payoffs. Dunlop and Radaelli provide new direction to policy learning studies by framing the literature in terms of its implications for policymakers, citizens and societies. They do so with reference to three key messages. First, although we may associate learning with positive change, it can actually be detrimental to politics and society. Learning is often the by-product of bargaining and the effort to secure compliance with the law, rather than the intended product of research to improve public policy. Second, we can develop categories to show how to help or hinder certain kinds of learning. For example, skepticism of science and low policy capacity mar the work of experts in governmental bodies, and incommensurable beliefs undermine deliberative forms of learning. Third, unless we design learning processes well, it is too easy for policymakers to learn the wrong lessons. In that context, learning scholarship helps us conceptualise the policy process and improve the process of learning within government.

Practical prescriptions for governing fragmented governments

Swann and Kim (2021) consolidate and take forward the Institutional Collection Action (ICA) literature to describe the problems that arise when public policy problems cannot be addressed effectively by a single, solitary government. Instead, many semi-autonomous organisations have to learn how to collaborate most effectively – across different scales of governance and institutional contexts – to reduce policymaking fragmentation. The main challenge is dealing with threats to collective action. Swann and Kim identify five main solutions for reducing collaborative risk and uncertainty: employ networking strategies that incorporate frequent, face-to-face interactions; design collaborative arrangements around service characteristics; partner with organisations with similar goals and values; increase inclusivity in collaboratives; and develop collaborative capacity incrementally.

Drawing practical lessons from punctuated equilibrium theory

Koski and Workman (2021) synthesise lessons from Punctuated Equilibrium Theory, which has become one of the most active research programmes in political science. One consequence of such conceptual and comparative expansion is diversity of scholarship under a single banner, and the need to step back to consider the meaning of key terms and relative benefits of many approaches. They focus primarily on conceptual advances in PET research on information processing, which builds scholarly and practical lessons on one key insight: policymakers and governments face an oversupply of information and the need to produce effective rules to maximise the use of the highest quality information. Koski and Workman orientate their recommendations around finding the right balance between centralisation, which creates bottlenecks, and decentralisation, which leads to fragmentation. They signal to scholars the key findings from PET by focusing on possible solutions to those findings: design institutions to be information seeking (not merely attending to problems); encourage central units to listen to signals from multiple delegated units (rather than minimising dissent or ignoring outside experts); and, encourage issue bundling to challenge a tendency for issues to be tied up by narrow problem definitions.

Policy design and the added-value of the institutional analysis development framework

Heikkila and Andersson (2021) address collective action in the design of substantive public policy. Their chapter summarises key lessons generated by the Institutional Analysis and Development (IAD) framework. First, people are capable of – and often the best at – solving collective problems from the bottom-up, both outside and within government settings. Therefore, excluding these groups from the design stage leads to weakened legitimacy resulting in less compliance. Second, people have a natural tendency to engage in reactionary and emotional reasoning when they are passionate about an issue. Therefore, design frameworks to guard against the tendency toward biased analyses. A good framework provides a toolkit for identifying the factors that policymakers and stakeholders should consider when developing policies. Third, there are no silver bullets to policy designs and it is important to design contextually appropriate policy interventions. These types of recommendations may seem intuitive, which actually boosts the academic and practical value of IAD research. IAD studies show time and again that people ignore such solutions, prompting us to restate more vigorously the need to resist the temptation to rush policy analysis and design, and to document the unintended consequences of ignoring IAD advice.

Why advocacy coalitions matter and practical insights about them

Weible and Ingold (2021) focus less on public policy and governance and more on the political behaviour of those seeking influence in the policy process. One of the challenges in making sense of the literature on political behaviour is the varied ways in which we describe different forms of political associations. Basing their argument on the Advocacy Coalition Framework, Weible and Ingold respond to this challenge by comparing and contrasting advocacy coalitions with coalitions of convenience, interest groups, social movements, political parties, and epistemic communities. In contrast to these other terms, advocacy coalitions refer to informal political associations where policy actors work together over extended periods toward similar policy goals. Yet, knowing that coalitions exist is not the same as knowing how to get involved in them or how to form and maintain them. Weible and Ingold tackle these more practical challenges by offering ways to get involved in coalitions (auxiliary and principal members, brokers, and entrepreneurs), the forces that contribute to coalition formation and maintenance (different types of threats to beliefs), and the different approaches to identify coalitions (who are in key positions, who has decision authority, who has influential reputations, and who might be mobilised?). No single political strategy will work all the time, so Weible and Ingold provide a structured way to think about coalitions in this complexity given our bounded abilities to comprehend the world and capacities to act in it.

Concluding thoughts on advancing policy theory translations

The field of public policy has changed since Lasswell's (1951) initial vision. Unlike back then, today's field is now populated with numerous theoretical approaches and with methodologies that are far more sophisticated. These new theories and methods have opened the door for new ways to both construct and discover aspects of policy processes and have deepened the theory-based well of knowledge. Yet, successes have posed new challenges, particularly those around overcoming academic silos, esoteric lexicon, and knowledge that is not easily translatable.

In response, this book marks the start in an effort to draw practical lessons from policy theories. It challenges convention in striving to translate insights from the reservoirs of theory-based knowledge, communicate better the lexicon found in academia, and focus exclusively on the question of relevance. Thus, while the means by which we conduct our science have changed since Lasswell's initial vision about 70 years ago, our goals have remained the same in striving for greater human dignity through political equality (Cairney and Weible, 2017).

In directing us on the path for bridging theory and practice, this book certainly neither completes the journey nor can accomplish its goal on its own. We welcome your insights, reflections, and critical feedback in reading this book and encourage others to take on this same challenge and toward the same goal of bettering society.

References

Ayres, S, Marsh, A, 2013, Reflections on contemporary debates in policy studies, *Policy & Politics* 41, 4, 643–63

Cairney, P, 2015, How can policy theory have an impact on policymaking? The role of theory-led academic–practitioner discussions, *Teaching Public Administration* 33, 1, 22–39

Cairney, P, 2016, *The politics of evidence-based policy making*, London: Palgrave Springer

Cairney, P, 2021, Three habits of successful policy entrepreneurs, in (eds) Weible, C. and Cairney, P. (eds) *Practical Lessons from Policy Theories*, Bristol: Bristol University Press

Cairney, P, Oliver, O, 2020, How should academics engage in policymaking to achieve impact? *Political Studies Review*, 18, 2, 228–44

Cairney, P, Weible CM, 2017, The new policy sciences: Combining the cognitive science of choice, multiple theories of context, and basic and applied analysis, *Policy Sciences* 50, 4, 619–27

Crow, D, Jones, M, 2021, A guide to telling good stories that affect policy change, in (eds) Weible, C and Cairney, P (eds) *Practical Lessons from Policy Theories*, Bristol: Bristol University Press

DeLeon, P, 1997, *Democracy and the policy sciences*, Albany, NY: SUNY Press

DeLeon, P, Weible, CM, 2010, Policy process research for democracy: A commentary on Lasswell's vision, *International Journal of Policy Studies* 1, 2, 23–34

Dunlop, C, Radaelli, C, 2021, The lessons of policy learning: Types, triggers, hindrances and pathologies, in (eds) Weible, C. and Cairney, P. (eds) *Practical Lessons from Policy Theories*, Bristol: Bristol University Press

Flinders, M, 2013, The politics of engaged scholarship: Impact, relevance and imagination, *Policy & Politics* 41, 4, 621–42

Heikkila, T, Andersson, K, 2021, Policy design and the added-value of the Institutional Analysis Development Framework, in (eds) Weible, C and Cairney, P (eds) *Practical Lessons from Policy Theories*, Bristol: Bristol University Press

Heikkila, T, Cairney, C, 2017, Comparison of theories of the policy process, in CM Weible, PA Sabatier (eds) *Theories of the policy process* (4th edn), Boulder, CO: Westview Press, pp 301–28

Ingram, H, deLeon, P, Schneider, A, 2016, Conclusion. Public policy theory and democracy: The elephant in the corner, in G Peters, P Zittoun (eds) *Contemporary approaches to public policy: International series on public policy*, Basingstoke: Palgrave Macmillan, pp 175–200

Kingdon, J, 1984, *Agendas, alternatives and public policies* (1st edn), New York: Harper Collins

Koski, C, Workman, S, 2021, Drawing practical lessons from punctuated equilibrium theory. in (eds) Weible, C and Cairney, P (eds) *Practical Lessons from Policy Theories*, Bristol: Bristol University Press

Lasswell, HD, 1951, The policy orientation, in D Lerner, HD Lasswell (eds) *The policy sciences: Recent developments in scope and methods*, Stanford, CA: Stanford University Press, pp 3–15

Lasswell, HD, 1956, The political science of science: An inquiry into the possible reconciliation of mastery and freedom, *American Political Science Review*, 50, 4, 961–79

Ranney, A, 1968, The study of policy content: A framework for choice, in A Ranney (ed) *Political science and public policy*, Chicago, IL: Markham Publishing Company, pp 3–21

Sabatier, PA, 1992, Political science and public policy: An assessment, in W Dunn, RM Kelly (eds) *Advances in policy studies, 1950–1990*, Brunswick, NJ: Transaction Books

Sabatier, PA, Jenkins-Smith, HC, 1993, *Policy change and learning: An advocacy coalition framework*, Boulder, CO: Westview Press

Schneider, AL, Ingram, HM, 1997, *Policy design for democracy*, Lawrence, KS: University Press of Kansas

Shipan, CR, Volden, C, 2012, Policy diffusion: Seven lessons for scholars and practitioners, *Public Administration Review*, 72, 6, 788–96

Simmons, R, 2021, Using cultural theory to navigate the policy process, in (eds) Weible, C and Cairney, P (eds) *Practical Lessons from Policy Theories*, Bristol: Bristol University Press

Swann, W, Kim, S, 2021, Practical prescriptions for governing fragmented governments, in (eds) Weible, C and Cairney, P (eds) *Practical Lessons from Policy Theories*, Bristol: Bristol University Press

Weible, CM, Heikkila, T, deLeon, P, Sabatier, PA, 2012, Understanding and influencing the policy process, *Policy Sciences*, 45, 1, 1–21

Weible, CM, 2017, Introduction: The scope and focus of policy process research and theory, in CM Weible, PA Sabatier (eds) *Theories of the policy process* (4th edn), Boulder, CO: Westview Press, pp 1–13
Weible, CM, Ingold K, 2021, Why advocacy coalitions matter and practical insights about them, in (eds) Weible, C and Cairney, P (eds) *Practical Lessons from Policy Theories*, Bristol: Bristol University Press

CHAPTER TWO

Three habits of successful policy entrepreneurs[1]

Paul Cairney

Introduction: how to improve the multiple streams narrative

The multiple streams approach (MSA) is one of policy scholarship's biggest successes. Kingdon's (1984) study is one the highest cited books in policy studies, there is a thriving programme of empirical application and theoretical refinement, its lessons are applied regularly in interdisciplinary studies, and it is relatively well known and enjoyed by practitioners and students (Herweg et al, 2015; 2017; Zahariadis, 2007; 2014; Jones et al, 2016).

Yet, its success is built on shaky foundations because its alleged strength – its flexible metaphor of streams and windows of opportunity – is actually its weakness. Most scholars describe MSA superficially, fail to articulate the meaning of its metaphor, do not engage with state of the art developments, and struggle to apply its concepts systematically to empirical research (Jones et al, 2016). These limitations create an acute scientific problem: most scholars apply MSA without connecting it to a coherent research agenda. Consequently, it is difficult to produce new knowledge systematically or describe with confidence the accumulated wisdom of MSA. As the special issue on 'Practical lessons from policy theories' shows, this problem is a feature of many policy theories which have expanded far beyond their original intentions (Weible and Cairney, 2018).

There have been some recent attempts to solve this problem by encouraging conceptual clarity via hypothesis production and testing (Cairney and Jones, 2016; Cairney and Zahariadis, 2016; Herweg et al, 2015). However, this solution only appeals to a niche audience of MSA scholars. Most readers and users of MSA draw on Kingdon's (1984) classic metaphor without taking their research to the next level by engaging with over 30 years of subsequent research and theoretical refinement. Kingdon's study of US federal politics in the 1980s can only take us so far. Therefore, we need a more profound solution that draws the attention of *all MSA users* to state of the art research, its applications, refinements and contemporary implications. Its success will provide benefits to everyone, from the expert scholar to the new student. I solve this problem in three ways. First, I turn lessons from individual studies and systematic and qualitative reviews of the literature into a coherent MSA narrative. If successful, this narrative will become the primary reference point for policy scholars seeking to conduct new empirical research and explain MSA to new audiences such as students, practitioners and scholars from other disciplines. It will therefore serve as a valuable heuristic: if they have not read this chapter, they have not done their homework.

Second, I apply this narrative to a profoundly important topic for interdisciplinary scholars and policymakers – the politics of 'evidence-based policymaking' – to show how to make the MSA story as memorable, widely understood and correctly applied as possible. The result is a theory whose flexibility, undoubted popularity and wide application does not come at the expense of conceptual clarity.

Third, I focus primarily on 'policy entrepreneurs' as the heroes of the MSA story. Policymakers have to ignore most policy problems and most ways to understand and solve them. When their attention lurches to a problem, it is too late to produce a new solution. Their motive to select any solution is fleeting, during a brief 'window of opportunity'. So, I structure the chapter around the three strategies that effective policy entrepreneurs combine to adapt to these limitations in their complex and unpredictable environment:

1. telling a good story to grab the audience's interest;
2. producing feasible solutions in anticipation of attention to problems; adapting their strategy to the specific nature of each 'window'. In large systems, they are like surfers waiting for the 'big wave', but in small subsystems they can be like Poseidon moving the 'streams'.
3. Therefore, a focus on the MSA story and the strategies of entrepreneurs helps consolidate the research agenda for specialist policy scholars *and* explain real world policymaking to anyone hitherto attached to romantic stories of 'evidence-based policymaking' in which we expect policymakers to produce 'rational' decisions in a policy cycle with predictable, linear stages.

How does the multiple streams story begin?

The MSA story begins as an antidote to the biggest work of fiction in policy studies: rational policymaking during a policy cycle. In an ideal-type world, policymaking would not seem so counterintuitive. 'Comprehensively rational' policymakers would combine their values with evidence to define policy problems and their aims, 'neutral' bureaucracies would produce multiple possible solutions consistent with those aims, and policymakers would select the 'best' or most 'evidence-based' solution. This act would set in motion a cycle of stages including legitimation, implementation, evaluation and the choice to maintain or change policy. The policy process would be predictable, and all actors would know how to engage with policymakers to translate their evidence into policy. We describe this fictional story of 'comprehensive rationality' and the 'policy cycle' as an ideal-type to compare with more realistic stories of complexity and unpredictable policymaking (Cairney, 2016, 16–19).

In the real world, policymaking often seems counterintuitive. There is too much information, and policymakers have to ignore most policy problems and most ways to understand and try to solve them. They use 'rational' and 'irrational' cognitive short cuts to help them pay attention to a manageable number of issues, and address policy problems without fully understanding them (Cairney and Kwiatkowski, 2017). When their attention lurches to a policy problem, it is too late to produce a new solution that is technically feasible and acceptable to policymakers. Their willingness and ability to select a policy solution is fleeting, during a brief 'window of opportunity' in which all key factors – heightened attention to a problem, an available and feasible solution and the motive to select it – must come together at the same time, or the opportunity is lost (Kingdon, 1984).

Our heroes are the successful 'policy entrepreneurs' who do not get discouraged by this more confusing story. The policy literature describes 'policy entrepreneur' in many ways (Beeson and Stone, 2013; Mintrom and Vergari, 1996, 431; Mintrom and Norman, 2009; Bakir and Jarvis, 2017; Jones, 1994, 196; John, 1999, 45; Christopoulos and Ingold, 2015; Laffan, 1997; Roberts and King, 1991). However, as described by our chosen narrator (Kingdon, 1984, 165–166), they are the agents for policy change who possess the knowledge, power, tenacity and luck to be able to exploit key opportunities. Entrepreneurs invest their time wisely for future reward, and possess key skills that help them adapt particularly well to their environments (Cairney, 2012, 272).

Entrepreneurs use three strategies to maximise their impact in crowded, complex and often unpredictable policy environments. First, they know that agenda setting is about exercising power to generate attention for some issues over others, and establishing one way of thinking about problems at the expense of the others. To that end, entrepreneurs identify how to manipulate or reinforce the cognitive biases of influential policymakers. For example, they tell simple and persuasive stories combining facts with values and emotional appeals, engaging in coalitions and networks to establish trust in the messenger, and investing for the long term to learn the language of policy in key venues.

Second, they know that timing matters. There is not enough time to find a new policy solution during heightened attention to a policy problem. Instead, they develop technically and politically feasible solutions – in other words, they could work as intended and be acceptable to enough people in policy networks – and wait for the right time to present them to policymakers during a 'window of opportunity'.

Third, they know how to adapt to their environment to exploit, or help create, 'windows of opportunity' for action, in which policymakers have some motive to select a policy solution during heightened attention to a problem. The power of entrepreneurs can change markedly according to the scale of the policymaking environment. For Kingdon (1984), policy entrepreneurs in the US federal environment were 'surfers waiting for the big wave', suggesting that the environment is more important to explanation than the skills of individual actors. More recently, there have been hundreds of applications of MSA across the globe, generating new insights and practical implications (Jones et al, 2016). In particular, studies of subnational government, or policymaking in smaller countries or regions, suggest that entrepreneurs can – under particular conditions – be more influential than Kingdon (1984) suggested.

MSA tells a persuasive story about the role of timing and fleeting opportunity in politics. The attention of policymakers lurches frequently, but it is rare for them to possess a fully 'evolved' policy solution before their attention lurches elsewhere. Consequently, attention can rise and fall without producing major policy change.

MSA contrasts with the story of a linear policy cycle in which each stage appears in chronological order, and attention to the nature of a problem sets in motion the production and delivery of a solution. Instead, three key factors – *problem* definition, *policy* solution and *politics* (motive and opportunity) – are separate 'streams' which rarely 'couple' during a window of opportunity.

If described – rather confusingly – as water, the multiple streams metaphor suggests that, when streams come together, they are hard to separate. Or, if we describe the need for the 'stars to align' we overemphasise the role of serendipity and events completely out of the control of actors (in this scenario, 'no one can rewrite the stars'). Instead, a 'window of opportunity' is *best described as akin to a space launch* in which policymakers will abort the mission unless every relevant factor is just right. Some factors are not in the gift of humans (such as the environmental conditions), but others are (such as the choices we make on technology, resources and the rules governing lift-off). This metaphor suggests that the 'coupling' of streams is not inevitable, but entrepreneurs can help make things happen because they know the importance of framing problems to generate attention, to have a solution ready, and to help create and exploit infrequent opportunities to act.

Such strategies may be known to policy scientists, but scholars do not tell the same story. We should not underestimate the vulnerability of MSA to poor scientific practice if we do not tell its story consistently and accumulate knowledge systematically. Further, we should not underestimate the profound novelty and value of these insights to the researchers from many disciplines and professions, who are interested in the relationship between evidence and policy, but are more familiar with romantic stories of 'evidence-based policymaking' in which we should expect policymakers to produce 'rational' decisions in a policy cycle with predictable, linear stages. MSA provides an equally memorable and attractive story with more value to scholars and practitioners. It provides three ways to be more effective in politics and less disappointed in the gulf between real world and fantasy policymaking.

Entrepreneurs know why it is important to tell a good story about a policy problem

It is a truism in policy studies that 'the evidence' does not speak for itself. Someone needs to speak up for a policy problem in a way that sparks the attention and concern of their audience. This act does not involve providing more and more evidence, based on the misguided assumption that it will take us closer to the type of 'comprehensive rationality' associated with 'evidence-based policymaking' (EBPM) (Cairney, 2016, 15–18; Douglas, 2009). Rather, early post-war studies identified the implications of 'bounded rationality' when, for example, policymakers used 'rules of thumb' to limit their analysis and trial and error strategies to produce 'good enough' decisions (Simon, 1976, xxviii; Lindblom, 1959, 88). Then, modern theories took forward psychological insights (Kahneman, 2012; Haidt, 2001) to identify two drivers of agenda setting dynamics, whose implications are identified in Table 2.1.

First, policymakers can only pay attention to a tiny proportion of their responsibilities, so they ignore most evidence and promote very few issues to the top of their agenda (Baumgartner and Jones, 1993). They can only pay attention to one of many possible ways to understand and seek to solve problems, and this attention relates more to the beliefs of policymakers, and persuasion strategies of influencers, than the size of the problem or evidence base for its solution (Majone, 1989, 24; Dearing and Rogers, 1996). Second, policymakers draw on emotion, moral reasoning, gut instinct and habit as shortcuts to gathering information, to understand complex policy problems in simple ways (Lewis, 2013;

Table 2.1: Strategies for the 'problem stream': how to influence the policy agenda

Insight	Implication for strategy
Few problems reach the top of the agenda, and attention to problems is not dependent on the evidence of their size	Find ways to draw attention to problems by focusing on the beliefs of your audience more than your assessment of the evidence
Policymakers use 'rational' and 'irrational' ways to process a lot of information in a short space of time	Adapt to the cognitive biases of influential policymakers, and frame policy solutions as consistent with dominant ways to understand problems
There are many ways to frame any policy problem, and evidence often plays a limited role in problem definition	Combine evidence with framing strategies, persuasion, and storytelling
Limited time forces people to make choices before their preferences are clear	Adapt to 'rational' and 'irrational' ways in which policymakers short-cut decisions
Policymakers seek to reduce ambiguity as much as uncertainty	If you simply bombard policymakers with evidence, they will have little reason to read it. If you win the 'framing battle', policymakers will demand evidence on your problem and solution

Source: adapted from Cairney and Kwitakowski (2017)

Cairney and Kwiatkowski, 2017; Lodge and Wegrich, 2016). In other words, they pay attention to things they care about, or are already familiar with.

Consequently, entrepreneurs know not to bombard policymakers with more and more information as a way to generate attention, since it may have the opposite effect. Rather, they adapt to the ways in which policymakers combine 'rational' and 'irrational' thinking to sift large amounts of potentially relevant information. They perform the role of 'problem broker', to influence how policymakers understand a policy problem, *and* 'knowledge broker', to supply the concise evidence that is most relevant to this understanding (Knaggård, 2015, 453).

Agenda setters build on the issues 'already in the back of people's minds'(Kingdon, 1984, 103). As the wider public policy literature suggests, they combine evidence and emotional appeals (True et al, 2007), tell simple stories with heroes and morals (McBeth et al, 2014), romanticise their own cause while demonising their opponents (Sabatier et al, 1987), and/or exploit stereotypes of social groups to describe why governments should only give resources to the 'deserving' (Schneider and Ingram, 1993; 1997; 2005). These ways to exercise power – with reference to the beliefs and psychology of policymakers – can be as important as the material resources of actors (Kingdon, 1984, 131–33).

Entrepreneurs recognise the key distinction between the exercise of power to reduce *ambiguity* and the production of evidence to reduce *uncertainty* (Zahariadis, 2007, 66; Baumgartner and Jones, 1993, 31; Majone, 1989; Cairney, 2012, 234). Uncertainty describes a lack of knowledge. Scientists often focus on producing more high-quality evidence to reduce uncertainty, using evidence to measure the size of a known problem and the effectiveness of a relevant solution (Cairney et al, 2016; Cairney and Oliver, 2017).

More importantly, ambiguity describes the ability to support more than one way to understand and describe a policy problem. We reduce ambiguity by choosing one policy 'image'. That choice narrows our analysis and produces the conditions under which we can use evidence to reduce uncertainty. This is not a 'scientific' process, even if actors can use scientific evidence to make their case. Rather, agenda setting – or problem definition – is about 'framing' issues, or drawing the highest attention to one image by accentuating some facts and omitting others, linking problems to deeply held beliefs and values, using simple stories to assign cause and responsibility, exploiting crises or events, selecting the measures that produce the most supportive evidence of a problem, and tailoring these strategies to different audiences (Rochefort and Cobb, 1994, vii; Jones and Baumgartner, 2005, 8; Baumgartner and Jones, 1993, 107–8, 113; Hogwood, 1987, 30; Stone, 1989, 282–3; 2002, 191; Dearing and Rogers, 1996, 37–9; Birkland, 1997).

For example, tobacco control is often treated as a model for evidence advocates, in which the scientific evidence played a key role in debate at a national and international level (Cairney et al, 2012). Yet, the availability of evidence produced with scientific rigour was only one part of the agenda setting story, in which advocates of tobacco control also learned to: combine the scientific evidence on the harms of smoking, and harms of environmental tobacco smoke, with emotional appeals regarding the harms to children; challenge the frames of their competitors by quantifying the economic costs of smoking; reframe the implications of key values, such as the right to health and clean air over the right to smoke; and, generate a sense of crisis by describing smoking as a 'non-communicable disease' (NCD), 'epidemic', or public health 'crisis' (Baumgartner and Jones, 1993, 114; Cairney and Yamazaki, 2017; Cairney, 2016: 67–72).

Entrepreneurs have a solution ready to chase a problem

It is a major but temporary achievement to focus policymaker attention on one way of understanding a policy problem. It must be acted upon quickly, before attention shifts elsewhere. Further, since policymakers will not dwell on problems that cannot be solved, *a well thought out solution must already exist before a lurch of attention* (Kingdon, 1984, 103). So, entrepreneurs respond to the counterintuitive nature of the agenda setting process: politics is about well-established solutions chasing problems, not producing solutions when policymakers identify problems.

In other words, problem definition is only one part of the puzzle; a necessary but insufficient condition for major policy change. Instead of viewing agenda setting as one stage in a linear process in which problem definition is followed by formulation, legitimation and implementation, MSA draws on the 'garbage can model' of choice in which policymaking organisations are, 'collections of choices looking for problems, issues and feelings looking for decision situations in which they might be aired, solutions looking for issues to which they might be an answer, and decision makers looking for work' (Cohen et al, 1972, 1). This is 'organised anarchy' in which 'stages' should be viewed instead as 'relatively independent streams' which come together in a mess of activity: some actors articulate a poor or contested understanding of problems in relation to their vague aims, some have their preferred solutions and are looking to attach them to problems, and policymakers have unclear motives when selecting them (1972, 16).

Kingdon (1984) extended this focus on multiple streams to the US federal arena, to describe the conditions under which major policy change would take place. In particular, when policymaker attention lurches to a policy problem, a technically and politically feasible solution must already be available to address the problem defined by policymakers. Further, while attention lurches quickly from issue to issue, viable solutions involving major policy change take years or decades to develop. Kingdon describes ideas in a 'policy primeval soup', evolving or 'softening' as they are proposed by one actor then reconsidered and modified by a large number of participants (who may also have to be 'softened up' to new ideas). To deal with this disconnect between lurching attention and slow policy development, they try to develop widely-acceptable solutions in anticipation of future problems, then find the right time to exploit or encourage attention to a relevant problem (1984, 181).

This insight should not be understated, and the implications laid out in Table 2.2 can have a profound impact on people seeking policy influence. In particular, for people new to politics, who possess the reasonable expectation that we generate solutions *after* we identify problems, it will seem counterintuitive that there is not enough time to do so. Yet, attention lurches quickly from issue to issue, and the motive to act is temporary, so

Table 2.2: Strategies for the policy stream: how to develop and gain support for policy solutions

Insight	**Implication**
There is no linear policy cycle in which policymakers identify problems, formulate solutions, and make a choice	Generate technically and politically feasible policy solutions and seek opportunities to sell them during heightened attention
Solutions take time to 'soften' to become accepted within policy networks	Form coalitions with allies, and engage in networks, to identify how to modify and generate support for policy solutions

Source: adapted from Cairney and Zahariadis (2016) and Mintrom and Norman (2009).

'When the time for action arrives, when the policy window…opens, it is too late to develop a new proposal from scratch. It must have already gone through this process of consideration, floating up, discussion, revision and trying out again' (1984, 149). Therefore, 'advocates lie in wait in and around government with their solutions at hand, waiting for problems to float by to which they can attach their solutions, waiting for a development in the political stream they can use to their advantage' (Kingdon, 1984, 165–6).

MSA therefore helps clarify the role of 'timing' and idioms such as 'being in the right place at the right time' in policymaking. The absence of good timing is listed frequently as a major barrier to the use of scientific evidence in policy, prompting scholars to recognise the need for good networks to help spot opportunities, while recognising the 'serendipitous nature of the policy process' (Oliver et al, 2014a, 4). This emphasis on timing as serendipity is also reinforced in some studies of the policy implications of MSA (Avery, 2004; Howie, 2009; Pralle, 2009). Yet, entrepreneurs also *help create* windows of opportunity and have solutions ready when the time is right.

Just how long it takes to 'soften' a solution and wait for the right opportunity is unclear, but note the use of different metaphors. Smith (2013) describes the chameleon-like nature of ideas, suggesting they can potentially change quickly to adapt to a new environment. However, Kingdon (1984) uses a 'Darwinian' evolutionary metaphor, which suggests 'the slow progress of an idea towards acceptability' within policy networks, which might take decades (Cairney, 2013, 281). In such cases, evidence advocates should prepare for the long haul and expect limited short-term influence (Boswell and Smith, 2017). Indeed, even if they expect a new government to arrive with new ideas, or a new level of receptivity to solutions, they still need to be ready with a well worked out solution.

Entrepreneurs know when to 'surf the waves' or try to move the sea

To produce major policy change, policymakers have to possess the motive to pay attention to a problem *and* adopt the proposed solution. This motive is fleeting, during a 'window of opportunity'. Potential causes of a shift in receptivity to a policy solution include: 'Swings of national mood, vagaries of public opinion, election results, changes of administration…and interest group pressure campaigns' (Kingdon, 1984, 19). To return to the metaphor of a timely space launch out of the control of any single actor, our attention should shift to the importance of a 'policy environment'. In most modern policy theories, this 'environment' relates to the attitudes of many potentially influential audiences (actors at multiple levels of government or in key venues), the rules and norms of information gathering and behaviour in key venues, the supportive coalitions and networks, and the most relevant socioeconomic trends and key events (Heikkila and Cairney, 2017; Cairney and Weible, 2017).

In Kingdon's original study, Darwinian and environmental metaphors describe the vast scale of US federal-level politics and policymaking, in which it is difficult to imagine that one entrepreneur could do anything but adapt to rather than shape their environment.

Modern MSA studies help shift that image *somewhat* but we need to describe the nature of the modern literature to understand that shift. Jones et al (2016) identify 311 MSA applications published from 2000 to 2014, of which 132 are to the US, 205 to European countries or the EU, and 140 studies are outside both (many compare systems, so the number is above 311). The MSA has inspired applications in at least 65 countries and over 100 applications to subnational policymaking. This breadth of focus is also reflected in Zahariadis' (2014) 'illustrative list' of 41 texts, used by Cairney and Jones (2016, 44) to provide a more qualitative analysis of the modern insights generated by MSA studies. In it, there are national (20), subnational (13), and international (8) applications (including the EU and UN); and, while the US and Europe account for most, there are enough non-traditional applications – in countries such as China and Burkina Faso – to explore the extent to which practical lessons from the federal US extend to other countries or levels of government (see also Rawat and Morris, 2016).

Using these new studies, we can say that the insights from Tables 1 and 2 have a 'universal' quality, in which they can be applied to any time or place (Cairney and Jones, 2016, 39), but their implications can change markedly in different applications. To demonstrate, first consider key aspects of the context in which Kingdon generated his original analysis, and the new questions that arise if we shift our focus to other case studies:

- Few problems reach the top of the agenda because US federal policy can apply to almost all aspects of social and political life. What happens when some venues only consider a small number of issues?
- There are many ways to define issues, and the US 'macropolitical' level resembles an 'issue network' in which there are many actors competing to define issues (Baumgartner and Jones, 1993; Heclo, 1978). What happens in less competitive arenas where some definitions dominate debate for years or decades?
- Problems, policies, and politics are separate 'streams' partly as a function of the size of the US system and limits to key roles, such as when the President sets agendas but other actors generate solutions. What happens when key actors can become influential in more than one stream?
- The 'policy primeval soup' metaphor works for a US political system in which solutions take time to 'soften' and a piece of legislation may only gain traction when a large number of actors in a policy networks have engaged with and modified the original policy proposal. What happens when this initial process happens externally, such as in international organisations or networks or in other countries? The role of 'policy transfer' is discussed more in non-US or subnational US studies (Dolowitz and Marsh, 1996; see also Shephard et al 2020 on global and local policy entrepreneurs).
- MSA began as a study of a two-party political system with a division of powers between executive, legislative, and judicial branches. What happens in parliamentary systems in which the role of the executive and multi-party competition is more important (Herweg et al, 2015)?

Generally, outside of Kingdon's original study, there is often more scope for entrepreneurs to influence their environment or generate a wider range of strategies. Although the literature on this specific topic is patchy, and it is often difficult to compare cases (Jones et al, 2016; Cairney and Jones, 2016), key studies provide the following preliminary insights (Table 2.3).

Venue shop and frame issues to promote venue shift

MSA suggests that policy solutions only become feasible when they are acceptable to enough actors in key venues such as policymaking institutions or networks (Kingdon refers broadly to the 'policy community', but beware the potential for terminological confusion [Cairney, 2012, 179, 235]). Punctuated equilibrium theory modifies this expectation by focusing on the role of venue shopping, when actors are dissatisfied with progress in one venue and seek more sympathetic audiences elsewhere (Baumgartner and Jones, 1993, 35–7). If successful, they short-cut the

Table 2.3: Strategies for the 'politics stream' and to exploit 'windows of opportunity'

Insight	Implication for strategy
Actors dissatisfied with progress in one policymaking venue can seek more sympathetic audiences elsewhere	Engage in 'venue shopping' to encourage 'venue shift' and reduce the need to 'soften' policy solutions
Policymakers often import policy solutions from other political systems, which may reduce the need to 'soften' solutions in domestic networks	Engage in multi-level policy networks to seek opportunities to import 'pre-softened' policy solutions
Policy entrepreneurs can be more effective at a smaller scale of government	Recognise your potential role, as a surfer on the waves, or Poseidon moving them
In some systems, or during crises, the usual rules of MSA do not apply. Some MSA insights are not 'universal'	Do your homework on specific political systems, to understand the idiosyncrasies of the policy environment
The most frequent or predictable policy windows could be elections	Do not simply equate a 'window of opportunity' with unpredictable serendipity. Link problems to election debates, and seek solutions demonstrably popular with key parts of the public
Policymakers often select vague solutions to ill-defined problems during a policy window.	Do not put your faith in the policy cycle to ensure that broad intentions translate into the delivery of specific solutions

Source: adapted from Cairney and Jones (2016)

'softening' process in venues where audiences are more sympathetic to policy change (1993, 32–3; Cairney, 2013, 282).

Some modern MSA applications, particularly in the EU, use this insight to show that competition to reduce ambiguity relates simultaneously to problem definition and defining the most appropriate venue to address it (Ackrill and Kay, 2011; Sarmiento-Mirwaldt, 2013). In other words, the main definition of a policy problem can determine the venue held responsible for solving it: if tobacco is primarily a public health epidemic, rely on a health department; if it is a valuable commodity for trade and taxation, rely on trade and treasury departments (Cairney et al, 2012). However, we should be careful not to overstate the frequency and potential of such shifts, particularly if we assume that actors in each venue can be possessive about policy issues. Successful venue shift involves a level of energy not available to many actors. For example, Cairney (2006; 2007; 2009) initially described the reframing of a ban on smoking in public places – as a public health issue (a Scottish Parliament responsibility) rather than health and safety (Westminster) – as one of potentially many venue shifts, only to fail to see another example in the next 10 years.

Learn how to short-cut the softening process by importing pre-softened solutions

Non-US and subnational US studies identify the role of policy transfer and diffusion as a relatively quick way to shortcut the softening process. Policy transfer can be a response to 'bounded rationality': policymakers and influencers use external examples of successful policy innovation to set the agenda and present already-solved policy problems. Or, in some cases, federal, supranational bodies, and international organisations (or powerful countries like the US) put pressure on others to import policy solutions (Berry and Berry, 2014; Dolowitz and Marsh, 1996; Rose, 2005; Cairney, 2012, 108). Modern MSA studies identify many examples of the role of policy transfer in short-cutting the 'softening' process associated with Kingdon's original study (Bache, 2013; Bache and Reardon, 2013; Cairney, 2009; Liu et al, 2010; McLendon, 2003; Zahariadis, 2004).

Again, we should not overestimate the potential effect of policy transfer. External policymakers provide the source of new solutions, but MSA helps explain the conditions under which they would be accepted during a 'policy transfer window' (Cairney, 2012, 269–71). For example, most countries agreed to the same package of policy solutions in the WHO Framework Convention on Tobacco Control, but very few have the environments conducive to the adoption of those policy instruments during subsequent policy windows. Consequently, the implementation of imported policy solutions is highly uneven (Cairney and Yamazaki, 2017) and, in some countries, almost non-existent (Mamudu et al, 2015).

Identify the conditions under which entrepreneurs emulate Poseidon

Subnational MSA studies suggest that policy entrepreneurs can be more effective at 'a smaller and/or more local scale of government' (Cairney and Jones, 2016, 46). Henstra (2010), Oborn et al (2011), and Dudley (2013) identify examples of scales small enough for an entrepreneur to influence all three streams successfully: $100k funding for a Canadian municipal emergency management policy, healthcare reform inside London, and the London mayor as framer and audience for a road congestion charge (see also Mintrom, 2019). Robinson and Eller (2010) also find that, in Texas schools policy, the streams are not separate in the way Kingdon describes, since key actors are involved in all three. Each example raises the possibility that the coupling of streams by entrepreneurs is more straightforward in smaller and more manageable issues (even if their analytical separation began as a way to explain 'organised anarchy' in a small, single organisation (Cohen et al, 1972)).

Identify the times when the usual rules of MSA seem not to apply

Hall (1993) identifies the rare occasions in one political system (UK) in which the rules of policy softening and feasibility no longer apply: during crisis leading to paradigm change, the old ideas and their proponents are no longer relevant (albeit, Hall was not engaging with MSA (see Cairney, 2013, 283)). Zhu's (2008) MSA case study of China adds the possibility that, in some political systems with very different procedures to the US, the rules of softening may also not apply. Zhu identifies the role of technical *infeasibility*: actors can propose a politically acceptable solution that cannot be dealt with routinely by the governing bureaucracy, prompting high external and government attention, and potentially major policy change. The case study implication is so different to Kingdon's that it reminds us to question the 'universal' applicability of any practical solution generated by MSA.

Be realistic about the frequency and cause of windows of opportunity

Howlett's (1998) quantitative analysis of Canadian politics suggests that elections represent the most frequent source of a window of opportunity for policy change. He provides a way to challenge the idea of a serendipitous aligning of the stars which can happen at any moment, suggesting that planning for an election may be more sensible than for a random event. Herweg et al (2015, 437) identify more specific drivers for policymakers: to *pay attention to problems*, including when it 'puts the policy makers' re-election at risk'; and, *become receptive to solutions*, including when the solution is popular among the public and key interest groups, or when the governing political party is seen as competent in this field and has made an ideological commitment to a particular approach. Such statements remind us of the important role of party competition in salient issues (since policy studies often downplay such dynamics).

Note the difference between a window of opportunity for a broad idea or specific solution

Cairney et al (2017, 118) suggest that, in the case of 'prevention' policy in the UK, policymakers 'paid attention to an ill-defined problem and produced a solution which often proves to be too vague to operationalize in a simple way'. There was high support and enthusiasm to prompt a shift from reactive public services towards earlier intervention in people's lives, but limited discussion of the specific ways in which they would deliver well-defined solutions (Cairney and St Denny, 2020). Such experiences remind us of the absence of a policy cycle with linear and ordered stages. If a cycle existed, this initial resolution of a problem at the agenda setting stage would be followed by more detailed solution production, formulation and implementation. If not, an idea's time may come and go without any meaningful resolution, beyond this broad commitment to do something.

Conclusion

It is important to tell the MSA story well. A concise and coherent theoretical story aids metaphorical and conceptual clarity, encourages a coherent research programme, and allows all relevant audiences – from expert policy scholars to scientists and practitioners in other fields and new students – to understand and communicate its insights in similar ways.

To that end, I told the well-established story of MSA in relation to new debates on 'evidence-based policymaking'. In that context, MSA provides insights which might seem counterintuitive to actors less familiar with policy theories and still hoping for EBPM. Modern EBPM debates seem to be built on renewed hopes for comprehensive rationality and a linear policy cycle. In contrast, I describe policymaking in the real world by identifying the three strategies used by successful policy entrepreneurs.

First, *entrepreneurs tell a persuasive story to frame a policy problem*. Few problems reach the top of the agenda, and attention to problems is not dependent on the evidence of their size. Instead, policymakers face too much information, use 'rational' and 'irrational' ways to process a lot of information, and make choices in a short space of time without being fully aware of their preferences. Policymakers seek to reduce *ambiguity*, by focusing on a simple definition of a complex problem, and *uncertainty*, by gathering information relevant to that definition. Entrepreneurs focus on the beliefs of their audience more than their assessment of the evidence. They reinforce the cognitive biases of influential policymakers by combining facts with values and emotional appeals, and by framing policy solutions as consistent with dominant ways to understand problems. If you simply bombard policymakers with evidence, they will have little reason to read it. If you win the 'framing battle', policymakers will demand evidence on your problem and solution.

Second, *entrepreneurs make sure that their favoured solution is available before attention lurches to the problem*. There is no policy cycle in which policymakers identify problems, formulate solutions, and make a choice in that order. Instead, by the time policymakers pay attention to a problem it is too late to develop a technically and politically feasible solution from scratch. Solutions take time to 'soften' and become accepted within policy networks, and entrepreneurs seek opportunities to sell their solutions during heightened attention, by forming coalitions and engaging in networks to identify receptivity to policy solutions and an opportunity to act.

Third, *entrepreneurs exploit a 'window of opportunity' during which policymakers have the willingness and ability to adopt their policy solution.* The role of entrepreneurs changes at different scales and in different systems. Further, modern studies highlight a wider range of strategies for entrepreneurs seeking to influence windows of opportunity, including: 'venue shopping' to seek more sympathetic audiences, encourage 'venue shift', and reduce the need to 'soften' policy solutions; engaging in multi-level policy networks to seek opportunities to import 'pre-softened' policy solutions; adapting to the idiosyncrasies of the policy environments in different political systems; as well as the more obvious value of linking problems to election debates and seeking solutions demonstrably popular with key parts of the public.

This story may seem familiar to people who have read Kingdon (1984), but MSA has come a long way since his foundational text was published. We need to incorporate three decades of empirical application and conceptual refinement into a coherent modern MSA story and, while doing so, make sure that the meaning of its attractive metaphor remains clear. Only then can policy scholars be sure that their empirical applications of MSA form part of a far larger narrative of the policy process.

Acknowledgement

To Benj Pasek and Justin Paul.

Note

1 The article which this chapter is based on is available via Open Access here: https://doi.org/10.1332/030557318X15230056771696

References

Ackrill, R, Kay, A, 2011, Multiple streams in EU policy-making: The case of the 2005 sugar reform, *Journal of European Public Policy* 18: 72–89

Avery, G, 2004, Bioterrorism, fear, and public health reform: Matching a policy solution to the wrong window, *Public Administration Review* 64: 274–288

Bache, I, 2013, Measuring quality of life for public policy: An idea whose time has come? Agenda-setting dynamics in the European Union, *Journal of European Public Policy* 20, 21–38

Bache, I, Reardon, L, 2013, An idea whose time has come? Explaining the rise of well-being in British politics, *Political Studies* 61, 4, 898–914

Bakir, C, Jarvis, DSL, 2017, Contextualising the context in policy entrepreneurship and institutional change, *Policy and Society*, 36, 4, 465–78

Baumgartner, F, Jones, B, 1993, *Agendas and instability in American politics*, Chicago, IL: Chicago University Press, 2009

Beeson, M, Stone, D, 2013, The changing fortunes of a policy entrepreneur: The case of Ross Garnaut, *Australian Journal of Political Science* 48, 1, 1–14

Berry, F, Berry, W, 2014, Innovation and diffusion models in policy research, in P Sabatier, C Weible (eds) *Theories of the policy process* (3rd edn), Chicago, IL:Westview Press

Birkland, T, 1997, *After disaster: Agenda setting, public policy, and focusing events*, Washington, DC: Georgetown University Press

Boswell, C, Smith, K, 2017, Rethinking policy 'impact': Four models of research–policy relations, *Palgrave Communications* 3, 44, 1–10, doi:10.1057/s41599-017-0042-z

Cairney, P, 2006, Venue shift following devolution: When reserved meets devolved in Scotland, *Regional and Federal Studies* 16, 4, 429–445

Cairney, P, 2007, Using devolution to set the agenda? Venue shift and the smoking ban in Scotland, *British Journal of Politics and International Relations* 9,1, 73–89

Cairney, P, 2009, The role of ideas in policy transfer: The case of UK smoking bans since devolution, *Journal of European Public Policy* 16: 471–488

Cairney, P, 2012, *Understanding public policy*, Basingstoke: Palgrave

Cairney, P, 2013, What is evolutionary theory and how does it inform policy studies?, *Policy and Politics* 41, 2, 279–298

Cairney, P, 2016, *The politics of evidence-based policy making*, London: Palgrave Springer

Cairney, P, Jones, M, 2016, Kingdon's multiple streams approach: What is the empirical impact of this universal theory?, *Policy Studies Journal* 44, 1, 37–58

Cairney, P, Kwiatkowski, R, 2017, How to communicate effectively with policymakers: Combine insights from psychology and policy studies, *Palgrave Communications* 3, 37, doi:10.1057/s41599-017-0046-8

Cairney, P, Oliver, K, 2017, Evidence-based policymaking is not like evidence-based medicine, so how far should you go to bridge the divide between evidence and policy?, *Health Research Policy and Systems* 15, 35, https://doi.org/10.1186/s12961-017-0192-x

Cairney, P, St Denny, E, 2020, *Why isn't government policy more preventive?* Oxford: Oxford University Press

Cairney, P, Weible, C, 2017,The new policy sciences, *Policy Sciences* 50, 4, 619–627
Cairney, P, Yamazaki, M, 2017, A comparison of tobacco policy in the UK and Japan: If the scientific evidence is identical, why is there a major difference in policy?, *Journal of Comparative Policy Analysis*, https://doi.org/10.1080/13876988.2017.1323439
Cairney, P, Zahariadis, N, 2016, Multiple streams analysis: A flexible metaphor presents an opportunity to operationalize agenda setting processes, in N Zahariadis (ed) *Handbook of public policy agenda-setting*, Cheltenham: Edward Elgar
Cairney, P, Studlar, D, Mamudu, H, 2012, *Global tobacco control: Power, policy, governance and transfer*, Basingstoke: Palgrave
Cairney, P, Oliver, K, Wellstead, A, 2016, To bridge the divide between evidence and policy: Reduce ambiguity as much as uncertainty, *Public Administration Review* 76, 3, 399–402, doi:10.1111/puar.12555
Cairney, P, Harvey, M, St Denny, E, 2017, Constitutional change, social investment and prevention policy in Scotland, in M Keating (ed) *A wealthier, fairer Scotland*, Edinburgh: Edinburgh University Press
Christopoulos, D, Ingold, K, 2015, Exceptional or just well connected? Political entrepreneurs and brokers in policy making, *European Political Science Review* 7, 475–498
Cohen, M, March, J, Olsen, J, 1972, A garbage can model of organizational choice, *Administrative Science Quarterly* 17, 1, 1–25
Dearing, JW, Rogers, EM, 1996, *Agenda setting*, London: Sage
Dolowitz, D, Marsh, D, 1996, Who learns what from whom: A review of the policy transfer literature, *Political Studies* 44, 343–357
Douglas, H, 2009, *Science, policy, and the value-free ideal*, Pittsburgh, PA: University of Pittsburgh Press
Dudley, G, 2013, Why do ideas succeed and fail over time? The role of narratives in policy windows and the case of the London congestion charge, *Journal of European Public Policy* 20, 1139–1156
Haidt, J, 2001, The emotional dog and its rational tail: A social intuitionist approach to moral judgment, *Psychological Review* 108, 4, 814–834
Hall, P, 1993, Policy paradigms, social learning, and the state: The case of economic policymaking in Britain, *Comparative Politics* 25, 2, 275–296
Heclo, H, 1978, Issue networks and the executive establishment, in A King (ed) *The new American political system*, Washington, DC: American Enterprise Institute
Heikkila, T, Cairney, P, 2017, A comparison of theories of the policy process, in C Weible (ed) *Theories of the policy process* (4th edn), Chicago, IL: Westview Press

Henstra, D, 2010, Explaining local policy choices: A multiple streams analysis of municipal emergency management, *Canadian Public Administration* 53, 2, 241–258

Herweg, N, Huß, C, Zohlnhöfer, R, 2015, Straightening the three streams: Theorising extensions of the multiple streams framework, *European Journal of Political Research* 54, 3, 435–449

Herweg, N, Zahariadis, N, Zohlnhöfer, R, 2017, The multiple streams framework: Foundations, refinements, and empirical applications, in C Weible, P Sabatier (eds) *Theories of the policy process* (4th edn), Chicago, IL: Westview Press

Hogwood, B, 1987, *From crisis to complacency*, Oxford: Oxford University Press

Howie, WO, 2009, Mandatory reporting of medical errors: Crafting policy and integrating it into practice, *Journal for Nurse Practitioners* 5, 9, 649–654

Howlett, M, 1998, Predictable and unpredictable policy windows: Institutional and exogenous correlates of Canadian federal agenda setting, *Canadian Journal of Political Science* 31: 495–524

John, P, 1999, Ideas and interests. Agendas and implementation: An evolutionary explanation of policy change in British local government finance, *British Journal of Politics and International Relations* 1, 1, 39–62

Jones, B, 1994, *Reconceiving decision-making in democratic politics: Attention, choice and public policy*, Chicago, IL: Chicago University Press

Jones, B, Baumgartner, F, 2005, *The politics of attention*, Chicago, IL: University of Chicago Press

Jones, MD, Peterson, HL, Pierce, JJ, Herweg, N, Bernal, A, Raney, HL, Zahariadis, N, 2016, A river runs through it: A multiple streams meta-review, *Policy Studies Journal* 44, 1, 13–36

Kahneman, D, 2012, *Thinking fast and slow*, London: Penguin

Kingdon, J, 1984, *Agendas, alternatives and public policies*, New York: Harper Collins, 1995

Knaggård, A, 2015, The multiple streams framework and the problem broker, *European Journal of Political Research* 54, 3, 450–465

Laffan, B, 1997, From policy entrepreneur to policy manager: The challenge facing the European Commission, *Journal of European Public Policy* 4, 3, 422–438

Lewis, P, 2013, Policy thinking, fast and slow: A social intuitionist perspective on public policy processes, *American Political Science Association 2013 Annual Meeting*, http://ssrn.com/abstract=2300479

Lindblom, C, 1959, The science of muddling through, *Public Administration Review* 19, 79–88

Liu, X, Lindquist, E, Vedlitz, A, Vincent, K, 2010, Understanding local policymaking: Policy elites' perceptions of local agenda setting and alternative policy selection, *Policy Studies Journal* 38, 1, 69–91

Lodge, M, Wegrich, K, 2016, The rationality paradox of nudge: Rational tools of government in a world of bounded rationality, *Law & Policy* 38, 3, 250–267

McBeth, M, Jones, M, Shanahan, E, 2014, The narrative policy framework, in P Sabatier, C Weible (eds) *Theories of the policy process* (3rd edn), Chicago, IL: Westview Press

McLendon, MK, 2003, Setting the governmental agenda for state decentralization of higher education, *Journal of Higher Education* 74, 479–516

Majone, G, 1989, *Evidence, argument and persuasion in the policy process*, New Haven, CT: Yale University Press

Mamudu, H, Cairney, P, Studlar, D, 2015, Global public policy: Does the new venue for transnational tobacco control challenge the old way of doing things?, *Public Administration* 93, 4, 856–873

Mintrom, M, 2019, *Policy entrepreneurs and dynamic change*, Cambridge: Cambridge University Press

Mintrom, M, Norman, P, 2009, Policy entrepreneurship and policy change, *Policy Studies Journal* 37, 4, 649–667

Mintrom, M, Vergari, S, 1996, Advocacy coalitions, policy entrepreneurs and policy change, *Policy Studies Journal* 24, 3, 420–434

Nutley, S, Walter, I, Davies, H, 2007, *Using evidence: How research can inform public services*, Bristol: The Policy Press

Oborn, E, Barrett, M, Exworthy, M, 2011, Policy entrepreneurship in the development of public sector strategy: The case of London health reform, *Public Administration* 89, 2, 325–344

Oliver, K, Innvar, S, Lorenc, T, Woodman, J, Thomas, J, 2014a, A systematic review of barriers to and facilitators of the use of evidence by policymakers, *BMC health services research* 14, 1, 2, www.biomedcentral.com/1472–6963/14/2

Oliver, K, Lorenc, T, Innvær, S, 2014b, New directions in evidence-based policy research: A critical analysis of the literature, *Health Research Policy and Systems* 12, 34, www.biomedcentral.com/content/pdf/1478-4505-12-34.pdf

Parkhurst, J, 2017, *The politics of evidence: From evidence based policy to the good governance of evidence*, London: Routledge

Pralle, SB, 2009, Agenda-setting and climate change, *Environmental Politics* 18, 5, 781–799

Rawat, P, Morris, J, 2016, Kingdon's 'streams' model at thirty: Still relevant in the 21st century?, *Politics and Policy* 44, 4, 608–638

Roberts, N, King, P, 1991, Policy entrepreneurs: Their activity structure and function in the policy process, *Journal of Public Administration Research and Theory* 1, 2, 147–175

Robinson, SE, Eller, WS, 2010, Testing the separation of problems and solutions in subnational policy systems, *Policy Studies Journal* 38, 2, 199–216

Rochefort, DA, Cobb, RW, 1994, Problem definition: An emerging perspective, in DA Rochefort, RW Cobb (eds) *The politics of problem definition*, Kansas City, KS: University Press of Kansas

Rose, R, 2005, *Learning from comparative public policy: A practical guide*, London: Routledge

Sabatier, P, Hunter, S, McLaughlin, S, 1987, The devil shift: Perceptions and misperceptions of opponents, *The Western Political Quarterly* 40, 3, 449–476

Sarmiento-Mirwaldt, K, 2013, Can multiple streams predict the territorial cohesion debate in the EU?, *European Urban and Regional Studies*, doi: 10.1177/0969776413481984

Schneider, A, Ingram, H, 1993, Social construction of target populations: Implications for politics and policy, *American Political Science Review* 87, 2, 334–347

Schneider, A, Ingram, H, 1997, *Policy design for democracy*, Lawrence, KS: University of Kansas Press

Schneider, A, Ingram, H (eds), 2005, *Deserving and entitled: Social construction and public policy*, Albany, NY: State University of New York Press

Shephard, DD, Ellersiek, A, Meuer, J, Rupietta, C, Mayne, R Cairney, P, 2020, Kingdon's multiple streams approach in new political contexts: Consolidation, configuration, and new findings,. *Governance* (Early View) https://doi.org/10.1111/gove.12521

Simon, H, 1976, *Administrative behavior* (3rd edn), London: MacMillan

Smith, K, 2013, *Beyond evidence based policy in public health: The interplay of ideas*, Basingstoke: Palgrave Macmillan

Stone, D, 1989, Causal stories and the formation of policy agendas, *Political Science Quarterly* 104: 281–300

Stone, D, 2002, *Policy paradox: The art of political decision making* (revised edn), London: Norton

True, JL, Jones, BD, Baumgartner, FR, 2007, Punctuated equilibrium theory, in P Sabatier (ed) *Theories of the policy process* (2nd edn), Cambridge MA: Westview Press

Weible, CM, Cairney, P, 2018, Practical lessons from policy theories, *Policy & Politics*, vol 46, no 2, 183–97

Zahariadis, N, 2004, European markets and national regulation: Conflict and cooperation in British competition policy, *Journal of Public Policy* 24, 1, 49–73

Zahariadis, N, 2007, The multiple streams framework, in P Sabatier (ed) *Theories of the policy process*, Cambridge, MA: Westview Press

Zahariadis, N, 2014, Ambiguity and multiple streams, in P Sabatier, C Weible (eds) *Theories of the policy process* (3rd edn), Chicago, IL: Westview Press

Zhu, X, 2008, Strategy of Chinese policy entrepreneurs in the third sector: Challenges of 'technical infeasibility', *Policy Sciences* 41, 315–334

CHAPTER THREE

Narratives as tools for influencing policy change[1]

Deserai Crow and Michael Jones

Introduction

There is plenty of science, philosophy, and literature pointing to the importance of narrative in human affairs. One way to understand the findings and arguments presented is that people, by nature, are inclined to impose meaning on the world and that when they do, they rely on information shortcuts (heuristics) to develop quick and easy emotional renderings of the world that fit with who they think they are and what they know. People's preferred way of meaning-making is through story (see Jones et al, 2014b). The essence of these interdisciplinary findings is captured by Hardy:

> For we dream in narrative, daydream in narrative, remember, anticipate, hope, despair, believe, doubt, plan, revise, criticise, construct, gossip, learn, hate and love by narrative. In order to really live, we make up stories about ourselves and others, about the personal as well as the social past and future. (1968, 5)

If this is true of individuals, it should not be surprising that narrative also matters in public policy. Public policy is navigated by a system of actors who are vying for their preferred policy goals. Within this system, policy actors wield narratives to help achieve their goals, communicate problems and solutions, and citizens use them to communicate their preferences to policy elites, among other uses. However, much of this storytelling is governed by intuition, anecdote, and ad hoc theorising, which is not to malign policy actors – there is little else to go on. Here we try to improve the intuitive ad hoc nature of policy narration by drawing upon extant narrative research in public policy to offer theoretically based and useful storytelling advice. The advice is intended for scholars who may teach or conduct research about policy processes, but who may not be familiar with recent innovations in policy scholarship focused on the role of narrative in policy processes or potential applications of these theoretical innovations for their students. The advice may also be relevant for practitioners who seek to influence policy, and for whom applied lessons from theoretical knowledge can help improve practice.

Our contributions here are twofold: first, we use a recent theoretical innovation in policy scholarship – the Narrative Policy Framework – to build a guide for applied understanding of theory. Second, in service to our general aim, we outline two key pitfalls that can lead to ineffective policy communication. The first, the knowledge fallacy, is likely to be familiar to many readers versed in the science communication literature. The second, which we entitle the empathy fallacy, is, to our understanding, novel and has not before been identified within policy narrative research. Finally, we bridge narrative policy theory with specific intervention points in the policy process, providing illustrations along the way.

Policy narrative pitfalls

A good place to begin grappling with effective narrative communication in public policy is to identify general orthodoxies often associated with policy communication. In this section we detail two common fallacious approaches to policy communication, only the first of which is acknowledged in social science scholarship: (1) the knowledge fallacy and (2) the empathy fallacy. We argue that these approaches to communication all too often fail to meet communicator expectations and should be avoided and should also be incorporated into our scholarly understanding of types of communication failures.

The knowledge fallacy

There can be little doubt that most western democracies are products of the Enlightenment (Rakove, 1997, 18) – a philosophical orientation that built a hopeful, agential, and progressing model of the individual founded upon the ideas that there are inalienable truths and that reason and science light the way to these truths. Behind all of this is a simple idea: there is truth in the world.

A contemporary manifestation of this seventeenth century Enlightenment notion is found in what has been termed the knowledge deficit approach (for example, Kellstedt et al, 2008). The central ideas of this approach are that policy is complex and ambiguous, people do not understand policy in the way that experts do, and that individuals need to be educated on the relevant facts. Once educated, people will then 'reasonably' accept the position of the expert(s). A host of studies across many policy areas have assessed the knowledge gap between experts and lay people (for example, Sterman, 2008; Qin and Brown, 2006) that the knowledge deficit approach aims to rectify.

The failures of the knowledge deficit approach are most likely derivative of the assumptions it makes about how people think and reason. Kahneman (2011) describes two modes of human cognition: system 1, where people's unconscious thought process is driven by quickly determined emotional assessments of incoming stimuli without much thought; and, system 2, where people think carefully – some might say rationally – through their decisions. Not surprisingly, when communicating science or policy expert information, scientists and experts are communicating using and assuming system 2. People, however, are usually receiving the information emotionally, in system 1. The differences, then, between experts and laypeople may erect barriers if experts are using types of logic and communication aimed at influencing individuals using system 2 thinking.

Kahan (2014) sheds light on the dichotomy of emotion-driven versus logic-driven thinking, arguing that common assumptions about the link between knowledge and evidence-based decisions are simply wrong. He describes what he calls the 'motivated reasoning hypothesis' wherein people make decisions based upon cultural beliefs rather than evidence or knowledge. Knowledge, then, has to be processed by people, who come to that knowledge carrying considerable baggage in terms of how they understand the world, and they are hardwired to protect that baggage.

The empathy fallacy

Suffering from what one might call an 'Enlightenment hangover', the knowledge deficit approach is, in our estimation, the dominant communication model of policy actors. A popular but less pervasive alternative to this approach is probably best articulated by a community of researchers in policy studies loosely characterised as interpretivists (see Yanow, 2007). Interpretivists presume to not believe in any authoritative objective truths; for this community, there are multiple truths, as we all understand the world individually. Narrative is frequently a centrepiece of their approach (for example, Fischer, 2003).

The interpretive approach to narrative in policymaking has had its successes (see for example the success of using personal stories of sex workers in South Africa and marginalised individuals from the LGBTQ community in the US and other countries to elevate marginalised groups on government agendas and, in some cases, policy changes were observable (Open Society, 2016)). When stories are rendered as understood by people affected, context specific policy outcomes are attainable. However, the often-unstated assumption of this approach is that audiences influenced by authentic stories have a common sense of empathy that is emotionally appealed to by an authentic narrative. That is, if the narrator can just project to the audience an emotive human story through narrative, the audience will be persuaded by our universal human empathy. This is a seductive approach because there can be little doubt that generating empathy matters. However, empathy appeals, like knowledge appeals, are filtered through people's biases and this means that how people respond to the appeals is hardly universal.

The lesson of these two fallacies for policy communicators is found in a common underlying characteristic of both. While the knowledge fallacy relies upon the veracity of 'objective' facts and relationships, and the empathy fallacy relies on 'authentic' emotion to communicate policy consequential information, both approaches share commitments to the assumption that a message can be unassailably true independent of all else. It is this commonality among the two approaches that we label as fallacious because they can produce ineffective communication.

The Narrative Policy Framework

Policy actors need a mechanism by which they can narrate in a way that accounts for their own biases, the audience's biases, and the structure of the story itself. The mechanism to understand good storytelling has most recently been assessed using an approach titled the Narrative Policy Framework (NPF). The goal of the NPF is to examine characteristics of narratives, their influence, and other policy-relevant attributes. In many ways the NPF is derivative of previously described interpretivist approaches (Smith and Larimer, 2016), openly embracing interpretivism within research (for example, Gray and Jones, 2016; Jones and Radaelli, 2015) while simultaneously examining the use of science and evidence in strategically constructed narratives used by policy advocates (for example, Smith-Walter et al, 2016). However, the major difference between the NPF and interpretive narrative approaches is in the NPF's focus on scientific method and empirical observation to unearth generalisable findings. Since people do universally narrate, the NPF begins from the premise that understanding narrative is the best way to understand meaning-making within the policy process.

The NPF begins by dividing narratives into the two categories of content and form. The content of a policy narrative refers to the highly variable ideas and concepts within a narrative, which is specific to a policy area. Climate change narratives are about climate change. Campaign finance narratives are about campaign finance. Form, on the other hand, refers to the structure of narrative and is generalisable across narratives, regardless of content. The NPF identifies four major narrative form elements (Jones et al, 2014a):

1. *Setting* The setting consists of policy consequential features such as geography, laws, evidence and other facets of the policy subsystem. Many parts of the settings appear fixed (such as the US Constitution); others are highly contested (for example, the science on LGBT parenting).
2. *Characters* Characters are typically defined as victims who are harmed or potentially so, villains who are responsible for the harm or threat, and heroes who promise relief for the victim.
3. *Plot* Plots are organising devices that link characters to each other via motive and relationships and situate the story and its occupants in time and space.
4. *Moral of the story* This is the point of the story, usually manifesting as a policy solution or a call to action.

One of the most consistent NPF findings is that whether or not a narrative is congruent with an individual's values or beliefs matters in terms of how the narrative influences the recipient's interpretation of the narrative. What we mean is that if a person is, for example, conservative and they encounter a narrative that has content that they recognise as conservative, it is generally more favourably received. Congruent narratives are found to strengthen policy beliefs (for example, Shanahan et al, 2014), increase the likelihood of accepting new policies (for example, McBeth et al, 2014), favourably structure how people recall policy consequential information (Jones and Song, 2014), and lead to increased empathy (Niederdeppe et al, 2015). While we introduce and discuss other relevant NPF and narrative findings in what follows, congruence is a major theme that runs throughout the remainder of our discussion of good storytelling in public policy.

Good storytelling in public policy: understanding it and constructing it

In the previous sections, we have spelled out two potential policy communication fallacies and summarised relevant findings from a recently developed approach to studying narrative in public policy. Similarly structured to Peterson and Jones' (2016) advice for climate change policy narrators, here we summarise some of the insights from the previous sections as well as conclusions from other relevant literatures into steps policy actors should consider prior to crafting their policy narratives. While we present the following as steps, in practice the process tends to be nonlinear. Policy actors should expect to move back and forth between the steps as they build their narrative. Before building a narrative, the narrator must first establish her goals, her audience, and her purpose for constructing the narrative. Scholars can use these steps to better understand how narratives are constructed, the component parts of such narratives, and the intervention points where narratives might be observed and therefore studied. The construction of narratives is discussed below from the perspective of how a communicator would wisely construct a narrative. It should be stated, however, that communicators include policy actors as well as scholars. Similarly, scholars should understand the process by which a communicator constructs a narrative in order to best analyse those narratives.

Step 1: Tell a story

Foremost is the need for the policy actor to recognise that they are telling a story. It might be a boring fact-filled objectively neutral story devoid of emotion or a hyperbolic emotional polemic that ignores facts and evidence, but it is still a story – just probably a bad one. The goal then for any communicator is to tell a good story.

Step 2: Set the stage

Determine the staging materials

This starts with a deep reading of the academic and advocacy literature available for a policy area, supplemented by talking to people and conducting independent research (circumstances permitting). Without understanding the facts, the emotions, and the strategies used to influence policy, even the most knowledgeable expert will be at a loss for the tools of effective communication. A primary goal in this step is to identify the motivating beliefs or values of the audience as they relate to the issue. Ideology is often easily observed to play a role in many policy areas, but a literature review may point to more refined beliefs such as cultural types (Thompson et al, 1990) or environmental beliefs (Dunlap et al, 2000), which may do a far better job of getting at what people actually believe. Additionally, it is important for communicators to do a bit of introspection about their own beliefs. Know the boundaries in belief systems held by stakeholders. Know the audience. Since a good story is the goal, it is necessary to select content that is both favourably received by the audience and true to stakeholder values.

Arrange the props on the stage

The next step is to select the most important information– from the vast array collected above – to include in the story. Note what is commonly referenced: evidence, legal parameters, geography, and so on. Examine these props carefully in light of the intended audience's beliefs and values. Some of these props will inspire negative emotions and some will inspire positive emotions. Both types of emotions can help your cause, but the evidence suggests positive emotions are more beneficial (for example, Pidgeon and Fischhoff, 2011). The trick in setting the stage is to faithfully narrate the best assessments of the empirical reality of the policy environment – leveraging science, evidence, and best practices – but doing so in a way that inspires people to feel something about the policy narrative, while simultaneously avoiding the pitfalls of knowledge and empathy fallacies.

Step 3: Establish the plot

Public policies always exist because of a problem. Plots include this definition either as a starting point or to help tell the evolution of a problem (for example, Stone, 2011). The problem definition establishes real or potential harm. It sets up the cause of the harm. Establishing the cause necessarily points to what can be done. If poverty is the cause of crime, then reducing or eliminating poverty is the solution; if individually bad choices cause crime, then a solution will focus on the decisions of individuals, perhaps by restructuring incentives. In establishing causality, the plot must also link characters to the setting, noting what elements of the setting are important and the ends to which they are employed. We discuss problem definition in more detail below.

Step 4: Cast the characters

The literature on policy narratives can offer guidance on casting characters. The problem definition has already established the relationship between the setting and characters. The point now is to illustrate those roles to maximum effect. Victims should be sympathetic and the narrator should portray singular human beings where possible and appropriate, only using abstract statistics as supporting evidence for the plight of the victim (Small et al, 2007). Protagonists have been consistently found to play a driving role in policy narratives. The more a hero is liked, the more agreement with the narrative (Jones, 2014) and emphasising heroic action (for example, the solution) and ignoring or downplaying the opposition also appears to be a winning strategy (Shanahan et al, 2013). The NPF has identified a complicated role for villains as sometimes their effect is inconsistent (for example, Jones, 2014), other times divisive (McBeth et al, 2017), and their role has been shown to be a moderating one, where they exercise indirect effects on opinions (Zanocco, Song, and Jones, 2017). In any case, there can be little doubt that villains are important as they establish the nature of the blame in a problem definition, even if their potential effects must be understood in a nuanced fashion in terms of the specific context.

Step 5: Clearly specify the moral of the story

While stories with no point might be interesting to avant-garde cinema critics, we counsel against such an approach with policy narratives as they are best kept as straightforward as possible. Whether the policy narrative culminates in a call to action or a specific policy solution, the point of the story should be clear.

Public policy narrative intervention points

Above, we outlined the importance of narratives. With this as our foundation, we can make a number of statements about the importance of narratives to human communication and to policy. Next, we present several lessons that practitioners can employ in their work within policy-relevant organisations and debates and that scholars can employ to analyse strategically constructed narratives used to influence policy debates. We tackle this section through the lenses of the above steps, the type of actor who is constructing the narrative, and the type of narrative intervention they might use to influence the policy process. It is important to note here that using narrative to communicate, and perhaps influence policy outcomes, is not necessarily an act of political advocacy, nor should the use of narrative be seen as an ethical pitfall for experts. Just as a journalist is trained to tell a compelling story so that an audience's attention is captured and held so that facts of a story can be relayed to a reader or viewer (Keller and Hawkins, 2009), so too do scientists or policy experts need to capture attention and communicate both the importance and complexity of issues to their audiences (Krulwich, 2008). A communicator, especially a communicator of complex issues or facts, must make the audience care and pay attention before the audience is primed to accept the more complicated facts that might follow. Narrative can help communicators do these things, but they also, of course, can be strategically deployed by advocates.

Policymakers and policy advocates

Elected officials, public administrators, and professionals who work within the advocacy sector all share goals related to promoting what they believe are 'good' policies to achieve solutions to specific societal problems. Depending on their role and sector, they may use different strategies to achieve their goals, but each of these categories of actors works largely within a set of formal and informal institutions (Birkland, 2014), including legislatures, executive agencies, courts, and the public sphere. The narrative strategy used by these policy actors will differ depending on the audience and their goals. These actors are the focus of most of the attention of policy scholars who attempt to understand the resources and strategies used to influence policy (Baumgartner and Jones, 1993; Ostrom, 1990; Sabatier and Jenkins-Smith, 1993), but there are two additional categories of policy actors worth exploring here.

Policy experts

Policy experts include actors such as scientists, policy analysts, economists, and others who work to understand the problems that society faces, potential solutions to those problems, and trade-offs made in the policy decision process. These actors work most often within formal institutions such as legislatures and executive agencies, but may also contribute more on the periphery, such as serving as a consultant or informal adviser to decision makers. Their role is to help understand the problems that society faces, the causes of those problems, and the potential solutions to such problems (Kingdon, 2003). As such, these actors play influential roles shaping public policy and are almost always restrained by having the expectation of adhering to scientific and professional standards. Thus, these actors are likely to shy away from overly rhetorical approaches to communication (see Krulwich, 2008). They are also the policy actors most prone to the knowledge fallacy.

Citizens and voters

Citizens are the hardest to pin down in terms of their policy goals. Most are driven by culture, beliefs, or personal experiences that they bring to bear on policy considerations. Citizens can serve as voters in the political process, but also are often viewed by other policy actors as latent resources that can be tapped to pressure policymakers and others through protest, public opinion, or similar pressure tactics (Zaller, 2003: Zaller, 1992).

These individuals often possess lower levels of expertise and therefore may be prone to the empathy fallacy.

Public policy intervention points explored

We next specify several policy intervention points where narrative is likely to play a prominent role, drawing from a commonly used teaching framework to integrate narratives with policy practitioner intervention points (Smith, 2005). For each intervention, we describe how a narrator could benefit from the insights offered by the NPF to tell good stories. All of these interventions require the narrator to acknowledge steps 1 and 2 above – recognise that you are telling a story, and to set the stage by understanding the audience's beliefs and your own in order to best navigate any divergence between those sets of beliefs. Beyond these points, each of the interventions below discusses where the intervention fits into the typology introduced above (casting characters, plot, and so on). The rules that govern each intervention are important to consider, as each has different lengths, professional or evidence inclusion norms, and similar constraints. A Twitter post will inherently be different from a policy analysis or witness testimony but perhaps can be a useful policy narrative medium as well (Merry, 2016). Despite these constraints, within the various contexts more or less effective narratives can be constructed by paying attention to the steps outlined above. While the examples below are drawn from a number of different American media, storytelling according to the guidance outlined here is certainly not constrained by nationality – humans are storytellers and examples will be found in any policy context.

Problem definition

How we understand and label societal problems is central to the policies we select (or fail to select) to solve them. Kingdon (2003), Stone (2011), and other scholars have long focused on the power of defining policy problems as central to policy outcomes. When policy advocates or experts successfully define a problem in a compelling and accurate manner, the problem can take on increased salience and increased policy attention, leading to a higher likelihood of action to solve the problem (Baumgartner and Jones, 1993). Part of defining a problem includes assigning blame or causality for the problem (Stone, 2011). *How* the problem is defined, then, is essential to understanding the policies leveraged to solve it. *Who* is to blame for the problem is a role played by one or more characters cast in the narrative.

Defining a problem in order to persuade policy actors, the public, and others to solve said problem can draw on multiple aspects of what we know from narrative research. If, for example, the problem of climate change is defined primarily according to a national security message associated with refugee populations, then we are likely to see solutions offered that tend more towards military solutions or humanitarian aid abroad as the following example suggests:

> Starting in 2006, Syria suffered its worst drought in 900 years; it ruined farms, forced as many as 1.5 million rural denizens to crowd into cities alongside Iraqi refugees and decimated the country's livestock. Water became scarce and food expensive. The suffering and social chaos caused by the drought were important drivers of the initial unrest. Climate scientists have argued that global warming very likely exacerbated the historic drought, thanks to potentially permanent changes to wind and rainfall patterns.
>
> But climate change will impact more than access to water. The Pentagon recognizes global warming as a significant strategic threat, saying that it could cause 'instability in other countries by impairing access to food and water, damaging infrastructure, spreading disease, uprooting and displacing large numbers of people, compelling mass migration…' the US military fears such disruptions could 'create an avenue for extremist ideologies and conditions that foster terrorism'. (Mansharamani, 2016)

This example uses empathy to create a vivid story, and effectively ties climate change to displaced populations, international instability, and terrorism. It then uses that empathetic narrative to transport the audience, opening them up to receive evidence from scientists and military experts about the consequences of climate change for global security. On the other hand, if we define the problem of climate change as being about potential economic impacts and gains, as US President Obama did in his 2016 State of the Union address, we may see solutions aimed at encouraging renewable energy development and green jobs programmes.

> Look, if anybody still wants to dispute the science around climate change, have at it. You'll be pretty lonely, because you'll be debating our military, most of America's business leaders, the majority of the American people, almost the entire scientific community, and 200 nations around the world who

> agree it's a problem and intend to solve it. But even if the planet wasn't at stake; even if 2014 wasn't the warmest year on record – until 2015 turned out even hotter – why would we want to pass up the chance for American businesses to produce and sell the energy of the future? Seven years ago, we made the single biggest investment in clean energy in our history. Here are the results. In fields from Iowa to Texas, wind power is now cheaper than dirtier, conventional power. On rooftops from Arizona to New York, solar is saving Americans tens of millions of dollars a year on their energy bills, and employs more Americans than coal – in jobs that pay better than average. (Obama, 2016a)

Both of these definitions of the climate change problem are true in the sense that they are supported by ample scientific evidence. The first narrative of climate change does not include blame for the underlying problem of climate change. We are introduced to victims of climate change, however. The second example narrated by President Obama introduces heroes in his narrative including businesses, politicians, and implicitly his administration. President Obama also implies that climate deniers are the villains of the narrative and that climate change is an opportunity for economic progress. The second narrative is also tied to more specific policy prescriptions while the first is more about consequences of a changing climate.

Public policies

Closely related to – and drawing upon – the problem definition discussed above, the actual wording and codifying of public policies is considered an intervention point where narratives can play an important role. Public policies translate ideas, values, and rules into law. These policies, however, also draw upon emotive stories of problems as well as evidence that indicates a solution is warranted. The audience (Step 2) for public policies is often the general public writ large, but specific constituencies can be appealed to directly through the writing of effective policies in narrative form. By using condensation symbols, lawmakers frequently appeal to lofty values while speaking to specific groups in the rules or laws passed. Public policies always include a plot (problem – Step 3) and a moral or solution (Step 5), but constructing these components effectively can help the policy appeal to specific groups or to broad publics.

For example, the US Endangered Species Act (ESA) of 1973 beautifully states a clear problem, cause, and solution:

The Congress finds and declares that –

(1) various species of fish, wildlife, and plants in the United States have been rendered extinct as a consequence of economic growth and development untempered by adequate concern and conservation;
(2) other species of fish, wildlife, and plants have been so depleted in numbers that they are in danger of or threatened with extinction;
(3) these species of fish, wildlife, and plants are of esthetic, ecological, educational, historical, recreational, and scientific value to the Nation and its people;
(4) the United States has pledged itself as a sovereign state in the international community to conserve to the extent practicable the various species of fish or wildlife and plants facing extinction.[2]

The ESA is a strict command-and-control approach to environmental protection and includes penalties for non-compliance. In this way, the narrative about the importance of environmental protection is a persuasive segue to a stringent moral of the story – the regulatory solution. This example illustrates how public policies themselves are codified narratives that bring values, problems, causes, and morals (solutions) together.

Media outreach and construction

The less formal, but perhaps more widely influential venues such as media or social media are vitally important for constructing narratives, particularly among those constituents considered part of the support base. Policymakers, advocates, and experts often interact with the press, but in differing ways. Policymakers and advocates are likely to view media outreach and communication as a mechanism for advancing their political goals. For experts, on the other hand, the onus is to communicate scientific or technical 'facts' in clear, accurate, and compelling ways so that laypeople understand and care.

Media outreach can take the form of providing interviews to journalists, issuing press releases, holding events to capture press attention, or engaging in social media activity to directly communicate with supporters without mediation of journalists or other gatekeepers. Of particular importance is Step 2 of the NPF typology wherein the narrator seeks to understand the audience, as well as Step 4 which includes assigning blame or causality. This is often aided by casting effective characters (Step 3) as heroes, villains, or victims. Because the characters can be particularly polarising in some political scenarios, knowing the audience and casting appropriate

Figure 3.1: American Health Care Act Twitter Narratives

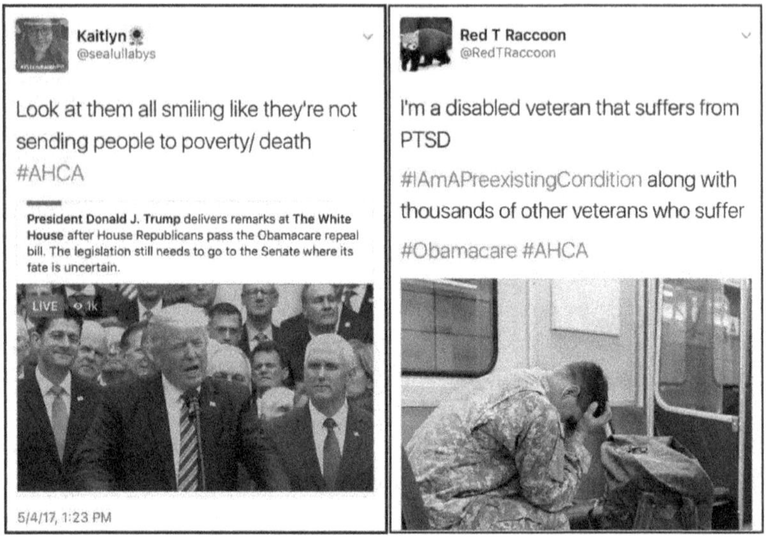

characters who align with what the audience already knows about the characters is important for creating an effective narrative.

In both traditional and social media, the construction of narratives requires clarity, simplicity, and consistency. The two images in Figure 3.1 were posted on Twitter on 5 May 2017 and reference the American Health Care Act (AHCA) vote in the US House of Representatives that took place on 4 May 2017. Both Twitter users are telling stories that argue against the passage of the AHCA, but using different characters in their social media narratives. The image on the left uses the villain character to depict the House Republicans and President Trump as villains, while the image on the right uses a veteran to depict victims of the AHCA policy. The veteran or soldier in American political discourse is also, of course, a hero, so this combination of hero as victim makes the Twitter narrative potentially powerful.

These examples illustrate how characters can be used effectively, even in minimalist social media narratives to not only clearly communicate a policy goal, but also elicit emotion from the audience (either anger or sympathy in the images depicted). NPF research indicates that the hero character can be the most effective at persuading audiences to support the policy goals of the narrator. It is conceivable, however, that when the audience is narrow and the narrative is targeted, the villain can be compelling, perhaps most so when the narrative is intended to mobilise supporters.

Policy briefings and statements

Policy narratives get told in numerous venues, some more formal than others. Some of these formal venues are akin to political theatre, as preferences in many macro institutions (such as the US Congress) are relatively fixed (for example, Baumgartner and Jones, 1993) and there simply is not much persuasion going on; but that does not mean that narrative is unimportant. It still can play the role of drawing attention

– attention in general or attention to specific facets of a problem, all of which play a role in setting the political agenda (Peterson and Jones, 2016).

Using policy briefings or statements such as testimony before committees, advocates and policymakers work to outline their version of the evidence related to the problem (plot), the source of the problem (villain, blame), and solutions to said problem. These actors can most effectively create such narratives by capturing attention both inside the formal venue as well as outside (often through capturing media attention). An example of formal congressional narratives involves US Senator James Inhofe. Washington, DC, experienced an unseasonably cold spell during which Senator Inhofe spoke on the Senate floor holding a snowball to attempt to dispute climate science. As reported in the *Washington Post*:

> While 'eggheads' at 'science laboratories' were busy worrying about how the increase in heat-trapping gases in the atmosphere was leading to a long-term upward shift in temperatures and increased atmospheric moisture, Inhofe happened to notice that it was cold outside. Weirdly cold outside. So cold, in fact, that water falling from the sky had frozen solid. So he brought some of this frozen water into the Capitol and onto the Senate floor to show everyone, but mostly to show the eggheads. (Bump, 2015)

Senator Inhofe cast scientists and former Vice President Al Gore – a vocal climate change activist – as villains, while implicitly casting himself as a hero by calling these individuals out for perpetrating the 'greatest hoax' in American history. This 'hoax' and the blame associated with it directed towards scientists and environmental advocates is a consistent narrative that Senator Inhofe employs, which resonates with his audience and frequently captures media attention to heighten his profile and his narrative outside of the formal venues of the Senate.

Policy evaluation

Policy evaluation – the point where a policy is examined to understand if it is 'working' or not – comes in many forms such as the highly technical evaluations of policy experts, economists, and some policy advocates, but it can also be as rudimentary as an opinion piece to a newspaper. Regardless, inherent in any policy evaluation are several underlying constructs (Bardach and Patashnik, 2015): (1) a policy problem, which as outlined above is a fundamental aspect of narratives associated with developing a story's plot; (2) evidence to support the problem as defined and that leads to the associated policy solutions offered; (3) criteria by which the policy or policies will be analysed, such as equity or efficiency (Stone, 2011).

One such example is former President Obama's evaluation of the Affordable Care Act in the *Journal of the American Medical Association* in 2016. Obama (2016b) wrote:

> Health care costs affect the economy, the federal budget, and virtually every American family's financial well-being. Health insurance enables children to excel at school, adults to work more productively, and Americans of all ages to live longer, healthier lives. When I took office, health care costs had risen rapidly for decades, and tens of millions of Americans were uninsured. Regardless of the political difficulties, I concluded comprehensive reform was necessary.

In setting the stage, he articulated the urgency and severity of the problem of the prior health care system in the United States. He also casts characters such as families, children, and Americans of all ages as victims. He casts himself as the hero in the final sentence. Later in this paper, he narrates his policy recommendations and warns of the villains lurking to destroy progress. He calls upon policymakers to:

> build on progress made by the Affordable Care Act by continuing to implement the Health Insurance Marketplaces and delivery system reform, increasing federal financial assistance for Marketplace enrollees, introducing a public plan option in areas lacking individual market competition, and taking actions to reduce prescription drug costs. Although partisanship and special interest opposition remain, experience with the Affordable Care Act demonstrates that positive change is achievable on some of the nation's most complex challenges. (Obama, 2016b)

This example illustrates that policy evaluation can also be a mechanism for effective storytelling.

Expert testimony

Whether before a decision venue such as a legislature, or in a courtroom, experts are essential to communicating to the less knowledgeable the complex and often technical details of a given policy issue or problem. Telling a good story in these situations will no doubt improve knowledge transfer.

In March 2016 as the drinking water contamination crisis in Flint, MI, gained national attention in the US, the US Congress held hearings to determine what happened and who was to blame. One expert witness used the formal congressional venue and audience as an opportunity to point blame at high profile individuals and agencies.

> Virginia Tech Prof Marc Edwards said in his opening statement that he was dumbfounded by top EPA officials' inability to take responsibility for the lead contamination of Flint's drinking water supply. (Dolan and Spangler, 2016)

By capturing attention through the use of narrative tools such as casting villainous characters, clearly laying blame on those characters, and arguing that their actions were at least negligent if not criminal, Professor Edwards captured external media attention and wrestled part of the narrative away from the political actors who dominated the series of hearings.

Public comment

In democracies, citizens who are not generally players in public policy will often find themselves attempting to translate their preferences into policy outcomes. To translate those preferences, citizens have several mechanisms by which they can tell their stories to policymakers, experts, and advocates who might take up the fight on their behalf. Telling stories is important for citizens to participate, otherwise the expertise and jargon of experts can marginalise citizen voices (Schneider and Ingram, 1997). Citizens may possess the most compelling stories to tell about policy effects, societal problems that must be solved, and the impacts of political decisions on their everyday lives. In the policy narrative about the AHCA discussed above, citizens told their compelling stories to evoke empathy and attempt to persuade public opinion and congressional policymakers. Comedian Jimmy Kimmel told the story of his newborn son's congenital heart defect on his late-night show on Monday, 1 May 2017, prior to the House vote. Other citizens began a social media campaign organised around the #IAmAPreexistingCondition hashtag. These types of citizen narratives can effectively evoke emotion from the audience and provide evidence from the lives of policy beneficiaries as illustrated in Figure 3.2.

Good Faith Actor Assessments

Organisations must often wrestle with questions about whether they accurately represent their mission and values to the public. Particularly for mission-oriented organisations such as those in the non-profit and public sectors, this is an essential component of ensuring buy-in from constituents including funders, members or citizens, staff, and external supporters. By periodically conducting Good Faith Actor Assessments using the NPF,

Figure 3.2: #IAMAPreexistingCondition

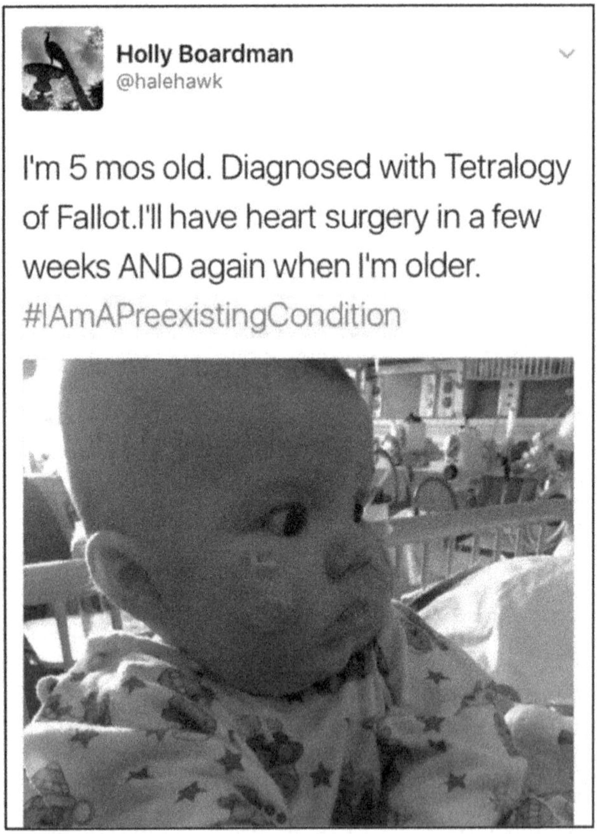

organisations can understand if their external messages map onto their internal goals, mission, and values. For example, a Cambridge, MA, non-profit organisation viewed itself as a passionate 'advocate for democracy' but was unsure whether their internal and external messages were consistent. With limited resources, the organisation sought to (1) assess the narratives it portrayed to the public relative to its defined mission; (2) determine where its mission fit relative to other organisations, especially those with greater resources; and (3) locate potential ally organisations. Using the NPF's elements they compared internal and external narrative sources and found them consistent, concluding that they were in fact operating in good faith. What is important is that their analyses also identified the need to refine and target external messaging. Additionally, this organisation was able to identify 39 organisations focusing on narrower democratic advocacy issues and identified a 'value-added' role for itself in terms of facilitating cooperation among these groups.

Conclusion

Storytelling through narrative is how we humans naturally construct our lives. This instinct to tell stories illustrates why the Knowledge Fallacy is likely to fail most policy actors' goals of persuasion. When sharing our stories, we do not list facts. Rather, we use plot, characters, and morals to communicate. These narratives tend to be edited based on our audience – a very different narrative for our partner than for our 4-year-old child. At the same time, humans are not *only* storytellers, which is why the Empathy Fallacy is also likely to fail for most policy-oriented purposes. Humans not only tell stories to evoke emotion, but we also make arguments based on evidence to support our viewpoints. Through this same narrative construction process, policy actors build stories which they use to inform, influence, and evaluate policies. All policy narratives presumably have some goal of influencing policy outcomes or decisions. In essence, we want our policy narratives to matter in some meaningful outcome-oriented way.

Here we have bridged the NPF literature, providing a clear and applied discussion of the framework so that scholars can effectively understand and apply the framework to their own research and teaching. In so doing, we have also articulated two fallacies – one drawn from the literature and one unique to our discussion. We have also endeavoured to provide useful guidance to practitioners who engage in the various policy interventions discussed herein. The template we present here and the examples of intervention points outlined above are intended to provide practitioners with mechanisms for translating the literature and theory on policy narratives into actionable guidelines to use in their own practices. Our hope is that both scholars and practitioners can use the knowledge and guidance provided to improve upon their work, whether that work is aimed at influencing policy processes or understanding them.

Notes

1 The article which this chapter is based on is available via Open Access here: https://doi.org/10.1332/030557318X15230061022899

2 The entire Act can be found at www.fws.gov/endangered/esa-library/pdf/ESAall.pdf

References

Bardach, E, Patashink, EM, 2015, *A practical guide for policy analysis: The eightfold path to more effective problem solving*, Washington, DC: CQ Press

Baumgartner, FR, Jones, BD, 1993, *Agendas and instability in American politics*, Chicago, IL: University of Chicago Press

Birkland, TA, 2014, *An introduction to the policy process: Theories, concepts and models of public policy making*, New York: Routledge

Bump, P, 2015, Jim Inhofe's snowball has disproven climate change once and for all, *Washington Post*, 26 February

Dolan, M, Spangler, T, 2016, Five takeaways from congressional hearing on Flint, *Detroit Free Press*, 15 March

Dunlap, RE, VanLiere, KD, Mertig, AG, Jones, RE, 2000, Measuring endorsement of the New Ecological Paradigm: A revised NEP scale, *Journal of Social Issues* 56, 3, 425–42

Fischer, F, 2003, *Reframing public policy: Discursive politics and deliberative practices*, Oxford: Oxford University Press

Fischer, F, Forester, J, (eds) 1993, *The argumentative turn in policy and planning*, Durham, NC: Duke University Press

Gray, G, Jones, MD, 2016, A qualitative Narrative Policy Framework? Examining the policy narratives of US campaign finance regulatory reform, *Public Policy and Administration* 31, 3, 93–220

Hardy, B, 1968, October. Towards a poetics of fiction: 3) An approach through narrative, *Novel: A forum on fiction* 2, 1, 5–14

Jones, MD, 2014, Cultural characters and climate change: How heroes shape our perception of climate science, *Social Science Quarterly*, 95, 1, 1–39

Jones, MD, Radaelli, CM, 2015, The Narrative Policy Framework: Child or monster? *Critical Policy Studies* 9, 3, 339–55

Jones, MD, Song, G, 2014, Making sense of climate change: How story frames shape cognition, *Political Psychology* 35, 4, 447–76

Jones, MD, McBeth, MK, Shanahan, EA, 2014a, Introducing the Narrative Policy Framework, in MD Jones, EA Shanahan, MK McBeth (eds) *The Narrative Policy Framework and the practitioner: Communicating recycling policy*, New York: Springer

Jones, MD, Shanahan, EA, McBeth, MK (eds), 2014b, *The science of stories: Applications of the Narrative Policy Framework in public policy analysis*, New York: Palgrave Macmillan

Kahan, DM, 2014, Making climate-science communication evidence-based, in DA Crow, M Boykoff (eds) *Culture, politics and climate change: How information shapes our common future*, pp 203–20, Abingdon: Routledge

Kahneman, D, 2011, *Thinking, fast and slow*, New York: Macmillan

Keller, T, Hawkins, S, 2009, *Television news: A handbook for writing, reporting, shooting, and editing*, Scottsdale, AZ: Holcomb Hathaway

Kellstedt, PM, Zahran, S, Vedlitz, A, 2008, Personal efficacy, the information environment, and attitudes toward global warming and climate change in the United States, *Risk Analysis* 28, 1, 113–26

Kingdon, JW, 2003, *Agendas, alternatives and public policies*, New York: Longman

Krulwich, R, 2008, Tell me a story, *Engineering and science* 71, 3, 10–16

McBeth, MK, Lybecker, DL, Husmann, MA, 2014, in MD Jones, EA Shanahan, MK McBeth (eds) *The Narrative Policy Framework and the practitioner: Communicating recycling policy*, New York: Springer

McBeth, MK, Lybecker, DL, Stoutenborough, JW, Davis, SN, Running, K, 2017, Content matters: Stakeholder assessment of river stories or river science, *Public Policy and Administration*, 32, 3, 175–96

Mansharamani, V, 2016, A major contributor to the Syrian conflict? Climate change, *PBS*

Merry, M, 2016, Making friends and enemies on social media: The case of gun policy organizations, *Online Information Review* 40, 5, 624–42

Niederdeppe, J, Roh, S, Shapiro, MA, 2015, Acknowledging individual responsibility while emphasizing social determinants in narratives to promote obesity-reducing public policy: A randomized experiment, *PloS one* 10, 2, e0117565

Obama, B, 2016a, Remarks of President Barack Obama: State of the Union Address as delivered, Washington, DC: *The White House*

Obama, B, 2016b, United States health care reform: Progress to date and next steps, *Journal of the American Medical Association* 316, 5, 525–32

Open Society, 2016, Personal storytelling and advocacy: What works?, *Open Society Conference*, Manhattan, New York, 25–26 October

Ostrom, E, 1990, *Governing the commons: The evolution of institutions for collective action*, New York: Cambridge University Press

Peterson, HL, Jones, MD, 2016, Making sense of complexity: The Narrative Policy Framework and agenda setting, pp 106–33, *Handbook of public policy agenda setting*, Cheltenham: Edward Elgar, 106–33

Pidgeon, N, Fischhoff, B, 2011, The role of social and decision sciences in communicating uncertain climate risks, *Nature Climate Change*, 1, 1, 35

Qin, W, Brown, J, 2006, Consumer opinions about genetically engineered salmon and information effect on opinions: A qualitative approach, *Science Communication* 28, 2, 243–72

Rakove, JN, 1997, *Original meanings: Politics and ideas in the making of the Constitution*, New York: Vintage

Roe, E, 1994, *Narrative policy analysis: Theory and practice*, Durham, NC: Duke University Press

Sabatier, PA, Jenkins-Smith, HC (eds), 1993, *Policy change and learning: An advocacy coalition approach*, Boulder, CO: Westview Press

Schneider, AL, Ingram, H, 1997, *Policy design for democracy*, Lawrence, KS: University Press of Kansas

Shanahan, EA, Jones, MD, McBeth, MK, Lane, RR, 2013, An angel on the wind: How heroic policy narratives shape policy realities, *Policy Studies Journal* 41, 3, 453–83

Shanahan, EA, Adams, SM, Jones, MD, McBeth, MK, 2014, The blame game: Narrative persuasiveness of the intentional causal mechanism, in MD Jones, EA Shanahan, MK McBeth (eds) *The Narrative Policy Framework and the practitioner: Communicating recycling policy*, New York: Springer

Small, DA, Loewenstein, G, Slovic, P, 2007, Sympathy and callousness: The impact of deliberative thought on donations to identifiable and statistical victims, *Organizational Behavior and Human Decision Processes* 102, 2, 143–53

Smith, CF, 2005, *Writing public policy: A practical guide to communicating in the policy- making process*, New York: Oxford University Press

Smith, KB, Larimer, CW, 2016, *The public policy theory primer*, Boulder, CO: Westview Press

Smith-Walter, A, Peterson, HL, Jones, MD, Marshall, A, 2016, Gun stories: How evidence shapes firearm policy in the United States, *Politics & Policy* 44, 6, 1053–88

Sterman, JD, 2008, Risk communication on climate: Mental models and mass balance, *Science* 322, 5901, 532–3

Stone, D, 2011, *Policy paradox: The art of political decision making*, New York: Norton

Thompson, M, Ellis, R, Wildavsky, A, 1990, *Cultural theory*, Boulder, CO: Westview Press

Yanow, D, 2007, Interpretation in policy analysis: On methods and practice, *Critical Policy Analysis* 1, 1, 110–22

Zaller, JR, 1992, *The nature and origins of mass opinion*, Cambridge, UK: Cambridge University Press

Zaller, JR, 2003, Coming to grips with VO Key's concept of latent opinion, in M Mackuen, G Rabinowitz (eds) *Electoral democracy*, Ann Arbor, MI: University of Michigan Press

Zanocco, CM, Song, G, Jones, MD, 2017, *Fracking bad guys: Narrative character affect in public opinion about hydraulic fracturing*, Available at http://dx.doi.org/10.2139/ ssrn.3033321

CHAPTER FOUR

Using cultural theory to navigate the policy process

Richard Simmons

Introduction

Lasswell's (1951) seminal notion of effective policy analysis combines the 'technical' tasks of 'the scientific study of problems' and 'policymaking around these problems' (Turnbull, 2008). Yet uncertainty and complexity are widely acknowledged to structure contemporary policy-making environments (for example, Geyer and Cairney, 2015). Phenomena such as bounded rationality (Simon, 1955) and 'wicked' policy problems (Rittel and Webber, 1973) mean that sense-making often relies on more than simply scientific analysis. Grint (2005, 1473) therefore observes that to make progress in confronting often intractable problems, 'the task is to ask the right questions rather than provide the right answers'. Complexity therefore places a premium on not only evidence and judgement, but also the *ability to question, learn and adapt.*

In the face of this complexity, institutions matter. Policymakers use institutions to establish and prioritise particular values, norms, rules and roles, thereby reducing the complexity of choice. Sometimes this can be a very positive process, inspiring a flow of ideas and fast-thinking-type solutions to policy problems that 'fit' with the policy context. However, sometimes institutions can get in the way – reinforcing values, systems and practices that no longer fit so well, and acting as blinders to emerging issues. So how do policymakers develop effective policymaking strategies when they are so limited by bounded rationality? Do their 'cognitive frailties' make them over- reliant on a combination of rational and irrational informational shortcuts to act quickly and make adequate decisions? If so, should institutions be designed to limit their autonomous powers, or instead should their ability to develop such heuristics be celebrated, and work be undertaken with them to refine such techniques? This chapter mobilises Cultural Theory (CT) to address such questions, allowing researchers to examine the role of institutions in structuring how policy actors make sense of their environment.

The central problem addressed by this chapter is thus identified: policy is complex and mediated by institutions, and therefore 'institutional work' is needed to enhance the prospects of policy success. However, this raises some further key questions for policy researchers:

- What are the *dominant institutional patterns* that tend to structure policy problems and guide policymakers' response?
- How can *institutional analysis* assist in asking better questions in order to advance policy learning?
- How can research help identify and promote appropriate adaptations in particular policy contexts through the *institutional work* of 'creating, maintaining and disrupting institutions' (Lawrence and Suddaby, 2006)?

This chapter addresses these challenging questions through CT's parsimonious framework, which constitutes institutions in four, rivalrous 'cultural biases' (hierarchy, individualism, egalitarianism and fatalism). This theory is popular and has been applied across (i) a diverse range of empirical fields (see Swedlow, 2014 for a review), (ii) different elements of the policy-cycle (from tasks of problem definition, modelling, alternative selection and argument presentation to those of implementation and termination; Geva-May, 1997), and (iii) different levels and scales of activity (Mamadouh, 1999). In this way, the theory is claimed to provide some common frames of reference that benefit the work of policy scholars, including their engagement with practical policy actors (including professional advisors, commentators or other 'policy entrepreneurs' and those responsible for policy implementation – officials, managers and professionals).

Yet the alleged strength of CT's conceptual application can also prove a weakness if it results in superficiality. This includes what Mamadouh (1999) calls 'birdspotting' (whereby analysts spot illustrative examples of the four ideal-type categories while offering little by way of further explanation). This is grist to the mill of critics who claim that CT over-simplifies complex phenomena and so is insufficiently 'scientific' (for example, Boholm, 1996; Tansey and O'Riordan, 1999). Meanwhile, answers must also be found to the concerns of scholars seeking to use CT (who often struggle to systematically apply its theoretical refinements or engage with its state of the art), or practitioners who, anecdotally, sometimes struggle to get beyond the sense that, while 'somehow all this matters', it is hard in practical terms to 'know what to do' with the results.

Progress here has been further hampered by a lack of operationalisable measures. In response, this chapter places some new measurement tools at the heart of its discussion (see Simmons, 2016). These measures allow researchers to build a 'map' of institutional (in)congruence, comparing how things 'actually are' with how they 'should be' as a way of generating creative institutional dialogue and avoiding counterproductive institutional conflicts. They further allow researchers to understand the implications of policymakers following their 'internal compass' (based on informational and institutional shortcuts). In this way, these measures show the direction in which the compass is pointing and compare this with the guidance provided by the 'map'. Key tensions here provide researchers with better interpretive tools that promote more informed institutional analysis in particular policy environments. In turn, this enables researchers to consider policymakers' ability and willingness to ask better questions as they navigate their policymaking environment, as well as providing practical opportunities for research impact through more grounded discussions about practical action and 'institutional work'.

In short, this chapter uses CT to shine a light on these institutional dynamics and provide policy researchers with some useful heuristics to navigate this terrain. In what follows, the chapter first introduces the CT framework and some of the tools it provides in helping researchers make sense of institutions; framing different institutional logics and how they relate to one another. The problems of measurement in CT and how these are addressed by the new measurement tool are then discussed. Next, the chapter's key metaphors of a 'map' and a 'compass' are used to set out a key distinction between how cultural patterns are both 'internalised' in individuals and 'institutionalised' in policy contexts. Discussion follows on how this helps researchers to understand the navigation of both *change* and *obstacles to change*. Finally, the chapter addresses a further key distinction: between more abstract and intangible 'institutional' understandings and their more grounded and material 'practical' applications. This considers the added value of this analysis for asking better questions, and learning from the answers to suggest adaptations that fit better with today's complex policy contexts. In combination, the above analysis aims to provide a memorable 'route map' for policy scholars seeking to conduct new empirical research as well as new audiences such as students, practitioners, and scholars from other disciplines.

Understanding cultural theory

Cultural theory (CT) has emerged as an important tool for policy analysis (Hood, 1998; Geva-May, 2002; Klitgaard, 1997; Hoppe, 2011; Swedlow, 2002; 2011; 2014; 2017; 6 and Swedlow, 2016). Following Mary Douglas' exposition of the theory (1970; 1982; 1992) and Thompson et al's (1990) seminal refinement of it, there have been numerous attempts to develop its insights into the *institutional* factors governing policy effectiveness (for example, Wildavsky, 1987; Thompson, 2008; 6, 2003). Links between culture and institutions are important; in short, 'culture consists in institutions, which preserve cultural values and norms and give them authority' (Brett, 2000; see Douglas, 1987). In turn, this provides the context for social interaction, shaping people's preferences and justifications so that 'everything human beings do or want is *culturally biased*' (Mamadouh, 1999, 396) (see Figure 4.1). Yet how do people acquire 'cultural bias'? And what types of bias are we talking about?

For its proponents, the CT framework provides parsimonious answers, in a clear and comprehensive set of dimensions and propositions that are together claimed to 'grasp the fundamental nature of sociality' (Mamadouh, 1999, 396). CT's success derives from the intuitive importance of these two high-level dimensions and empirical resonance of the four cultural 'biases' or 'worldviews' that result from their juxtaposition.

The two *high-level dimensions* are represented as the vertical and horizontal axes in Figure 4.2. Each may be strong or weak. In *strongly-regulated* cultures actors are heavily constrained by rules and ascribed behaviour; in weakly-regulated cultures much less so. Meanwhile, in *strongly-integrated* cultures

Figure 4.1: Constituting institutions: reciprocal effects between CT's core elements

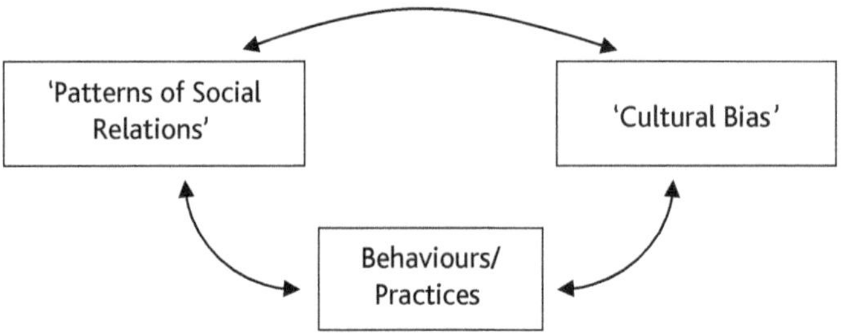

Figure 4.2: The dimensions and cultural biases of CT

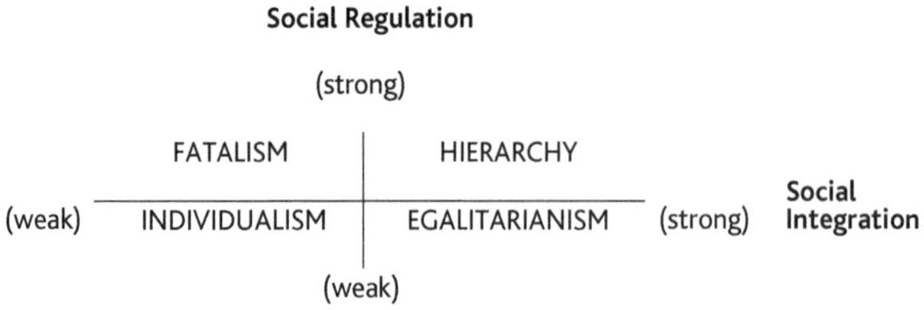

actors are connected and included in group membership; in weakly-integrated cultures much less so. As is now widely- known, when these high-level dimensions are combined, the CT framework reveals four 'cultural biases' or 'worldviews', each of which describes different ideal-typical patterns of social relations:

Hierarchy (strong regulation, strong integration) sums up a bureau-professional relationship in which the policy process and policymakers' behaviour are defined by strict rules and procedures that govern particular roles.

- *Individualism* (weak regulation, weak integration) constructs policymakers (and the targets of policy) as more autonomous, utility-maximising individuals, who need to be incentivised by appeals to their self-interest.
- *Egalitarianism* (weak regulation, strong integration) is represented by 'mutualistic' forms of relationship, in which policy may be co-produced through more collective norms and processes (but may yet flounder in the face of excessive homophily/groupthink or intra-/inter-group conflict).
- *Fatalism* (strong regulation, weak integration) sees social relations as imposed by external structures, and pressures to conform with any social group are weak. This leaves individuals isolated and withdrawn within a policy system where 'co-operation is rejected, distrust widespread, and apathy reigns' (Hood, 1998, 9).

Researchers have applied CT readily to define some key battlefields for policy debate. A classic exemplar is the well-known conundrum of the 'tragedy of the commons' (Hardin, 1968; see Wildavsky, 2006, 228; Buck, 1989). Here, in the absence of regulation to prevent the over-grazing of common-land, is the best answer *hierarchical* oversight and regulation by formal authorities (as Hardin suggests)? Or the peer oversight and moral regulation of *egalitarian* institutions (as suggested by Ostrom, 1990)? Should the land be privatised and regulated by the 'invisible hand' of a market in which motivated *individualists* are left to maximise their own utility? Indeed, is there any point in actively attempting to regulate, or should another hand – that of *'fate'* – be left to prevail? Or, finally, should some 'hybrid' solution be constructed? While each scenario is theoretically possible, acceptance of each provokes a different set of detailed prescriptions for policy action, for which the relative advantages and disadvantages would need to be considered. Similar variations in the realms of possibility exist for myriad other policy issues, many of which are complex in modern policy contexts.

Beyond this, CT has developed various tools and resources of use to scholars in their struggles for more reflective research and analysis:

1. 'static' CT analysis (what life looks like from *within* each ideal-type)
2. 'dynamic' CT analysis (what to look for when ideal-types *interact*)
3. measurement tools (to strengthen such analysis).

With regard to 'static' analysis, CT is now established as much more than a cultural classification scheme, yet its value as such should not be underestimated. Numerous ideal-type comparisons, often in the form of tables, have been compiled in CT research (see Figure 4.3 for a well-known example). Such 'static' analysis is an essential part of sensitising researchers to the fundamental, ideal-type building blocks of CT

- allowing insights into what life looks like from *within* each ideal-type. However, it says nothing of the prevalence of particular ideal-types in a particular context, nor of the dynamics resulting from their interdependence. Many scholars are aware of this, yet 'birdspotting-type' accusations still persist in discussions and peer review. Cultural analysis should not stop here.

By contrast, 'dynamic' CT analysis examines what happens when ideal-types interact. Such analysis is accommodated in some key theoretical propositions (Thompson et al, 1990). Two in particular are considered here. First, the 'requisite variety condition' states that elements of all four ideal-types should be expected to be present within a policymaking system at any time. Second, the 'compatibility condition' states that viable patterns arise when social relations and cultural biases are mutually supportive of each other – and vice-versa (Thompson et al, 1990).

Together, these propositions explain two important patterns between the four ideal-types: those of relative *dominance and subordinacy*, and those of relative *congruence and dissonance*. With regard to the former, the four ideal-types' continuous rivalry in any policy context means that anomalies can breed and grow (6, 2003). This risks the system becoming unstable and the 'destructive potential of the inevitable tensions and conflicts' being released (6, 2003, 402). Such perspectives develop those of the currently-dominant prescriptive approach for policy analysis using CT, namely that of 'clumsy solutions' (Verweij and Thompson, 2006; Verweij, 2011) in which the voice of different ideal-types is able to be heard and responded to (as opposed to one voice being dominant and drowning out the others (Thompson, 2008)). Achievements here involve the cultivation of a 'polyrational imagination' that, by embracing more than a single ideal-type, takes institutional pluralism seriously (Davy, 2016). In terms of institutional analysis, this involves standing back to reflect on how the weaknesses of one worldview might be compensated by the strengths of another (Hoppe, 2011), so that 'the impossible becomes possible when you see it from a different point of view' (Stewart, 1996). The lesson here is that failing to recognise other perspectives can cause considerable problems – wearing 'institutional blinkers' is not an option. For scholars interested in robust CT analysis, this requires careful critical reflection to avoid the selective acknowledgement and reporting of (i) particular cultural voices, or (ii) conversations between them.

For example, in relation to climate change, Thompson (2003) identifies three competing 'stories' associated with different worldviews. In what he calls the 'egalitarian story', protagonists point to the profligate consumption and production patterns of the global North as the fundamental cause of global climate change. By contrast, the 'hierarchist' story asserts that uncontrolled population growth in other regions of the world places local and global eco-systems under pressures that quickly become dangerously uncontrollable. Meanwhile, the 'individualist' story suggests that the price of natural resources is the most important factor in both controlling demand and footing the bill for environmental protection. In sum, while each story contains its own internal logic, it stands in tension with the others and holds only part of the solution to this policy problem. Institutional pluralism ensures that the institutional blinkers are removed and that appropriate attention and weight is attached to each of these stories in allowing more effective policy solutions to emerge.

When a state of *congruence* is achieved in a balance of perspectives, the above tensions and conflicts are minimised. Congruence is about the 'fit' between perceptions of how much of each ideal-type there *actually is* in any given context, and how much there *should be* for the system to be optimally viable (Simmons, 2016). A key task for research here is to understand how any incongruence can be successfully measured and managed. For example, to what extent does analysis indicate an excess or deficit of hierarchy? Or of individualism, egalitarianism or fatalism? And how might we address significant excesses or deficits? CT provides a way of framing more critically

-reflective research on these issues – whether this is reflection '*in-action*' (thinking carefully about the situation that is unfolding), '*on-action*' (thinking retrospectively about the effects of how a situation was handled), or '*for-action*' (thinking about future actions with the intention of making changes or improvements) (Schon, 1983; Killion and Todnem, 1991). In other words, CT research not only has to show that its information is valid

Figure 4.3: An example of static CT analysis for conceptual sensitisation

Fatalist	Individualist	Hierarchist	Egalitarian
Low co-operation Rule-bound approach to organisations	Atomized approach Stress on negotiation and bargaining	Socially cohesive Rule-bound approach to organizations	High-participation structures Every decision 'up for grabs'
Ad hoc, minimalist response to crises **Watchword**: resilience	Responds to crisis through resort to competition and self- interest **Watchword**: enlightened self- interest	Relies on expertise and tighter procedures in response to crises **Watchword**: steering	Based on participation and whistle-blowing **Watchword**: community participation
Weakness: Excessive inertia or passivity	**Weakness**: Individual put before collective benefit; lack of co-operation and corruption	**Weakness**: Tendency towards over-ambitious projects; misplaced trust in expertise	**Weakness**: Unwillingness to accept higher authority, can lead to unresolved feuds, degenerating into co-existence
Control Approach 'Chancism' Organisation as gaming machine	**Control Approach** 'Choicism' Organisation as arena	**Control Approach** 'Bossism' Organisation as a ladder of authority	**Control Approach** 'Groupism' Organisation as collegial
Prone to a vicious cycle whereby public cynicism, rejection of public participation, lack of checks on office holders and inefficiency/corruption of office holders reinforce each other	Prone to rivalry and competition, plus the problems of relying on market-mechanisms for policy delivery	Prone to prioritising the interests of the organisation above all; needs well-understood rules; and tends to blame deviants in case of problems, not the organisation	Four alternative modes: – traditional collegia – transformational – radical alternative – elite democratic community

Source: Hood (1998)

(at the nexus between 'data', 'questioning' and 'reflection in-action'), but that it is insightful (at the nexus between 'interpretation', 'learning' and 'reflection on-action') and of practical use (at the nexus between 'findings', 'adaptation' and 'reflection for-action'). Hence, it is highly feasible for scholars to ask, for a particular policy context:

> *'Reflection in-action'*
> 'How would things appear if I were to look at them through the lens of hierarchy, individualism, egalitarianism, or fatalism?'
> 'How much does what I actually observe around me look more or less like one or other – or some combination – of these possibilities?'
> *'Reflection on-action'*
> 'To what extent does that reflect a pattern of dominance and subordinacy, or of congruence and dissonance?'
> 'What effects does that produce in terms of behaviours, or "operational practices"?'
> *'Reflection for-action'*
> 'Should any action be taken as a result?' 'If so, what should be done?'

In sum, sensitisation to each of CT's four worldviews (through static analysis) is an important step towards deeper reflection about their (dynamic) interaction. Static CT analysis increases the *power* of this reflection (allowing scholars to see things more clearly and quickly), while dynamic CT analysis determines the *direction* of it (allowing them to weigh the implications). What is important is that, as Swedlow (2002, 275) points out, this enables policy researchers to consider such things as:

> When policy change requires cultural change
> (for example, research examining 'experience-based design' shows that change from a hierarchical to a more egalitarian mindset was required before medical professionals would engage in a process of more person-centred and co-productive healthcare service design) (Bate and Robert, 2007);

1. When cultural change makes policy change more likely
   (for example, research shows that direct challenges to the appropriateness of traditional job classifications on the basis of stereotypical gender roles have led to the

deinstitutionalisation of this practice in many organisations) (Oliver, 1992);

2. Which policies are likely to reproduce and reinforce existing cultural configurations
(for example, research shows how self-regulating professions use codes of conduct and codes of ethics to clarify the responsibilities of members and articulate standards) (Perlis and Shannon, 2012);
3. Which policies are likely to challenge and reshape them
(for example, research shows how smoking laws and seat belt enforcement have established and reinforced new normative patterns in the UK) (Knott et al, 2008).

However, while CT's conceptual and theoretical tools travel easily across a wide range of contexts, levels and scales, the same cannot yet be said for its measurement tools (see Ripberger et al, 2015 for a review). Although this may seem curious, some brief explanations are offered here before a way forward is suggested.

Measurement to support *static CT analysis* is difficult for at least two reasons. First, there are issues of (de)contextualisation. For example, early attempts to produce generalised measures of cultural bias used a survey instrument that was free of any social context (Dake, 1991; 1992). These attempts were largely unsuccessful (Ripberger et al, 2015). Critics were unsurprised, arguing that cultural biases must be considered in combination with contextualised patterns of social relations (for example, Rayner, 1992). However, contextualised measures bring problems of their own; both in lacking wider comparability and in the cost and effort of developing bespoke measures that accurately capture the necessary detail. To further complicate matters, Swedlow (2007; 2017) raises issues of what Douglas (1966) calls 'purity' and 'pollution'. In short, this means that any internal consistency in people's cultural ideal-type worldviews (that is, 'purity') may be compromised as it mingles with and is influenced by other worldviews (that is, 'pollution'). As it does, this pollution may again confound accurate measurement.

In contrast, Ripberger et al's (2015) review of the field suggests that the prospects of measurement to support *dynamic* CT analysis appear to have recently become more promising (including improvements in face, construct, concurrent and predictive validity). What is important is that a key factor in this is stronger recognition of the theoretical justification for measuring *cultural bias* in ways that also take into account *patterns of social relations* and *actual behaviours*.

Overcoming challenges of measurement

One new approach, developed by this author (Simmons, 2016), seeks to overcome the above challenges of measurement. This approach uses CT to 'map' the degree of cultural congruence in different policy contexts. It is re-presented briefly here as a way to both operationalise CT and to build on the 'map' and 'compass' metaphors outlined in the introduction (to which we also return in the next section of the chapter). In short, Simmons' (2016) research was conducted in a public administration context, focusing on public service users' relationships with their service provider and the effects of this on their willingness and ability to 'voice' their opinions (see Hirschman, 1970). CT was used as a theoretical lens for understanding how cultural- institutional patterns serve to facilitate or constrain user voice. The results showed these effects to be considerable. In what follows, however, the focus is more on the approach taken by Simmons (2016) and how this helps overcome many of the objections made against earlier attempts to operationalise CT in survey research:

- First, the instrument was based on a deeply *contextualised* approach; namely, a preliminary phase of qualitative fieldwork in three locations from which detailed analysis of semi-structured interviews (N=80) elicited four key themes in the patterns of social relations that mattered most to service users (namely 'courtesy and respect'; 'how knowledge is valued'; 'how fairness and equity issues are resolved'; and 'how rules are set and policed').
- Second, issues of *purity and pollution* were addressed by taking an open, non- judgemental approach. Each of the four key dimensions was operationalised equally against each of the four CT ideal-types.This resulted in four statements being developed for each of the four key dimensions to assess users' normative perceptions of how things should be. Survey respondents in three different public service settings (social care (N=116); leisure services (N=318) and public housing (N=109)) were then invited to rate each individual statement on a 5-point Likert-type scale.
- Third, given that *congruence* is about the 'fit' between perceptions of how much of each ideal-type there 'actually is' in any given context, and how much there 'should be' for the system to be viable, each statement was re-worded according to the former in a second set of statements (see Figure 4.4). Ratings for each statement were then aggregated and presented on a radial plot (see Figure 4.5). Similarities in respondents'

Figure 4.4: Grouped statements measuring cultural congruence in public service organisations

Themes and Cultural Biases	How the service 'actually is'	How the service 'should be'
1: **How fairness and equity issues are resolved**		
Cultural bias: **Hierarchy**	'Day care/Leisure/Housing services are only be provided for those who need them most'	'Day care/Leisure/Housing services should only be provided for those who need them most'
Cultural bias: **Individualism**	'Individuals are given too little choice about the kind of service they get'	'Individuals should be given more choice about the kind of service they get'
Cultural bias: **Egalitarianism**	'Everybody in my community has the same chance of getting the service'	'Everybody in my community should have the same chance of getting the service'
Cultural bias: **Fatalism**	'It is a matter of chance or luckthat people get day care/leisure/housing services'	'People should not expect to get day care/leisure/housing services unless they are lucky'
2: **How knowledge is valued**		
Cultural bias: **Hierarchy**	'Users trust the experts to organise the service'	'Users should trust the experts to organise the service'
Cultural bias: **Individualism**	'The service gives priority to what individuals say they want'	'The service should give priority to what individuals say they want'
Cultural bias: **Egalitarianism**	'The service is run in line with the views of users as a whole'	'The service should be run in line with the views of users as a whole'
Cultural bias: **Fatalism**	'I am wary of those who claim to know what is best for the service'	'Users should be wary of anyone who claims to know what is best for the service'
3: **How rules are set and policed**		
Cultural bias: **Hierarchy**	'The Council imposes strict rules to tell users how to behave'	'The Council should impose strict rules to tell users how to behave'
Cultural bias: **Individualism**	'Individuals are free to use the service however they like'	'Individuals should be free to use the service however they like'
Cultural bias: **Egalitarianism**	'Users know how to behave without a lot of rules and regulations'	'Users should know how to behave without a lot of rules and regulations'

Themes and Cultural Biases	How the service 'actually is'	How the service 'should be'
Cultural bias: **Fatalism**	'There is no point having lots of rules because people don't obey them'	'There is no point having lots of rules because people won't obey them'
4: **Courtesy and respect**		
Cultural bias: **Hierarchy**	'Users respect the experts' decisions about the service'	'Users should respect the experts' decisions about the service'
Cultural bias: **Individualism**	'The staff accept that individuals know best what they need'	'The staff should accept that individuals know best what they need'
Cultural bias: **Egalitarianism**	'The service takes heed of what the user community has to say'	'The service should take heed of what the user community has to say'
Cultural bias: **Fatalism**	'In my experience, users do not have any power'	'Service users should not expect to have any power'

Source: Simmons (2016)

Figure 4.5: Key for radial plots in Figure 4.6

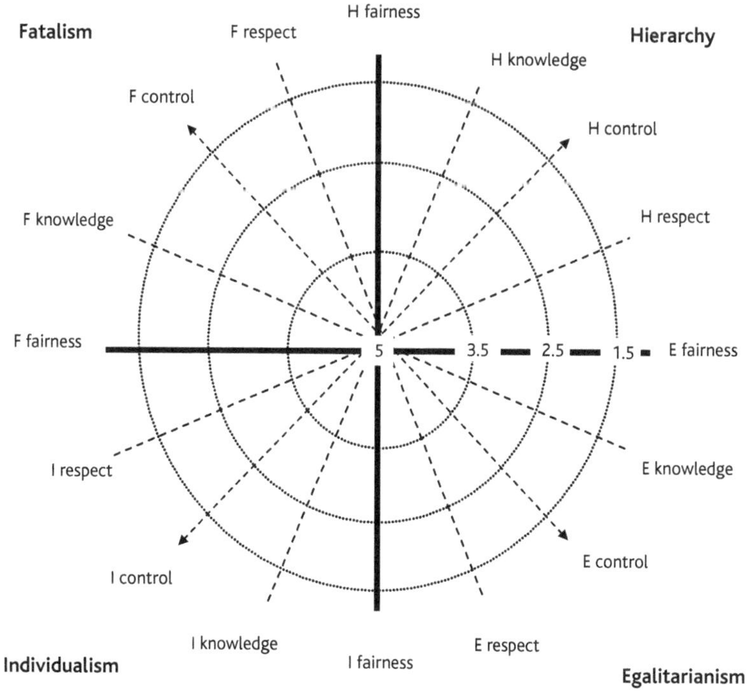

Figure 4.6a: 'User Perceptions of How the Service 'Is''

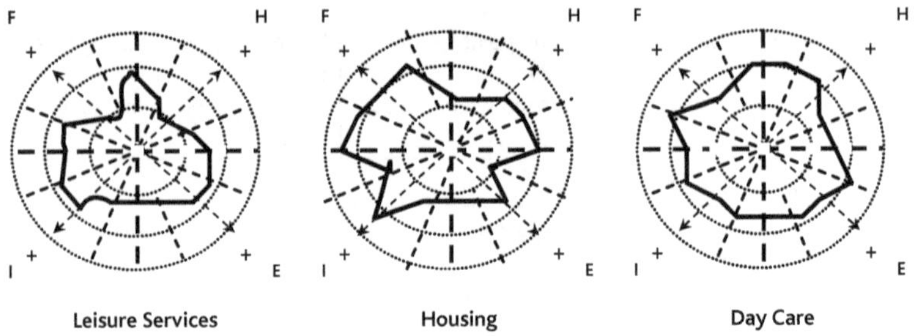

Source: Simmons (2016)

Figure 4.6b: 'User Perceptions of How the Service 'Is' vs How It 'Should Be''

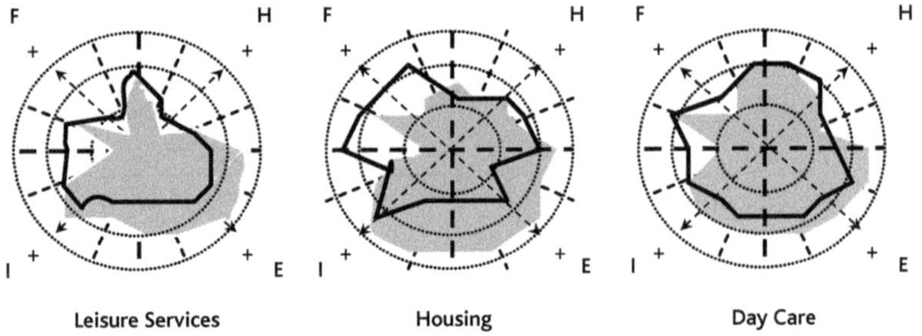

Source: Simmons (2016)

ratings of how things 'actually are' and how things 'should be' represent greater congruence; differences represent greater dissonance (see Figures 4.6a and 4.6b).

- Fourth, account was given to the theoretical justification for *measuring cultural bias in ways that also takes into account patterns of social relations and actual behaviours*. The statements were explicitly intended to capture the nature of a set of specific social relations rather than the essence of each cultural bias. In this way, differences in users' scores against these statements were used only in relative, rather than absolute, terms. Nevertheless, it is only these relative differences that are important in defining the extent of congruence and dissonance.
- Finally, adding to the 'face' and 'construct' validity in the above approach, Simmons (2016) was also able to show its *'predictive' validity* in terms of how notions of congruence correlated with other survey items measuring (i) respondents' perceptions of the quality of service relations, (ii) service performance and (iii) the availability of 'good opportunities' for user voice.

In defining conditions of cultural 'congruence' and/or 'dissonance', this map is able to identify the terrain in which researchers' and policy actors' attention might be productively focused, and where particular forms of action might be most appropriate (see Simmons, 2016). 6 and Swedlow (2016, 872) describe Simmons' (2016) approach as an 'innovative operationalisation' and 'methodological advance' for CT. Specifically, it allows a response to some key questions, such as: 'How would we know when the prevailing "institutional logics" have become suboptimal in the governance of problems in our particular context?' and 'How would we use CT to know which direction(s) to move in?'

For example, in Figure 6b congruence is most evident in the case of 'day care', where the shapes formed by the 'is' and the 'should be' statements are the most similar. By contrast, in the 'leisure' case there appears to be a particular blind spot in relation to egalitarianism (and to a lesser extent individualism). Meanwhile, in the 'housing' case there is work to do to close the gap on at least three dimensions – individualism, egalitarianism and fatalism. Knowing such things allows policy actors to understand more about what action to take. In this regard it should be noted that, even in the day care case, the relative congruence observed is an achievement that must be actively maintained. In the other cases, however, some form of change is required. Knowing this can spark the important process of 'questioning' (Turnbull, 2013). In the leisure case, for example, 'what might it look like to be more egalitarian?'

There remains at least one of the above objections that Simmons' (2016) approach does not overcome. This is the cost and effort of developing bespoke measures – even if these support more productive insights and reflections on the *institutional* factors governing policy effectiveness. In response, a purist might argue that 'organisations run surveys all the time on various issues; why not invest here?' However, in an environment of financial resource constraint, such contentions must be acknowledged. More fundamentally, there is another, more functional problem. As Argyris (1976, 365) observes, effective learning requires both 'valid information' and 'receptivity to corrective feedback'. However, while the CT 'map' claims to provide valid information, there is no guarantee that policy actors will be receptive to this feedback. This brings back into the discussion how these actors are influenced by their 'internal compass'. An actor's 'internal compass' takes in the values and worldviews that are compatible with their approach toward particular policy issues (6 and Swedlow, 2016). As a reference point from which everything can be checked to determine a sense of 'rightness' (Smythe and Norton, 2007, 74), this internal compass directs their 'judgement' (Vickers, 1965) and 'fast-thinking' (Kahneman, 2011). No bad thing, perhaps – unless this starts sending them off-course. Yet faulty compass readings arise when thought-styles become 'cultural blinkers', plotting a course ahead that blocks out other constructions of the problem. In this way, the patterns of relations and cultural bias that are internalised in individuals sometimes form such 'credible commitments' that they hold actors back from exploring alternatives or distort their policy orientation and navigation. Examples abound, such as commitments to market principles of 'value for money' in public procurement that ignore other policy goals such as carbon emission issues, or commitments to restrictive planning regulations and/or protection of the green belt that ignore other policy goals such as the provision of affordable housing.

A helpful addition to Simmons' (2016) measures of the degree of *institutionalisation* of cultural biases in the 'map' would therefore be a measure of the extent of people's *internalisation* of such perspectives in their 'internal compass'. Value may be claimed here for comparability in the 'framing of cultural configurations' – or how policymakers use institutions – in both 'compass' and 'map'. Arguably, measurement of the compass therefore might therefore involve a relatively straightforward extension of Simmons' (2016) methodology by simply asking respondents to both 'rank and rate' the competing attitude statements in each section of Figure 4.3. Nevertheless, a more reliable technique might be using Q methodology with these statements (Brown, 1993; Durning, 1999). A robust method for combining the sorting and ranking of statements with factor analysis and hierarchical cluster analysis, this approach has the potential to add further insights.

In combination, having a means of 'measuring' the compass as well as the map provides a more detailed understanding of the dynamics governing the 'tension-field' in particular policymaking contexts. This includes the directions in which 'receptivity to corrective feedback' is lacking, thereby moving towards or away from particular patterns of social relations and facilitating/constraining particular movements on the map that might be needed to effect appropriate adaptations and change. These issues form the focus for the next section of this article.

Using the 'map' and the 'compass' for policy analysis and policy navigation

CT researchers' ability to measure differences in the extent to which patterns of social relations and cultural bias are both 'internalised' in individuals (that is, in their 'internal compass') and 'institutionalised' in particular policy contexts (that is, in ways that can be 'mapped') is important. Earlier we asked how policymakers develop effective policymaking strategies when they are so limited by bounded rationality, and whether their 'cognitive frailties' make them over-reliant on a combination of rational and irrational informational shortcuts to act quickly and make adequate decisions. Measurement helps researchers to answer these questions and reduce the need for such shortcuts. Indeed, given that policy actors rarely possess an infallible 'internal compass', a reliable 'map' provides them with an invaluable tool against which to check they are on track. As Turnbull (2013, 125) asserts, 'individuals hold the capacity to reflect upon and problematise their place within a field, for example by reflecting upon their own entrenched ways of doing things'. CT analysis supports this by helping scholars to demonstrate the extent to which policy actors are able to *orientate* themselves 'appropriately' toward policy problems and *navigate* the actions that might be taken to address them. In this sense, this chapter addresses questions raised in the introduction about the extent to which institutional patterns tend to structure policy problems and guide policymakers' response, and how institutional analysis can help by identifying better questions to promote policy learning.

However, two questions remain. First, if policy actors are both over-reliant on their internal compass and unreceptive to corrective feedback, how might institutions be designed to limit their autonomous powers? Meanwhile, if they are more receptive, how might work be undertaken with them to recalibrate their compass readings? In either case, CT measurement can be used to help ensure that the direction in which their internal compass points them is not too far away from where their attention is most needed. The fit between their compass readings and the problem context is therefore significant. If there is a good fit, fast thinking is more likely to lead to successful action strategies and policy navigation. However, if this is not the case, a different approach may be demanded. In this way, the 'map' and 'compass' are each useful tools but must be harnessed and used in conjunction for effective navigation. Relatedly, in his highly influential text *Beyond Rational Management*, Quinn (1988: xv) distinguishes between one decision-making frame that is 'purposive, static and entropic', and another that is 'holistic, dynamic and generative'. Policymakers' 'purposive frame' is the equivalent of their 'internal compass'; in their 'holistic frame' they map a wider range of perspectives. What is important is that Quinn (1988) observes that 'exceptional individuals' do not achieve excellence by using one or other frame but by using both in conjunction.

While this may be so, if one or other of the 'compass' or 'map' is perceived to be unreliable, it is likely to be disregarded. So how do relationships between the two play out? Notions of 'purity' and 'pollution' (see Swedlow, 2017) are invoked here to explore the field of relationships between the compass and map. This centres particularly on their different 'purity claims'. Moreover, in assessing how the nature of the boundary between the compass and map may vary at different times in the policy process, Stirling's (2008: 278–79) distinction between the 'opening up' or 'closing down' of policy discourse is also informative:

> If it is about 'closing down' the policy process, then the aim is to assist decision-making by cutting through the messy, intractable and conflict prone diversity of views and develop in a clear authoritative prescriptive recommendation…On the other hand, if it is about 'opening up' the process, the focus is on revealing wider policy discourses and interpretations of the available evidence.

How might we encapsulate and understand these distinctions? In short, the 'internal compass' is careful to keep its boundaries high, as both a reference point and a container for 'principled' judgement. In Quinn's (1988) terms, it is 'purposive, static and entropic'. The map's 'polyrationality' can therefore feel confrontational and its 'corrective feedback' challenging, which in turn affects 'receptivity'. At the above point of 'closure' of the policy process, where a clear decision is needed, it therefore filters this polyrationality, which it views as 'noise pollution'. This practice of filtering underpins its purity claim; that it enables decision-makers to see and think more clearly in the sense-making process.

By contrast, the 'map' maintains more open boundaries to develop an overview of the policy context. It is a checkpoint for patterns of congruence and dissonance, remaining open to all perspectives and possibilities without placing a judgement on them. It filters this information using polyrationality. This practice of filtering underpins its purity claim of providing 'valid information' (Argyris, 1976), thereby simplifying complexity and providing clarity for 'better-informed' decisions. In Quinn's (1988) terms, this process is 'holistic, dynamic and generative', providing useful 'corrective feedback' to the process of 'reflection for-action'.

It should be noted here that 'objections to' or 'acceptance of' each other's claims can provoke either conflict or co-operation. Hence, the discourse from compass to map may be: 'Don't stay open! Decisions have to be made sometime and scanning the environment is no longer helpful!' The response may be: 'OK, but we need to have confidence in those decisions. Show that you have taken our inputs seriously if you want us to quieten down.' Conversely, the discourse from map to compass may be: 'Don't stay closed! Things are complex and uncertain and you need to stay aware!' Yet here, the response may be: 'OK, but we need to have confidence that you have "valid information" if we are going to be convinced to open up.'

At the heart of this are the key issues of questioning, learning and adaptation. In sum, (i) each perspective asks and answers *questions* differently, and (ii) each holds the key to different influences on the effectiveness of *learning*: that is, 'valid information' (map) and 'receptivity to corrective feedback' (compass). In learning to co-operate, as successful policy navigation necessitates, *adaptation* therefore becomes a 'dance', with at least two elements: first, as either the 'holistic' frame (map) or 'purposive' frame (compass) is pulled forward, so the other is pushed into the background; Second, at times when the policy process is 'opened up' the map is more likely to be foregrounded, and vice-versa. For conflict to be avoided and greater co-operation to be made possible, the focus therefore must be on greater acceptance of each other's 'purity claims'.

In sum, researchers' knowledge of policy actors' compass bearings are important. This can show how open or closed actors are to particular forms of corrective feedback. This might lead to productive discussions with policy actors about engaging in critical reflection of how well their compass readings 'fit' with the policy context. However, such conversations require researchers to also ensure that institutional maps are as accurate as possible and that findings of institutional (in)congruence are communicated clearly as a way to help actors in navigating the policy terrain. For 'research with impact', this task could include identifying opportunities for change through more grounded 'institutional work'.

This brings us to the final question identified in the introduction: that of how research can help identify and promote appropriate adaptations in particular policy contexts through the institutional work of 'creating, maintaining and disrupting institutions' (Lawrence and Suddaby, 2006). For some, this is a sticky question: if institutional issues underpin the policy context, in real terms what can be done? 'Culture' is notoriously difficult to change, and 'institutionalisation' notoriously difficult to overcome. However, as Pellizzoni (2001, 59) observes, 'seemingly intractable controversies may often be faced at the level of [discourse and] practices'. Perhaps the answer therefore lies in CT's core reciprocal interrelations between cultural bias, patterns of social relations and 'operational practices' (Figure 4.1) (see 6, 2011; 2015; 2016). In this way, 'learning-by-thinking' strategies (that is, reflection) may be supplemented or even usurped in the process of adaptation by practical 'learning-by-doing' strategies.

This links notions of 'the institutional' to those of 'the practical' in institutional work. What is important is that Lawrence and Suddaby (2006,

219) recognise institutional work as 'intelligent, situated institutional action'. In recognition of this, for example, Simmons (2016) was able to use the above findings from his research to sit with public service managers, staff and user representatives, and discuss significant differences on the 'map' and how they might be reduced. This involved 'such purposive actions as the redrafting of standard operating procedures, establishment of new mechanisms for stakeholder 'voice', provision of new staff training opportunities, and new, 'nudge'- type activities in the phrasing and presentation of communications' (Simmons, 2016, 949). Specific *practical remedies* that are applied in different policy contexts need to be bespoke to the policy issues they face. However, the tools of CT analysis can provide a guide for the deeply practical, situated 'institutional work' from which they might emerge. Effective navigation, particularly in an environment of complexity and ambiguity, therefore might be said to depend on greater reflection and the acquisition of such 'practical wisdom' through 'practical learning' (Rhodes, 2015).

Conclusions

Linking operational practices and systems back to institutionalised cultural biases and patterns of social relations, CT allows researchers to shine a light on new possibilities for addressing policy problems. Key reference points range from the relatively fast (for example, following the direction given by our 'internal compass'), to the relatively slow (for example, deeper 'reflection on values and norms and, by implication, the social structures which were instrumental in their development': Greenwood, 1998, 1049). In short, it is argued here that dangers lie in wait if policy actors lean too heavily and uncritically on their 'internal compass' when navigating policy problems, and that deeper reflection is important for developing greater capacities for questioning (Turnbull, 2013), learning (Argyris, 1976) and adaptation (Lawrence and Suddaby, 2006).

CT provides a useful framework for structuring research inquiry that leads to better institutional questioning, learning and adaptation in different (and especially complex) policy contexts. Yet this chapter argues that insufficient thought is given to such institutional issues. In particular, the chapter has sought to examine some of the evidence of this theory's potential and explain why it remains controversial. This has involved an attempt to move beyond the banality of 'birdspotting'-type narratives in CT analysis, and to lay some of myths about CT's practical value. The chapter raises the particular importance of operationalising CT using 'map' and 'compass' measurements as a way to make sense of these contexts. Relations of relative (in)congruence are particularly worthy of policy attention, whether to generate a creative institutional dialogue or to help avoid counterproductive institutional conflicts. Yet patterns of (in) congruence are not always readily visible. Researchers can therefore play an important role in robustly mapping out this terrain and providing this map as 'valid information' for policy debate. Meanwhile measurements of the compass show how likely it is that policy actors will engage on this terrain.

This chapter makes three further assertions: (i) that current prescriptive approaches for policy analysis using CT, such as the notion of 'clumsy solutions', generally lack the precision of measurement, (ii) that in conjunction, the 'map' and 'compass' provide researchers with the tools to support more effective policy navigation, and (iii) that more detailed understandings of the dynamics governing particular movements on the map are needed to effect appropriate institutional adaptations and change. As noted above, given that policy actors rarely possess an infallible 'internal compass', a reliable 'map' provides an invaluable tool against which to check they are on track. To conclude, then, this chapter suggests that in the face of considerable complexity and uncertainty, orientation and navigation are demanding and ongoing tasks. However, by adding a map to policymakers' internal compass, researchers can provide a sense of where they are going and direction about how to find their way. There remains a need to connect these things with a detailed engagement of the terrain in order to align this research with practical action and institutional 'work'. It is hoped that through the 'map' and 'compass' approach outlined in this chapter there is a potential basis for moving further forward, and more speedily, in this direction.

References

Argyris, C, 1976, Single-loop and double-loop models in research on decision-making, *Administrative Science Quarterly* 21, 363–75

Argyris, C, Schön, D, 1974, *Theory in practice*, San Francisco, CA: Jossey-Bass

Bate, P, Robert, G, 2007, *Bringing user experience to healthcare improvement*, Oxford: Radcliffe

Boholm, A, 1996, A critique of cultural theory, *Ethos* 61, 64–84

Brett, J, 2000, Culture and negotiation, *International Journal of Psychology* 35, 2, 97–104

Brown, S, 1993, A primer on Q methodology, *Operant Subjectivity* 16, 91–138

Buck, S, 1989, Cultural theory and management of common property resources, *Human Ecology* 17, 1, 101–16

Dake, K, 1991, Orienting dispositions in the perception of risk, *Journal of Cross Cultural Psychology* 22, 61

Dake, K, 1992, Myths of nature, *Journal of Social Issues* 48, 4, 21–37
Davy, B, 2016, *Land policy*, London: Routledge
Douglas, M, 1966, *Purity and danger*, London: Routledge & Kegan Paul
Douglas, M, 1970, *Natural symbols*, London: Barrie and Rockliff
Douglas, M, 1982, *In the active voice*, London: Routledge
Douglas, M, 1987, *How institutions think*, London: Routledge & Kegan Paul
Douglas, M, 1992, *Risk and blame*, London: Routledge
Durning, D, 1999, The transition from traditional to postpositivist policy analysis: A role for Q-methodology, *Journal of Policy Analysis and Management* 18, 3, 389–410
Geva-May, I, 2002, Cultural theory: The neglected variable in the craft of policy analysis, *Journal of Comparative Policy Analysis: Research and Practice* 4, 3, 243–65
Geva-May, I with Wildavksy, A, 1997, *An operational approach to policy analysis*, Boston, MA: Kluwer
Geyer, R, Cairney, P, 2015, *Handbook on complexity and public policy*, Cheltenham: Edward Elgar
Greenwood, J, 1998, The role of reflection in single and double loop learning, *Journal of Advanced Nursing* 27, 1048–53
Grint, K, 2005, Problems, problems, problems: The social construction of 'leadership', *Human Relations* 58, 11, 1467–94
Hardin, G, 1968, The tragedy of the commons, *Science* 162, 3859, 1243–8
Hirschman, A, 1970, *Exit, voice, and loyalty*, Cambridge, MA: Harvard University Press
Hood, C, 1998, *The art of the state*, Oxford: Oxford University Press
Hoppe, R, 2011, *The governance of problems*, Bristol: Policy Press
Kahneman, D, 2011, *Thinking, fast and slow*, New York: Farrar, Strauss and Giroux
Killion, J, Todnem, G, 1991, A process for personal theory building, *Educational Leadership* 48, 6, 14–16
Klitgaard, R, 1997, Applying cultural theories to practical problems, in R Ellis, M Thompson (eds) *Culture matters: Essays in honour of Aaron Wildavsky*, Boulder, CO: Westview Press
Knott, D, Muers, S, Aldridge, S, 2008, *Achieving culture change*, London: Cabinet Office
Lasswell, H, 1951, The policy orientation, in D Lerner, H Lasswell (eds) *The policy sciences*, Stanford, CA: Stanford University Press
Lawrence, T, Suddaby, R, 2006, Institutions and institutional work, in S Clegg, C Hardy, T Lawrence, W. Nord (eds) *Handbook of organizational studies*, London: Sage
Mamadouh, V, 1999, Grid-group cultural theory, *GeoJournal* 47, 395–409

Oliver, C, 1992, The antecedents of deinstitutionalization, *Organization Studies* 13, 563–88

Ostrom, E, 1990, *Governing the commons*, Cambridge: Cambridge University Press

Pellizzoni, L, 2001, The myth of the best argument, *British Journal of Sociology* 52, 1, 59–86

Perlis, C, Shannon, N, 2012, Role of Professional organizations in setting and enforcing ethical norms, *Clinics in Dermatology* 30, 2, 156–9

Quinn, R, 1988, *Beyond rational management*, San Francisco, CA: Jossey-Bass

Rayner, S, 1992, Cultural theory and risk analysis, in S Krimsky, D Golding (eds) *Social theories of risk*, Westport, CT: Praeger

Rhodes, R, 2015, Recovering the 'craft' of public administration in Westminster government, paper for *Political Studies Association Conference*, Sheffield, March–April

Ripberger, J, Swedlow, B, Silva, C, Jenkins-Smith, H, 2015, Operationalizing cultural theory in survey research, paper for *European Consortium for Political Research (ECPR) Annual Meeting*, Montreal, August

Rittel, H, Webber, M, 1973, Dilemmas in a general theory of planning, *Policy Sciences* 4, 155–69

Schön, D, 1983, *The reflective practitioner*, London: Temple Smith

Simmons, R, 2016, Improvement and public service relationships: Cultural theory and institutional Work, *Public Administration* 94, 933–52

Simon, H, 1955, A behavioral model of rational choice, *Quarterly Journal of Economics* 69, 1, 99–118

6, P, 2003, Institutional viability: a neo-Durkheimian theory, *Innovation* 16, 4, 395–415

6, P, 2011, *Explaining political judgement*, Cambridge: Cambridge University Press

6, P, 2015, Structure and political agency, thought style and strategy schedules in government, Paper for *Political Studies Association Conference*, Sheffield, March–April

6, P, 2016, How 'natives' work, *Public Administration* 94, 4, 1005–22

6, P, Swedlow, B, 2016,An institutional theory of cultural biases, public administration and public policy, *Public Administration* 94, 4, 867–80

Smythe, E, Norton, A, 2007, Thinking as leadership/leadership as thinking, *Leadership* 3, 1, 65–90

Stewart, J, 1996, Moving partnerships forward, Paper for *Policy and Performance Review Network Conference*, Warwick

Stirling, A, 2008 Opening up and closing down, *Science, Technology, & Human Values*, 33, 2, 262–94

Swedlow, B, 2002, Toward cultural analysis in policy analysis, *Journal of Comparative Policy Analysis* 4, 3, 267–85

Swedlow, B, 2007, Using the boundaries of science to do boundary-work among scientists: Pollution and purity claims, *Science and Public Policy* 34, 9, 633–43

Swedlow, B, 2011, Cultural theory's contributions to political science, *PS: Political Science & Politics* 44, 4, 703–10

Swedlow, B, 2014, Advancing policy theory with cultural theory, *Policy Studies Journal* 42, 4, 465–83

Swedlow, B, 2017, Three cultural boundaries of science, institutions, and policy, *Review of Policy Research* 34, 6, 827–53

Tansey, J, O'Riordan, T, 1999, Cultural theory and risk: A review, *Health, Risk & Society* 1, 1, 71–90

Thompson, M, 2003, Cultural theory, climate change and clumsiness, *Economic and Political Weekly* 38, 48, 5107–12

Thompson, M, 2008, *Organising and disorganising*, Axminster: Triarchy Press

Thompson, M, Ellis, R, Wildavsky, A, 1990, *Cultural theory*, Boulder, CO: Westview Press

Turnbull, N, 2008, Harold Lasswell's 'problem orientation' for the policy sciences, *Critical Policy Studies* 2, 1, 72–91

Turnbull, N, 2013, The questioning theory of policy practice, *Critical Policy Studies* 7, 2, 115–31

Verweij, M, 2011, *Clumsy solutions for a wicked world*, Basingstoke: Palgrave MacMillan

Verweij, M, Thompson, M, 2006, *Clumsy solutions for a complex world*, Basingstoke: Palgrave MacMillan

Vickers, G, 1965, *The art of judgment*, New York: Basic Books

Wildavsky, A, 1987, Choosing preferences by constructing institutions, *American Political Science Review* 81, 1, 3–21

Wildavsky, A, 2006, *Cultural analysis*, New Brunswick: Transaction

CHAPTER FIVE

The lessons of policy learning: types, triggers, hindrances and pathologies[1]

Claire A Dunlop and Claudio M Radaelli

Introduction

The literature on policy learning has generated a huge amount of heat (and some light) producing policy learning taxonomies, concepts and methods, yet the efforts to demonstrate why we should think about policy processes in terms of learning have been rare and mostly in the past (Dunlop, Radaelli and Trein, 2018). Additionally, policy learning has progressed in different sub-fields, such as the study of diffusion, transfer, individual and collective learning, social learning, and knowledge utilisation (see the family tree of learning in Dunlop, Radaelli and Trein, 2018; and the fragmentation in sub-fields portrayed in Goyal and Howlett, 2018). This has discouraged the tasks of communicating, comparing and combining insights that, the editors of this special issue remind us, are fundamental to translate research to a wider audience, avoiding jargon and obfuscation.

We offer this chapter to both an audience of academics and to actors involved in policy-processes, be they elected politicians, public managers, activists or pressure groups. We address the academic audience made up of specialists in policy analysis by arguing that the quality of our findings should be judged in terms of 'translation reach'. We set out to show how we can combine and integrate research on learning so that it can be translated to a wider audience of social scientists looking for cumulative findings, typical lessons, concepts that travel across fields.

The concept of 'wider audience' means, however, that a useful assemblage, synthesis and communication of findings should also assist social scientists in carrying a conversation with those who are directly involved or affected by policy processes. Our central proposition is that these two readerships (social scientists and practitioners) can be combined if we fine-tune our effort to maximise the reach of translation around exemplary lessons. Thus, we answer the following questions: what are the lessons of thinking about policy processes in terms of learning? What are their triggers and hindrances? What can go wrong with learning, that is, what are the pathologies? Answering these particular questions shows to social scientists the value and explanatory leverage of drawing on learning theory to analyse public policy. But it also points practitioners towards usable knowledge: lessons that can be applied to real-world policy processes. This particular focus brings us close to another important goal of the special issue: to bridge the theory–practice divide.

Of course, to translate theory into practice does not mean to supply a menu of policy recommendations for concrete problems and cases. Different actors need diverse translations. Learning is the process of updating beliefs about public policy. This can of course refer to beliefs on how to make policy more efficient, legitimate, democratic. It can also, however, mean learning how to use public policy to win consensus, to promote one's strategy, to humiliate the opposition – without necessarily improving on efficiency or effectiveness. Thus, there are too many practical translations of learning into recommendations, unless we answer the question 'learning for whom and what purposes'.

Indeed, a recommendation may empower an actor but disempower another. Rather than recommendations, theory-driven lessons, based on significant accumulation of findings, show typical ways in which theory can become relevant. They inspire large audiences rather than directing a specific actor towards a strategy. They frame reality in a way that is creative and illuminating.

This stance, finally, allows us to reconnect policy learning with the ambition of the founding studies: Karl Deutsch, Herbert Simon and Charles Lindblom, were inspired by theories that would produce practical insights. In John Dewey's pragmatism, education, policy and the publics are profoundly related. Dewey's 1927 classic *The Public and its Problems*, reprinted in 2012, concerned engaging a public distracted and uninterested in public policy problems with the essence of democracy – a prophecy of the current mood of anti-politics. Dewey's utopia was to turn the *Great Society* into the *Great Community* (Dewey, 2012: 141). To achieve this, he even thought of mobilising the arts to draw the attention of the public towards the assimilation of 'accurate investigation' (Dewey, 2012: 140). Of course, the founding father of policy inquiry, Harold Lasswell, was aware of Dewey's lessons about bridging the gap between academic knowledge and society: '[O]ne thing Lasswell learned from the pragmatists, and Dewey in particular, was that inquiry requires community' (Torgerson, 1992: 231). Given this, we do not need additional motivation to explore the lessons of learning in public policy. Our analysis will be selective. We, and others, have produced reviews of the literature (Dunlop and Radaelli, 2013; Heikkila and Gerlak, 2013; Moyson, Scholten and Weible, 2017). Here, instead of drawing on a particular method to extract findings, we illustrate this with examples rather than covering a broad range of the field.

We will make use of Dunlop and Radaelli (2013) more than other reviews because this is a concept-driven analysis of a vast number of empirical studies (our initial population was 833 articles) and therefore suits our purpose of combining, integrating and assembling the field into a limited number of clear propositions. One way to navigate our contribution is the following: the features, triggers, hindrances and pathologies of learning depend on the policy process context in which actors interact: are the policy actors engaged with bargaining or are they trying to understand what works on the basis of science and evidence? Are they finding solutions within a pre-established hierarchy or rules and procedures? Or, instead, is this a policy process with the main goal of fostering participation? The 'tone' of the policy process shapes the style and nature of learning.

Our first lesson is therefore that learning has different qualities and logics depending on this tone. We will refer to four process-related contexts: epistemic (or knowledge- driven), reflexivity, bargaining and compliance with hierarchy. The second lesson is that learning has its own triggers and hindrances. It does not simply happen. The third lesson concerns dysfunctional learning – learning that is 'bad'. The question 'bad for whom, or for what?' allows multiple answers. Learning can be 'bad' for the organisation in question, or because it violates some normative standards like pluralism, accountability, or legitimacy. Finally, we conclude with what this type of research agenda can deliver to social scientists and practitioners.

Lesson 1: Learning has different qualities

Let us start again from our definition of learning as 'the updating of beliefs based on lived or witnessed experiences, analysis or social interaction' (Dunlop and Radaelli, 2013: 599). It follows that *policy* learning is about how knowledge that comes from these experiences, analysis and social interaction is considered and acted upon by policy actors. This centrality of the *process* of knowledge acquisition and belief updates reveals an important practical insight: learning may be unintentional, but it does not occur randomly – not all policy processes carry the same probability of producing learning outcomes. Thus, any answer to the question 'why does learning happen?' requires a specification of the contexts by which learning outcomes are facilitated. We argue that social scientists can communicate more effectively and more widely if they abandon an exclusive focus on learning and open their peripheral vision to these contexts. This is where our analysis aids communication among ourselves: university-based researchers and social scientists in general. Let us see why and how. A vast literature on modes of governance and decisions in public policy

(Dente, 2014) and learning types (Dunlop and Radaelli, 2013) has pinned down four predominant contexts in which policy decisions are made. These four contexts are hierarchy, bargaining, reflexivity and finally the expert-driven or epistemic. How do actors, problems, interactions fall into one category or the other? This can be the result of institutional choice – for example the decision to create an independent regulator. But often the same policy domain (for example, environment, housing, transportation) manages decisions in different contexts, depending on the concrete issue at stake and how actors are socially perceived as legitimate and knowledgeable. Two dimensions matter, then. One is *uncertainty* or *issue tractability* (Jenkins-Smith, 1990) and the other is the *certification of actors* associated with the issue (McAdam et al, 2001).

Uncertainty is low when there are ways to find a solution to a policy problem, although these ways may be costly, require a lot of evidence and time, and so on. We know how to govern the quantity of money in a country and to collect data on public expenditure in a number of policy domains. But, we do not have established ways to build regulatory budgets. Yet another set of problems exhibit radical uncertainty. The latter results in either reliance on epistemic experts or being opened up to widespread social debate. And here, we see that the social perception of actors matters. At a given time and in a given society, some actors are perceived as competent, technically skilled, independent, or all of these. That's the concept of social certification. Institutional choice may nudge social perception, for example by allocating certain powers to an independent regulator or level of governance. More generally though, we can think of all cases when a socially certified actor (institutional or not) enjoys a privileged position in the decisional context. Hence, expert groups, courts, regulators, or standard setting bodies may possess such certification. Where an issue lacks an agreed set of 'go-to' actors, policy participants are plural. Just how plural depends on the level of issue tractability. When this is high we have interest-driven actors; where both tractability and certification are low we have the most plural and social of policy arenas. Taken together, these two dimensions provide the policy-making contexts along which we situate our analysis of learning (see Figure 5.1).

Learning epistemically

Recall that in epistemic contexts there is high uncertainty: actors need to learn. When this is coupled with the existence of an authoritative body of knowledge and experts who are willing and able to interact with policy-makers and take a proper role in the policy process, for example by sitting on statutory consultative bodies, we have conditions that facilitate

Figure 5.1: Learning in decision-making contexts

		PROBLEM TRACTABILITY	
		LOW	HIGH
CERTIFICATION OF ACTORS	LOW	Learning in reflexivity	Learning as by-product of bargaining
	HIGH	Learning in epistemic contexts	Learning in hierarchy

Source: Adapted from Dunlop and Radaelli, (2013, Figure 1: 603)

the transmission of problem-solving ideas. With caution, we can use the metaphor of teaching in the sense that the expert brings to the decision-making table evidence that effectively mitigates uncertainty.

How the lesson is understood or manipulated, and whether it is the right lesson to learn, is another question. Indeed, a necessary condition for successful learning is that experts must have authoritative knowledge which is policy-relevant. Consider Peter M Haas's (1990) landmark case study, United Nations (UN) decision-makers learned that the Mediterranean needed to be and could be 'saved' because the epistemic community had both exclusive access to specialist knowledge *and* had a credible policy plan that made the knowledge real to decision-makers. Where experts are politically ignorant, the rejection of scientific knowledge often follows (see the cases of the EU and hormone growth promoters (Dunlop, 2010, 2017c) and the difficult relationship between economists and the European Commission in the early days of EU corporate tax policy (Radaelli, 1997).

We can add to this. The most skilled teachers have more than just cognitive authority. They have the soft skills – notably, communication, leadership and entrepreneurship – to hold the attention of powerful elites (Cross, 2013; Dunlop, 2014: 216–17). Boehmer-Christiansen's (1994) work on the early years of the Intergovernmental Panel on Climate Change (IPCC) highlights the role of the panel chair – Bert Bolin – and his charismatic authority which was, in part, responsible for the step-change in learning on carbon emissions by governments in the 1990s.

Further, to absorb new knowledge, decision-makers must be in a 'ready to learn' state. In the conventional classroom, part of the teacher's role is to baseline their students to get a sense of their readiness: emotionally, physically, experientially and in terms of their knowledge (Novak and Gowin, 1984). In the policy arena, we think more in terms of how ready the system is to take on board new information. Here, the teaching mechanism is at its most potent where experts are willing and able to accommodate the often erratic and unpredictable timelines of policy-making.

What is being learned, and what is it good for? In an ideal typical manifestation, teaching mechanisms shed light on cause-and-effect relationships and how available evidence can be linked to desired policy outcomes. Of course, this is the world of evidence-based policy-making (EBPM) (Nutley et al, 2007) marked by the 'intended use by intended users' of science (Patton, 1997). Though (rightly) criticised as overly- functional (Cartwright and Hardie, 2012) and even at times mythological (Boswell, 2018), at the very least EBPM does afford a reduction in uncertainty. Moreover, this type of learning forces a forensic examination (if not always justification) of the logic and content of policies, and how these link to outputs (as opposed to focusing only on outcomes).

Learning from reflection

To approach learning in the context of reflection, think of dialogue. At the level of policy-sectors, this context triggers learning if there is a predisposition to listen to what the others have to say and to re-consider one's preferences. At the macro level of society, this is Dewey's utopia of the Great Society turning into the Great Community. Today, this type of learning is embedded in several instruments for policy choice, such as participatory policy analysis, experimental governance, deliberative polling and citizens' juries. But, dialogue doesn't just 'happen' and 'function' under any condition.

Radical uncertainty and the absence of a predominant actor mean this: we all know pretty much nothing (radical uncertainty), therefore we are likely to engage in public policy by blending our individual bits and pieces of incomplete evidence/ experience with arguments and values (Majone, 1989). This makes reason and social consensus possible (Habermas, 1984). Here, the 'how' of learning is more pertinent than the 'what' (Freeman, 2006).

Thus, to generate learning we need force-free deliberations involving a wide range of social actors of myriad backgrounds who bring a range of codified and un- codified knowledge types to bear on debate. Yet, for dialogue to deliver learning results, these debates must be convened in some way such as public engagement technologies. Deliberative tools are the most open allowing iterative processes of communication where what is learned and the possible ends to which those lessons are put are entirely open. In upstream policy engagement tools, citizens are invited to critique technological and policy prototypes in substantive and normative ways before any social roll-out is agreed (Wilsdon and Willis, 2004). Such early interactions are rare however. More commonly, public engagement is synonymous with tools such as consultation that fall some way short of a genuinely plural dialogue (Blanc and Ottimofiore, 2016).

One alternative is to facilitate reflexivity by building institutional architectures such as the experimental governance arrangements described by Sabel and Zeitlin (2008). The experimentalist architecture is essentially a network of multi-level governance units, such as the: European Commission, EU Member States, and industrial districts. In this network, there are policy problems for which no obvious solution is available at the centre. Thus, the centre's first task is to facilitate agreement on the objectives, for example via a system of indicators to measure progress. The second task is to encourage communication across the levels of the networks so that when a solution is found somewhere locally, by a certain constellation of actors, this solution can be validated via peer review within the network. If it passes validation, the solution can be imitated, adapted or hybridised by other actors in the multi-level network. Thus, the centre holds the measures and policy goals against which success can be gauged, but critically, lower-level policy actors have autonomy in how they achieve these policy ends and who in society they work with to get results. In exchange for this freedom, they participate in peer review exercises where they compare their approaches with European colleagues (Sabel and Zeitlin, 2010).

But what is learned in the context of reflexivity? Through open dialogue we learn about social norms (Checkel, 2005). This is a deep form of learning; by exploring and often re-defining social norms and the identities bound up within them, policy actors generate new consensus and new definitions of what is appropriate. They may even reframe their own identities – hence this deep learning is associated with paradigmatic policy change (Hall, 1993) and deutero learning (Argyris and Schön, 1978). Decision-makers learn about how to learn. What dialogue is good for and how to mainstream it into policy-making are the questions that follow. This is connected with ideals of Dewey's practical–moral deliberation (Sanderson, 2006), achieving the legitimacy of law through communicative rationality (Habermas, 1984) and the design of 'good' deliberative governance (Dryzek, 2010).

Learning as by-product of bargaining

When we turn to learning in the context of bargaining we enter the world of exchange, the craft of politics as compromise, give-and-take, exchange of resources, and 'making a deal'. To get into this mode, we need an issue that is eminently tractable and plural authority. 'Tractable' means that society (often public administration) has a repertoire of solutions, algorithms, or ways of doing things. Actors have to discover where the frontier of efficient bargaining lies, not how to cope with radical uncertainty. In terms of practical insights, understanding where a policy controversy is situated on this spectrum is crucial to success: one can pretend to bargain in a world of radical uncertainty, but it is like exchanging fake notes at the board game Monopoly® rather than making effective deals about what works.

Decision-makers, interest groups and civil society organisations need each other, they are inter-dependent. The mechanisms of exchange underpin interactions. Information is handled and changed during exchanges. Though decision-makers are not seeking truth (indeed they are bargaining), they select, acquire and trade information to inform their negotiating positions. This ultimately influences what they are willing to 'give' to competitors but it also generates a by-product: learning. In policy contexts where stable policy communities dominate, interaction will be routinised. Here, decision-making risk is calculable and exchange mechanisms underpinned by actors' probability judgements derived from long-standing experiences. While these calculations will be adjusted and re-calibrated over time, the lessons generated may be thought of as little more as the realisation of expectations as opposed to any new discovery. In such circumstances, though it is never complete, transparency will be sufficient for actors to be able to make an accurate prediction of other parties' stances. On the other hand, where interactions are novel or one-off, or a new actor enters the arena, risk increases and transparency reduces. In this context of incomplete information, interactions will be marked more by negotiation and bet-hedging. Here, exchanges do not simply create lessons about the most efficient means to secure mutually beneficial outcomes. They may create new understandings about the issue entirely.

Our study on the Eurozone provides an instructive example (Dunlop and Radaelli, 2016: 117–19). Key episodes in the implementation of the European Semester fiscal surveillance system have been characterised by exchanges between Italy and France and the EU institutions. In one instance, Italy offered reforms in exchange of going beyond the deficit limits. France too played a similar game of offering offsets to the Commission, using the political leverage of a large member state to delay the reforms needed to exit the excessive deficit procedure. Here, we see a selective interpretation of policy and exchange mechanisms as the engine of learning about the boundaries of the negotiable.

What is learning via bargaining good for, then? Essentially, lessons about preferences and the costs of cooperation. Taking preferences first, through bargaining and negotiation, policy-makers, pressure groups, decision-makers learn about the composition of preferences on an issue, the salient outcomes around which parties can coalesce and about breaking points – the red lines, so to speak. Decision-makers also learn about the cost of reaching agreements. Where policy problems are time- sensitive, actors stand to lose if negotiation appears to be extending indefinitely and may radically adjust their stances to secure a quicker closure.

Bargaining in the end is good for certain things but not for others. Exchange generates important lessons both functionally and normatively. In terms of policy outcomes, ongoing negotiation uncovers the set of resource allocations required to ensure that no one gains at the expense of another. Once this is clear, decision- makers can work through the possible trade-offs implied by the resulting narrow set of choices. There are also normative gains. In a society, the many processes of repeated exchange encapsulate Lindblom's *Intelligence of Democracy* (1965) whereby policy stability is generated by increased appreciation and understanding of rivals' positions. This partisan mutual adjustment (PMA) (Lindblom and Woodhouse, 1963) has normative properties as well as empirical leverage: it claims that a society based on preferences is better than a society based on knowledge or 'intellectual cogitation' (Dente, 2014) – the opposite of epistemic learning.

Learning in hierarchies

Our exploration of learning in hierarchies starts with the acknowledgement that rules-based systems can be formal or informal, contained in institutions or simply believed and trusted by a society. Indeed, what matters for a hierarchical rule to have power is that someone is obeyed. In some societies, family norms and standards set by communities like the village, the tribe or the neighbourhood are much more important than laws and regulations (Putnam, 1993). This leads us to frame learning with the metaphor of compliance.

Often we think of hierarchy as instructions, commands, and everything else that seems the antithesis of learning. What's hierarchy to do with learning, then? Consider this: over time actors learn about the scope of rules, their flexibility, and what happens when they are not followed. In a sense, this is the shadow of hierarchy: the range of social phenomena projected by the existence of a system of rules. It may be a set of court decisions, or more generally the nature of the legal system (Kelemen, 2010) to illuminate the scope of rules, or the attitude of inspectors. The rule *per se* is an incomplete contract that is defined over time via implementation.

Three powerful explanations capture the essence of the shadow of hierarchy. One is Scharpf's analysis of decisional blockages set at different levels of governance, like in federal systems or in the EU (1988). Another is the institutional grammar tool (Crawford and Ostrom, 1995). The third is the veto-players approach by Tsebelis (2002), which does not deal explicitly with hierarchy but offers a template to analyse decision-making systems. The joint-decision trap sheds light on hindrances and pathologies, as we explain below. The institutional grammar pins down the conditions that lead a rule to generate social behaviour, and is explicit on what happens if that type of behaviour does not appear. Veto-players theory provides yet another way to look at hindrances – we talk about this in the next section.

Turning now to what this learning is good for, hierarchical rules are indispensable to organised societies. They define roles and stabilise expectations: an inspector has a role that is generally understood by companies and it is on the basis of expectations about this role that regulatory conversations between inspectors and firms take place (Blanc, 2016). Hierarchy also delivers on 'monitorability': some learning processes can be measured, compared, appraised because there is someone on top who sets the standards for monitoring compliance. Finally, this type of learning allows societies to sanction non-compliant behaviour. Sanctions and clear expectations about 'what happens if the rule is not followed' allow hierarchies to guide communities and societies. In international organisations, hierarchical learning is a common way to steer the behaviour of states and to allow the international society to affirm its norms.

Lesson 2: Triggers and hindrances

When learning 'works', it is because of some triggers that are activated – as we said earlier on, learning does not just 'happen'. But, learning processes can also be stymied, disrupted and de-railed. Thus, we need to look at both ends of the spectrum; the facilitating conditions as well as blocking factors. In this section, we consider triggers as well as hindrances.

Triggering and hindering epistemic learning

In epistemic contexts, an important learning trigger is the presence of statutory rights of consultation – meaning that an epistemic body ought to be consulted and listened to by policy-makers. A pluralistic approach to the use of expertise is another trigger. Some years ago, the European Commission launched a pan-European exercise on 'democratising expertise' with experts and policymakers. It culminated in the Liberatore report (2001). It is useful to recall the message of this report. For 'teaching' to be effective, expertise should be socially robust. This often implies a delicate balancing act between scientific quality and social, economic, and political preferences. Note that this trigger is not about 'majority voting in science', but rather about guaranteeing 'due process' in the way expertise is developed, used and communicated' (Liberatore, 2001: 7).

For other triggers, we recall the findings of the literature on Europeanisation (Börzel and Risse, 2003). Here, we find that 'norm entrepreneurs' (Finnemore and Sikkink, 1998) and cooperative informal institutions facilitate the mission of epistemic communities. New lessons are not simply taught *ex cathedra*. They require alignment between epistemic norms, on the one hand, and shared understandings and structures of social meaning, on the other. Norm entrepreneurs actively seek this alignment via persuasion and advocacy.

Turning to hindrances, one problem in public policy controversies is the fragmentation of epistemic communities. We mentioned the case of the Mediterranean (Haas, 1990), but other policy domains are fraught with epistemic controversies. A good example is economic policy in the EU since the crisis of 2008 – with equally strong epistemic arguments for and against 'austerity' among economists. Obviously, without consensus on the lesson to be taught, there cannot be a clear message on which decision-makers can act. In some contexts, experts are re-framed as 'facilitator'. They do not contribute to the definition of the preferences of the learner, rather they simply help with know-how and technical responses to precise questions. Obviously, there isn't much epistemic enlightenment in these cases, although normatively it is justifiable that elected decision-makers remain in control of the objectives of learning. No matter how accurate and well-understood the lesson is, low policy capacity is always a powerful barrier (Dunlop, 2015; see Regonini, 2017).

Enabling and disabling reflection

There are two important triggers for reflexivity. One is institutional and concerns the governance architecture of deliberative, co-productive spaces. The design of committees, the role assigned to the chair, the style of interaction have causal effects on the presence or absence of the mechanism of dialogue crucial to reflexivity (Joerges and Neyer, 1997). More generally, Risse and Klein (2010) identified a full range of institutional scope conditions that trigger reflexivity in negotiations. Precisely they point to: institutional settings that support overlapping role identities; the transparency of negotiation settings with actors uncertain about the preferences of their audience (or, at the opposite, low transparency with certainty about the preference of the audience whose consent is required); and, norms and institutional procedures that privilege authority based on moral competence rather than formal power roles and hierarchy. Always at the aggregate level (organisations and political systems), institutions that promote and support socialisation are a strong pathway to reflexive learning.

The other trigger operates at the individual level. Here, what matters is the predisposition of the actors. We must assume that, at least at some point in time during the course of a policy process, actors have the predisposition to listen and to 'move' and therefore change their preferences. A good set of case studies is included in *Frame Reflection*, where reflexive learning is triggered only when actors are prepared to go beyond the 'dialogue of the deaf' (Schön and Rein, 1994). Repeated failure and a deterioration of the status quo push actors into this predisposition. In her *Currency of Ideas*, McNamara (1999) illustrates how repeated failure with a certain paradigm of monetary policy opened-up the minds of policy-makers to new policy paradigms and ultimately reflexivity.

As for hindrances, they operate in organisational and political cultures where there is not a deliberative tradition, and compromise is considered almost like losing one's honour and reputation. Further, the presence of genuinely incommensurable arguments makes deliberation either fake or covers the aggressive attempt to silence an argument – hence, it is domination (Pellizzoni, 2001). Thus, deliberation can degenerate into pathological or dysfunctional learning. For Karolewski (2011) the conventional deliberative methods used in the EU have their own dark side, particularly the false will formation and rational hijacking of deliberation. Provocatively, Lynn Sanders (1997) in *Against Deliberation* lists reasons, broadly speaking concerned with domination, why deliberation can violate democratic standards.

Triggers and barriers to learning from bargaining

For exchange to take place in bargaining, barriers to contract must be low. This trigger is not just about the absence of legal or technological barriers.

It is also about the overall transparency of the negotiation settings and the circulation of information, so that actors can 'mutually adjust' on the basis of robust assumptions about what they exchange, with whom, and with what consequences. Partisan mutual adjustment is facilitated by Popper's (1945) open society with enforceable contracts and rule of law. Cultural, religious, technocratic dogmas limit learning via exchange.

If we move from the individual level to the organisational and social level, bargaining requires low barriers to aggregation of preferences. Eberlein and Radaelli (2010) distinguish between aggregation techniques and transformation techniques. Aggregation is particularly important for bargaining. It comes in two forms: one is issue-aggregation, the other is arena-aggregation. On the one hand, actors in organisations and political systems must be able to recombine issues to reach consensus and learn how to exploit cooperation. They should also be able to re-order issues temporarily, by exploiting delayed compensation and other classic ways of composing conflict. On the other hand, actors must be free to shift arenas and even to create a new arena, or break a complex conflict by allocating portions of the conflict to different arenas (Eberlein and Radaelli, 2010; for an empirical case see Radaelli and Kraemer, 2008 on the break-up of multi-dimensional conflict in different tax policy arenas in the EU).

The separation of procedures from substance reduces the friction in bargaining. If actors cannot successfully bargain on the outcome, they may find it easier to reach agreement on the procedure through which the outcome will be reached (Eberlein and Radaelli, 2010). It is the separation between procedure and substantive policy issues that is the trigger – not the procedure itself. There is another possible trigger based on de-coupling, that is, the separation between higher-level framework agreements and lower level policy issues. In this case the trigger is the possibility to agree on the framework agreement 'under the veil of vagueness' (Gibson and Goodwin, 1999, cited by Eberlein and Radaelli, 2010: 788).

Game theory suggests an important trigger – absent which we have the hindrance: exchange must be repeated, not one-shot, so that trust can be developed. The fuel of PMA, and more generally bargaining, is that the winners and losers are reshuffled in different iterations. No-one wants to play the same game if the result is always to be on the side of the losers. We illustrate empirically this point with the case of the negotiations on the excessive deficit procedure in the European Semester of the EU (Dunlop and Radaelli, 2016). The European Semester is an iterative mechanism of coordination of economic policy and promotion of structural reform. Bargaining deteriorates if there is ossification of winners and losers in the European Semester. Another hindrance is the low cost of defection, which makes partisan mutual adjustment and bargaining in general unstable.

Triggering and hindering hierarchy

It is not easy to pin down exactly the triggers for hierarchy. Studies of political culture suggest that habit-driven behaviour may best explain the variance between those who comply and those who violate. Such habits are underpinned by legitimacy, trust in authority, historical memories, and even deference as pre-conditions for political hierarchies to work (Dahl, 1971; Rothstein, 2000). Yet, this is only part of the story about the facilitating conditions. First, consider Tyler's famous question (2003): why do people pay taxes, obey and so on? Trust in authority is not a given; institutions must earn trust, and compliance must be socially deserved.

Second, consider Chayes and Chayes (1993): deterrence, sanctions, enforcement and, in short, interests represent only one side of compliance. The other is (yet again) trust, identity, beliefs and, in short, norms. Thus, the trigger to compliance can be found in both the logic of interests and in the logic of norms. It depends on how interest constellations are composed once a rule is enforced, how norms have developed in a given society or policy setting.

As for hindrances, we can revert to what we said about Scharpf (1988) and Tsebelis (2002). Tsebelis is eminently interested in agenda-setting and decision-making. But think about veto players at the stage of implementation – Héritier et al (2001) provide a good empirical example about the implementation of EU road haulage regulations and the structure of truck drivers' associations as veto players. A high number of veto players at the implementation stage hinders compliance. Actors may learn dysfunctionally how not to comply if there are low costs in exercising veto players power. The number of implementation arenas (low or high) is in itself a veto player variable – if your policy has to go through many hoops the probability of not getting to destination is high. In short, the presence of a high number of veto players makes the chain of compliance murky. It reduces the probability that actors will in the end really learn something about rules and rules-following.

Scharpf (1988) instead draws our attention to the joint-decision trap in systems of multi-level governance. Under joint-decision trap conditions, the very possibility of agreeing on rules to be enforced hierarchically is stymied. These are institutional hindrances. However, the hindrance may occur at the policy level: not always is the solution known in advance, or at least agreed on the top level of the hierarchy. Learning from the top (Radaelli, 2008) is possible only if there is a relatively clear, unambiguous, agreed-upon solution that can then be pushed down the chain of hierarchy.

Lesson 3: Watch out for learning pathologies

Finally, we turn to dysfunctional learning, or pathologies (Dunlop, 2017a). Here social scientists who are sceptical of the romantic or benevolent bias of learning (Radaelli, 2009: 1147) will find their comfort zone.

Dysfunctions of epistemic learning

Epistemic actors may teach the 'wrong' lesson (Dunlop, 2017b). It is difficult for elected politicians to understand that science is not about the ultimate truth, but a process of conjectures and confutations. Science is about discovery, not dogma. In this sense, the lessons provided by epistemic teachers are neither contingent arguments ready to be demolished nor ever-present truths. Absent this understanding of science, the epistemic mechanism degenerates into the pathology of the dialogue of the deaf (Schön and Rein, 1994), in this case the lack of understanding between the world of science and the world of public opinion and public policy. Alternatively, groupthink often results in situations where the paradigm laid out by experts has captured policy- makers' thinking (Janis, 1972). Finally, advocacy coalitions are good at mobilising counter-epistemic communities to politicise controversies and diluting the influence of experts and scientists (Rietig, 2018).

When reflexivity goes wrong

One problem with reflexivity is scale: the mechanisms of dialogue can be triggered in small-scale deliberative fora. However, we do not know exactly how to couple deliberation in, say, mini-publics with collective, nationwide decision-making fora, for example legislative committees (for this discussion see Hendriks, 2016). The research of appropriate institutional mechanisms to link sites of deliberation to real-world public choice is still going on. In the meantime, de-coupling remains a pathology. Papadopoulos asks whether attempts to empower citizens and promote reflexivity locally matter for decision-making and institutional choice. Until they do, they may distract us from fundamental issues of democratic governance, especially if they suffer from bureaucratisation and disproportionately favour specialised, professional non-governmental organisations over ordinary citizens (Papadopoulos, 2013: 143). To conclude, de-coupling between the local and the systemic levels, lack of inclusiveness, experto-cratic self-selection and domination are the main warning lessons for practitioners willing to go down the road of reflexive learning.

Dysfunctional bargaining

Bargaining may end up in dysfunctional learning. This happens when actors have widely different endowments of resources. The scale is tilted from the very beginning and inertia results. Further, incremental changes and PMA do not allow constellations of actors to produce radical policy change. And, learning without transformation of preferences is not desirable when sticky preferences are exactly 'the' problem from a normative point of view. If a system needs new beliefs, re-conciliation of trade-offs, and radical policy innovation to come out of a crisis, it may not benefit from the type of learning generated by bargaining.

Pathologies of hierarchy

The pathologies of hierarchy are clear. A perfect shadow of hierarchy system with full compliance has no breathing spaces. It does not adapt to the environment. It requires accurate coupling with democratic institutions and standards, otherwise it violates democratic norms by veering towards authoritarianism. It stifles innovation and deep learning. Once actors have learned how to comply, there is no room to explore learning in other ways.

Conclusions

Drawing lessons from policy learning has major benefits. We have drawn three lessons: on the contexts, on triggers and hindrances, and on pathologies of learning. To conclude, we show that these lessons bring four advantages.

First, the findings point to a distinctive set of advantages of looking at policy processes with a learning lens. This is more important than establishing when some conjectures about learning are supported by what kind of evidence. Our chapter defies the traditional judgement of the value of a contribution. (Is the empirical material new? Does it successfully test this or that conjecture?) Rather, we make the case for novelty on the criteria set by the editors of this special issue.

Second, we show that by opening up the peripheral vision on learning, and considering the four contexts in particular, social scientists can have a wider and more meaningful scientific conversation. Instead of collating data about who has tested what proposition about learning, we bring the findings on compliance, social norms, enforcement, Europeanisation, evidence-based policy and more to bear on learning. Ours is definitively not the standard review of the literature, but a synthesis that addresses the need of creating a wider social scientific audience for policy learning.

Turning to our other audience, the so-called practitioners, there are advantages too. Whether the problem is learning how to fight organised crime and corruption, or to re-launch growth in Europe or development in Africa, we suggest to start from capturing the context and then moving on to learning. This is equally important whether the objective is simply to exercise influence or to design a new process where a constellation of actors should reach some learning objectives over time. For social actors, our analysis shows when and how they should try to change the nature of the arena, or lobby for a re-design of the process – this lesson is often forgotten because social actors fight for a given policy objective, not for the parameters that define who does what and how in the policy process. As we said, it is important to understand the tone of the policy process in order to get learning right.

Third, triggers and hindrances add the fundamental scope conditions for learning to happen or not. Here our contribution shows to the audience of social scientists and the readership of practitioners that the general language of scope-conditions and middle-range theorising translates well into the world of policy learning. Some of the triggers and hindrances can be manipulated by design (like coupling a deliberative forum to public decision-making), others (like trust in institutions or attitudes towards science) are the product of historical memories and political culture. This is a lesson for those with the authority to design instruments and venues of learning (like consultation or a committee of enquiry) as well as for pressure groups. It is often the case that the problem is not learning *per se*, but activating the right mechanism or getting rid of the obstacles to learning.

The fourth advantage is to alert us that learning can be a failure. To demonstrate that learning can be dysfunctional brings back into the field of policy learning the classic orientation of many political scientists to focus on the difficulty of problem resolution, inertia, inefficiency, conflict and government failure. There are benefits for the audience of practitioners too. Private interests, non-governmental organisations and public managers themselves must be sufficiently critical in their engagement with learning. Depending on the context, they must be willing to unlearn lessons, push issues into arenas where learning types are different, or re-define their role (such as entrepreneur, teacher, and so on). To capture the strategic features of the context where learning takes place and whether the current approach to learning is functional or not is key.

Taken together, the lessons are useful to designers of public policy, but also to pressure groups and more generally non-state actors, including individual citizens who lobby directly by launching campaigns on specific issues (Alemanno, 2017). Typically, most of the attention is on the preferred solution and why learning does not take place, or takes place in a way that is not desirable. Our lessons direct us toward the profound insight of institutional analysis: learning responds to the tone of the interactions, to whether its mechanisms are activated or triggered or blocked, and to its quality: are we learning the good or bad lesson, for good or bad reason? Consequently, designers and social actors alike should get smarter, and direct their energy where it matters.

Note

1 Previous versions of this article were presented at Lee Kwan Yew School of Public Policy (LKYSPP) 16–17 February 2017, UK Political Studies Association (PSA) annual conference, Glasgow, 6–8 April 2017; workshop on 'Practical Lessons from Policy Theories' University of Colorado, Denver, 14–16 May 2017; and European Consortium of Political Research (ECPR) annual conference, Oslo, 6–9 September 2017. We are grateful to all the participants of these events for their criticisms and comments. Biggest thanks must go to our special issue editors Paul Cairney and Chris Weible for all their imaginative work, our anonymous reviewers and the editorial team of Policy & Politics for having faith in this innovative volume.The conceptual work was informed by two European Research Council (ERC) projects: Analysis of Learning in Regulatory Governance (ALREG) (grant # 230267) and Procedural Tools for Effective Governance (PROTEGO) (grant # 694632).The usual disclaimer applies. The article which this chapter is based on is available via Open Access here: https://doi.org/10.1332/030557318X15230059735521

References

Alemanno, A, 2017, *Lobbying for Change: Find your voice and create a better society*, London: Icon Books

Argyris, C, Schön, D, 1978, *Organizational learning: A theory of action perspective*, Reading, MA: Addison-Wesley

Blanc, F, 2016, *From chasing violations to managing risks*, PhD Thesis, Leiden: University of Leiden

Blanc, F, Ottimofiore, G, 2016, Consultation, in CA Dunlop, CM Radaelli (eds) *Handbook of regulatory impact assessment*, Cheltenham: Edward Elgar

Boehmer-Christiansen, S, 1994, Global climate protection policy: The limits of scientific advice. Parts 1 and 2, *Global Environmental Change* 4, 2, 140–59

Börzel, T, Risse, T, 2003, Conceptualising the domestic impact of Europe, in K Featherstone, CM Radaelli (eds) *The politics of europeanization*, Oxford: Oxford University Press

Boswell, J, 2018, What makes evidence-based policymaking such a useful myth? The case of NICE guidance on bariatric surgery in the UK, *Governance* 31, 2, 199–214

Cartwright, N, Hardie, J, 2012, *Evidence-based policy*, Oxford: Oxford University Press

Chayes, A, Chayes, AH, 1993, On compliance, *International Organization* 47, 2, 175–205

Checkel, JT, 2005, International institutions and socialization in Europe: Introduction and framework, *International Organization* 59, 4, 801–26

Crawford, S, Ostrom, E, 1995, A grammar of institutions, *American Political Science Review* 89, 3, 582–600

Cross, MKD, 2013, Rethinking epistemic communities twenty years later, *Review of International Studies* 39, 1, 137–60

Dahl, RA, 1971, *Polyarchy: Participation and opposition,* New Haven, CT: Yale University Press

Dente, B, 2014, *Understanding policy decisions*, New York, NY: Springer

Dewey, J, 1927, *The public and its problems*, New York, NY: Holt, 2012

Dunlop, CA, 2010, Epistemic communities and two goals of delegation: Hormone growth promoters in the European Union, *Science and Public Policy*, 37, 3, 205–217

Dunlop, CA, 2014, The possible experts: How epistemic communities negotiate barriers to knowledge use in ecosystems services policy, *Environment and Planning C – Government Policy* 32, 2, 208–28

Dunlop, CA, 2015, Organizational political capacity as learning, *Politics and Society* 34, 3, 259–70

Dunlop, CA, 2017a, Policy learning and policy failure: Definitions, dimensions and intersections, *Policy & Politics* 45, 1, 19–37

Dunlop, CA, 2017b, Pathologies of policy learning: What are they and how do they contribute to policy failure?, *Policy & Politics* 45, 1, 3–18

Dunlop, CA, 2017c, Epistemic communities and the irony of policy learning, *Policy and Society*, 36, 2, 215–32

Dunlop, CA, Radaelli, CM, 2013, Systematizing policy learning: From monolith to dimensions, *Political Studies* 61, 3, 599–619

Dunlop, CA, Radaelli, CM, 2016, Policy learning in the Eurozone crisis: Modes, power and functionality, *Policy Sciences* 49, 2, 107–24

Dunlop, CA, Radaelli, CM, Trein, JP, 2018, Introduction: The family tree of policy learning, in CA Dunlop, CM Radaelli (eds) *Learning in public policy: Analysis, modes and outcomes*, Basingstoke: Palgrave

Dryzek, JS, 2010, *Foundations and frontiers of deliberative governance*, Oxford: Oxford University Press

Eberlein B, Radaelli, CM, 2010, Mechanisms of conflict management in EU regulatory policy, *Public Administration* 88, 3, 782–99

Finnemore, M, Sikkink, K, 1998, International norm dynamics and political change, *International Organization* 52, 4, 887–917

Freeman, R, 2006, Learning in public policy, in M Moran, M Rein, RE Goodin (eds) *Oxford handbook of public policy*, Oxford: Oxford University Press

Goyal, N, Howlett, M, 2018, Lessons learned and not learned: Bibliometric analysis of policy learning, in CA Dunlop, CM Radaelli (eds) *Learning in public policy: Analysis, modes and outcomes*, Basingstoke: Palgrave

Haas, PM, 1990, *Saving the Mediterranean: The politics of international environmental co- operation*, New York, NY: Columbia University Press

Habermas, J, 1984, *The theory of communicative action volume 1*, Boston, MA: Beacon Press

Hall, PA, 1993, Policy paradigms, social learning and the state: The case of economic policy-making in Britain, *Comparative Politics* 25, 3, 275–96

Heikkila, T, Gerlak, AK, 2013, Building a conceptual approach to collective learning: Lessons for public policy scholars, *Policy Studies Journal* 41, 3, 484–511

Hendriks, CM, 2016, Coupling citizens and elites in deliberative systems: The role of institutional design, *European Journal of Political Research* 55, 1, 43–60

Héritier, A, Kerwer, D, Knill, C, Lehmkuhl, D, Teutsch, M, Douillet, A-C, 2001, *Differential Europe: The European Union impact on national policymaking*, London: Rowman & Littlefield

Janis, IL, 1972, *Victims of groupthink*, New York: Houghton Mifflin

Jenkins-Smith, HC, 1990, *Democratic politics and policy analysis*, Pacific Grove, CA: Brooks/Cole

Joerges, C, Neyer, J, 1997, From intergovernmental bargaining to deliberative political processes, *European Law Journal* 3, 3, 273–99

Karolewski, IP, 2011, Pathologies of deliberation in the EU, *European Law Journal* 17, 1, 66–79

Kelemen, RD, 2010, Globalising European Union environmental policy, *Journal of European Public Policy* 17, 3, 335–49

Liberatore, A, 2001, *Report of the working group on democratising expertise and establishing scientific reference systems*, Brussels: European Commission

Lindblom, CE, 1965, *The intelligence of democracy*, New York: The Free Press

Lindblom, CE, Woodhouse, EJ, 1963, *The policy-making process*, Engelwood Cliffs, NJ: Prentice Hall

McAdam, D, Tarrow, S, Tilly, C, 2001, *Dynamics of contention*, Cambridge, MA: Cambridge University Press

McNamara, KR, 1999, *The currency of ideas: Monetary politics in the European Union*, Ithaca, NY: Cornell University Press

Majone, G, 1989, *Evidence, argument, and persuasion in the policy process*, New Haven, CT: Yale University Press

Moyson, S, Scholten, P, Weible C M, 2017, Policy learning and policy change: Theorizing their relations from different perspectives, *Policy and Society*, 36, 2, 161–77

Novak, JD, Gowin, DB, 1984, *Learning how to learn*, Cambridge, MA: Cambridge University Press

Nutley, SM, Walter, I, Davies, HTO, 2007, *Using evidence: How research can inform public services*, Bristol: The Policy Press

Papadopoulos, Y, 2013, *Democracy in crisis? Politics, governance and policy*, Basingstoke: Palgrave Macmillan

Patton, MQ, 1997, *Utilization-focussed evaluation*, Thousand Oaks, CA: Sage

Pellizzoni, L, 2001, The myth of the best argument, *The British Journal of Sociology* 52, 1, 59–86

Popper, KR, 1945, *The open society and its enemies volume 2*, London: Routledge

Putnam, RD, 1993, *Making democracy work*, Princeton, NJ: Princeton University Press

Radaelli, CM, 1997, *The politics of corporate taxation in the European Union: Knowledge and international policy agendas*, London: Routledge

Radaelli, CM, 2008, Europeanization, policy learning and new modes of governance, *Journal of Comparative Policy Analysis* 10, 3, 239–54

Radaelli, CM, 2009, Measuring policy learning: Regulatory impact assessment in Europe, *Journal European Public Policy*, 16, 8, 1145–64

Radaelli, CM, Kraemer US, 2008, Governance areas in EU direct tax policy, *Journal of Common Market Studies* 46, 2, 315–36

Regonini, G, 2017, Governmentabilities without policy capacity, *Policy Sciences* 50, 2, 163–78

Rietig, K, 2018, The link between contested knowledge, beliefs and learning in European climate governance: From consensus to conflict in reforming biofuels policy, *Policy Studies Journal* 46, 1, 137–159

Risse, T, Klein, M, 2010, Deliberation in negotiations, *Journal of European Public Policy* 17, 5, 708–26

Rothstein, B, 2000, Trust, social dilemmas and collective memories, *Journal of Theoretical Politics* 12, 4, 477–501

Sabel, C, Zeitlin, J, 2008, Learning from difference: The new architecture of experimentalist governance in the European Union, *European Law Journal* 14, 3, 271–327

Sabel, C, Zeitlin, J, 2010, *Experimentalist governance in the European Union*, Oxford: Oxford University Press

Sanders, L, 1997, Against deliberation, *Political Theory* 25, 3, 347–76

Sanderson, I, 2006, Complexity, 'practical rationality' and evidence-based policy making, *Policy and Politics* 34, 1, 115–32

Scharpf, F, 1988, The joint decision trap: Lessons from German federalism and European integration, *Public Administration* 66, 3, 239–78

Schön, DA, Rein, M, 1994, *Frame reflection: Toward the resolution of intractable policy controversies*, New York, NY: Basic Books

Torgerson, D, 1992, Priest and jester in the policy sciences: Developing the focus of inquiry, *Policy Sciences* 25, 3, 225–35

Tsebelis, G, 2002, *Veto players: How political institutions work*, Princeton, NJ: Princeton University Press

Tyler, TR, 2003, Procedural justice, legitimacy, and the effective rule of law, *Crime and Justice* 30, 283–357

Wilsdon, J, Willis, R, 2004, *See-through science*, London: Demos

CHAPTER SIX

Practical prescriptions for governing fragmented governments

William L Swann and Seo Young Kim

Introduction

Collective action dilemmas, or the misalignment of individual incentives and desired collective outcomes, are prevalent across every scale of social interaction. These dilemmas are exacerbated in systems of fragmented authority or overlapping jurisdictions. The intractable, 'wicked problems' – climate change, global terrorism, health crises, crime, or poverty – facing governments are seldom contained within a jurisdiction and require interorganisational efforts to address them (Head and Alford, 2015; Martin and Guarneros-Meza, 2013), although even many common governing tasks are not suited to hierarchies. Whether contracting out social services, restoring an ecosystem in a shared watershed, lowering barriers to international trade, or coordinating sustainability activities across a municipality, policymakers confront obstacles to collaboration that hinder more efficient and effective governance.

As centralised versus decentralised approaches to deal with fragmentation have long been debated (Lyons and Lowery, 1989; Ostrom et al, 1961), collective action theories have explained how semi-autonomous governments can work together and overcome problematic externalities or 'spillovers' (that is, positive or negative consequences of an activity that affect third parties) that arise from fragmentation, while preserving local autonomy that can spur innovation and limit the expansion of bureaucracy.

The Institutional Collective Action (ICA) framework (Feiock, 2007; 2013) has emerged as an analytical lens for understanding collaboration in fragmented governance. 'ICA dilemmas', or situations in which an authority's incentives do not align with collectively desired outcomes, arise from spillovers of policy choice and design that transcend jurisdictions. ICA dilemmas stemming from fragmentation can lead to inefficient behaviour, such as free riding and service duplication, as well as normatively undesirable outcomes such as urban sprawl (Jimenez, 2016).

ICA dilemmas are ubiquitous in governance. They manifest *horizontally* between governmental units at the same level as the consequences of one unit's actions spill over to another's jurisdiction (for example, in interlocal relations); *vertically* as a governmental unit at one level pursues complementary or conflicting actions to those pursued at a higher or lower level (for example, in US state–local relations); and *functionally* between subunits of a unitary authority within a service provision area such as sustainability policy implemented by multiple departments within a municipal government (Feiock et al, 2017).

Extant research has identified key facilitators of collaborative governance, including power symmetry, incentive alignment, participant commitment, face-to-face dialogue, shared understanding and motivation, well-defined rules, effective leadership, flexible policy solutions, legitimacy and capacity for joint action (Ansell and Gash, 2008; Emerson et al, 2012; Huxham and Vangen, 2005; Sørensen and Torfing, 2009). The role of managerial strategies, networks and institutions in dealing with uncertainties associated with complex problems has also been underscored (Koppenjan and Klijn, 2004). However, few studies have considered how authorities mitigate collaboration risk and uncertainty and shape more self-organising arrangements for overcoming ICA dilemmas.

The ICA framework allows researchers and practitioners to compare alternative integrative mechanisms, ranging from self-organising informal networking to hierarchically imposed collaboration, and their ability more efficiently and responsively deliver public services. But what actionable steps can authorities take to lower barriers to collective action and utilise integrative mechanisms that enhance autonomy and reduce transaction costs? What can policymakers and scholars learn about collaborative governance from a deeper understanding of empirical research on overcoming ICA dilemmas? What practical and theoretical implications can we draw that transcend diverse institutional contexts and political systems?

In this chapter, we extract practical lessons and theoretical propositions from ICA research focused on fragmented arenas such as watershed management, environmental policy, emergency management and economic development. The narrative that unfolds through this literature is that policymakers can reduce collaboration risk and uncertainty with multiple strategies that can facilitate the adoption of more self- organised integrative mechanisms. However, these strategies involve nuanced tradeoffs and complexities that future research should consider. From a practical perspective, policymakers will find this chapter useful in that it provides a comprehensive guide for strategically reducing collaboration risk and uncertainty in fragmented arenas across different scales of governance. From a scholarly perspective, this chapter offers researchers a novel, integrative framework for understanding collaboration risk and uncertainty and begs new questions for empirical discernment.

We begin by outlining the intellectual foundations and assumptions of the ICA framework. We then systematically review the ICA empirical literature to tease out practical lessons and theoretical propositions for how authorities can strategically lower barriers to collective action. These lessons and propositions are organised around five fundamental collaborative governance themes: networking, contracting, partner selection, inclusivity and capacity building. We conclude with directions for future research focused on the relative effectiveness of integrative mechanisms, their impact on policy outcomes, and the extent to which they are generalisable across diverse institutional contexts.

Core assumptions and theoretical foundations

The ICA framework seeks to explain how semi-autonomous authorities can overcome barriers to collective action and improve policy outcomes in fragmented governance. While existing theories of collective action focus mostly at the micro level, the ICA perspective extends this logic to the decisions and behaviour of organisational actors such as local governments, public agencies, service delivery organisations and national governments. ICA is thus applicable across multiple scales and a variety of collaborative settings. In this section, we provide an overview of ICA's theoretical foundations and define key concepts in the framework.

Collective action

Figure 6.1 displays the five pillars of the ICA framework that the authors created based on the theoretical foundations described in Feiock (2013, 399–401). ICA rests on collective action theory, which concerns situations in which short-run individual incentives are misaligned with collective interests (Olson, 1965; Ostrom, 1990). Collective action theory assumes semi-autonomous actors will behave in accordance with the rational weighing of benefits and costs of strategies and their likelihood of producing desired results. ICA assumes actions are determined by benefit–cost analysis and contextual governing rules (Ostrom, 2005).

Local public economies

ICA also draws from work on local public economies (LPEs) (McGinnis, 1999; Oakerson and Parks, 2011; Ostrom et al, 1961), which contends that 'polycentricity', or having multiple autonomous authorities, offers

Figure 6.1: Five pillars of ICA, derived from Feiock (2013)

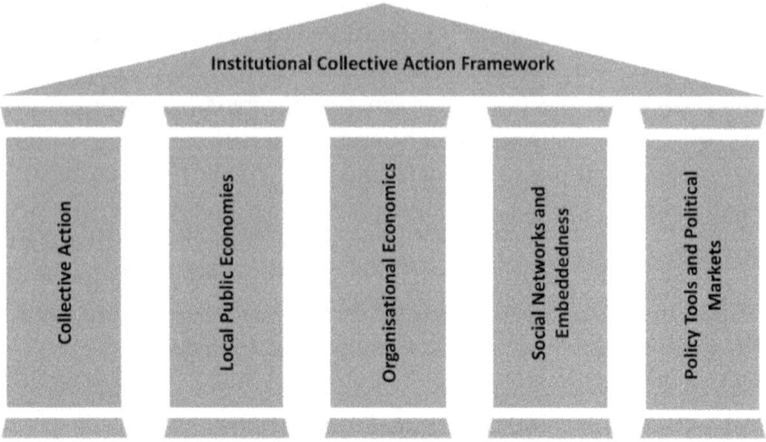

advantages in terms of expanding citizen choice, enabling self-governance, and producing public services more efficiently. However, polycentricity inevitably yields spillovers that create ICA dilemmas in policy arenas and can result in diseconomies of scale when there is a mismatch between citizen preferences and service provision.

LPEs frame the organisation of the policy arena, allowing analysts to specify the nature of the ICA dilemma, which concerns whether authorities face coordination or cooperation problems. Feiock and Scholz (2010) argue that coordination, or 'first-order', problems relate to information asymmetries and the inability of actors to identify joint opportunities, whereas cooperation, or 'second-order', problems involve incentivising actors to work collectively and refrain from opportunism. The nature of the problem also concerns the scale and complexity of collaboration needed to address the issue. For example, when issues are narrowly defined, and actors are connected through reciprocity and reputation, self-organising informal networking can be a more effective and efficient means of governance. However, when issues are broader and more disconnected actors are required to work together, more authoritative mechanisms such as delegated or imposed authority are likely to be needed for collective action (Feiock, 2013).

Organisational economics

ICA also incorporates organisational economics to understand how uncertainty or the 'transaction costs' associated with obtaining information, negotiating and enforcing agreements, and ensuring decision makers are dutiful democratic agents inhibits coordinated activity (Brown and

Figure 6.2: Mechanisms for overcoming ICA dilemmas, adapted from Feiock (2013, 404)

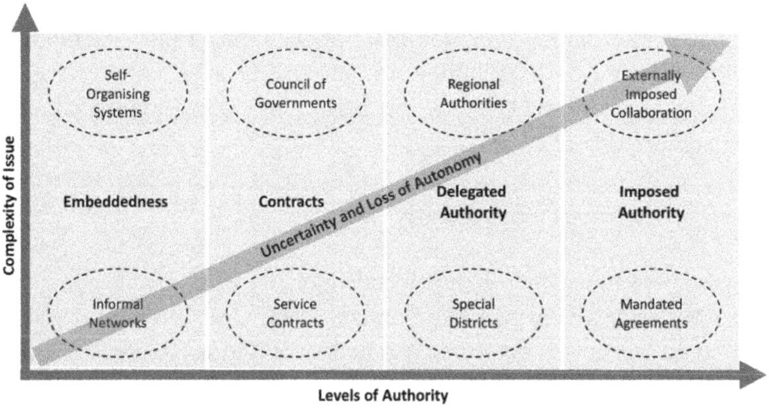

Potoski, 2005; Williamson, 1979). Uncertainty increases as collective decisions become more externally imposed and potentially deviate from local preferences (Buchanan and Tullock, 1962). Also, services having high 'asset specificity' (or narrow application) and/or 'measurement difficulty' (or the inability to gauge and monitor outputs and outcomes) are believed to be more prone to opportunism and thus more likely to be left to in-house production and provision (Williamson, 1981). However, such decisions in fragmented governments can lead to duplication and inefficient service delivery.

Figure 6.2 displays how uncertainty and autonomy relate to the integrative mechanisms for overcoming ICA dilemmas. While Feiock (2013, 404) organises these mechanisms into a 12-category taxonomy, we include only the mechanisms at the lowest and highest levels of complexity to maximise the generalisability of the framework. The vertical dimension captures the level of scope and complexity in collaboration; the horizontal dimension indicates the level of authority vested in the integrative mechanism, with more authoritative mechanisms to the far right; and the diagonal dimension shows how uncertainty increases and autonomy decreases as complexity becomes greater and authority moves away from local decision-makers. ICA assumes the preferred integrative mechanism is the one that imposes the least uncertainty and affords the most autonomy, while still overcoming the ICA dilemma. Organisational economics also introduces the concept of 'collaboration risk'.

Collaboration risk refers to actors' perceptions about whether collaborative efforts will fail (Feiock, 2013). Collaboration risk differs from transaction costs in that the former reflects actors' subjective assessment of collaboration, which reflects actors' interests, the nature of the underlying problem, and existing institutions, whereas the latter results from the integrative mechanism choice. ICA categorises collaboration risk into three types: 'coordination risk', or the inability to reconcile mutually beneficial opportunities; 'division risk', or the difficulty of establishing an agreement on the distribution of collective benefits and costs; and 'defection risk', or the likelihood that participants will not comply with an agreement (Maser, 1998).

Social networks and embeddedness

ICA also pulls from theories of embeddedness, networks and reciprocity (Axelrod, 1984; Coleman, 1988; Putnam, 1993; Uzzi, 1997) to explain how 'social capital' – or the shared resources such as trust, reciprocal norms and social structures that lead to either individual or collective action – can reduce the likelihood of opportunism and lower barriers to collaboration (Feiock and Scholz, 2010). ICA scholars have typically studied the effects of social capital on collaboration by comparing 'bonding' strategies, or establishing close relations based on shared norms and reciprocity, and 'bridging' strategies, or creating ties between heterogeneous groups for obtaining information and resources (Andrew and Carr, 2013; Berardo and Scholz, 2010; Jung et al, 2017).

Policy tools and political markets

Finally, research on policy tools (Salamon, 2002) and political markets (Feiock et al, 2014) informs ICA from the perspective of the interplay between governments and constituent groups. Integrative mechanism choice and design are considered a function of political negotiation between policy suppliers (governmental officials) and policy demanders (affected constituencies). ICA assumes government officials will provide the integrative mechanism, or configuration of mechanisms, desired by the most organised constituency groups in return for political contributions.

Empirical investigations: what we know about overcoming ICA dilemmas

Although a relatively new approach, the ICA framework has advanced our understanding of how semi-autonomous authorities in fragmented arenas lower barriers to collective action and strengthen collaborative governance. To systematically identify practical lessons from this literature, we first searched for all studies employing the 'institutional collective action framework', identifying and reviewing 68 empirical studies published during the 2006–2017 period. In addition, our literature review included some supporting and contradictory evidence from the broader networked governance literature that did not reference the ICA framework. Due to the overlap and unevenness in empirical attention across ICA's five theoretical foundations (Figure 6.1), we organised our literature review around the different levels of authority discussed in Feiock (2013): embeddedness, contracts and delegated/imposed authority (Figure 6.2).

Embeddedness and networks

Previous ICA research finds empirical support for the propositions that the emergence and durability of collaborations positively relate to embeddedness, or the extent of weak-tie relations (bridging ties), strong-tie relations (bonding ties), and reciprocity between actors (Feiock, 2007). Andrew and Carr (2013) find that public officials' informal bonding ties, or how quickly they can connect to all other actors in the network, relate positively to the level of formal organisational participation in regional emergency planning networks. But they find no evidence that public officials' informal bridging ties, or how much influence they have over network information sharing, influence such participation.

Berardo and Scholz (2010) take a different approach to measuring bonding and bridging ties. Analysing organisational dyads in US estuary policy networks, they find organisations tend to engage in bridging strategies by selecting popular actors as collaborative partners, which presumably increases access to information. This finding suggests that obtaining information about potential partners matters more in driving collaboration than the credibility of partners. However, Berardo and Scholz found actors use reciprocal bonding strategies to maximise credibility and lower the risk of defection particularly in dyadic relationships where collaboration risk is considered higher. Bonding strategies may also be more useful to buffer organisations against exogenous shocks such as natural disasters. Jung et al (2017) find bridging ties are easily broken during a disaster, as organisations tend to forge direct ties with those who have resources that can help them in emergency situations.

Informal social networking has also been linked to collaboration. Research finds a positive relationship between interlocal service agreements and municipal officials' informal networking in more frequent regional association meetings, but no evidence that networking in less-frequent professional associations matters (LeRoux et al, 2010). LeRoux et al conclude that more frequent, face-to-face, informal networking leads to greater interlocal collaboration. Similarly, Hawkins et al (2016) find that policymakers' informal network relations encourage formal collaborative agreements in regional economic development.

Research also suggests social capital enables authorities to overcome ICA dilemmas, lowering collaboration risk in joint ventures (Carr et al, 2017) and increasing the likelihood of forming regional partnerships in economic development (Park and Feiock, 2006). These findings are consistent with research on climate adaptation policy networks where collaborative benefits are more diffuse. While strong-tie, reciprocal collaboration in network formation leads to stronger collaboration over time, even weak-tie information exchanges can strengthen relational ties as networks mature (Ingold, 2017).

Homophily, or the tendency to form relational ties with those who are similar, is a concept closely related to embeddedness, which may also facilitate collaboration. ICA research finds political homophily presumably reduces risk and uncertainty and increases local governments' likelihood of collaborating in regional planning networks (Gerber et al, 2013) and emergency management networks (Song et al, 2017). Similarities in population size, racial composition, and geographical location have also been linked to interlocal collaboration (Lee, 2016). However, other research shows how the resources and professional competency of collaborators can be even more important than homophily, signalling a lower likelihood of collaboration failure (Calanni et al, 2015).

Contracts and agreements

To improve efficiency in service delivery, governments often contract out services but at the risk of suppliers failing to deliver in accordance with the agreement. Higher measurement difficulty of services makes reliance on provision from or with other local governments more likely, and reliance on nongovernmental providers less likely (Carr et al, 2009). Carr et al also find higher asset specificity of services increases the likelihood of external contracting with both governmental and nongovernmental service providers.

Bonding and bridging strategies also shape contracting decisions for activities high in measurement difficulty and asset specificity. Andrew (2009) observes how law enforcement agencies use bonding strategies to reduce collaborative risk and uncertainty. However, when specificity of the activity is high, such as in investigative services or financial transfers, agencies tend to avoid bonding strategies because they are likely to work to the disadvantage of gains from specialisation in the external provision market.

Governments also use adaptive multilateral agreements (MLAs) between three or more actors when services are difficult to measure and/or have narrower use. Andrew and Hawkins (2013) find MLAs are more likely to be formed when services are high in measurement difficulty and when asset specificity is either high or low.

ICA research has also empirically examined how transaction costs explain collaboration. Perceived and actual joint gains and lower information, agency and division costs tend to increase the likelihood that authorities will participate in joint agreements for economic development (Feiock et al, 2009). Research also finds at-large elections of city council members mitigate agency costs of aggregating the preferences of the citizen and facilitate interlocal collaboration for service delivery (Kwon and Feiock, 2010). However, all service contracts are not created equal and are influenced by the level of uncertainty that authorities face. Recent research finds that while cost savings explain shorter-term shared service agreements, longer-term agreements are better predicted by past experiences in service sharing and improved service quality and regional coordination (Aldag and Warner, 2017).

In some cases, restrictive monitoring mechanisms may be necessary to reduce collaboration risk and ensure stability in interorganisational collaboration. Restrictive contracting features, such as a financial reporting system and having financial records available for audit by a third party, are more likely to be used in vertical interlocal agreements (ILAs) with higher-level governments than in horizontal ILAs (Andrew et al, 2015). Looser collaborative arrangements appear better suited for more complex problems. For example, governments can address intractable problems by facilitating local partnerships through 'soft steering' approaches such as providing funding and expertise, as opposed to setting restrictive performance targets (Martin and Guarneros-Meza, 2013).

Delegated and imposed authority

ICA dilemmas can also be addressed with more authoritative mechanisms such as delegated and imposed authority. Delegated authority emerges from principals' desire to delegate power to other actors such as external service providers, other governments, or special districts. Under delegation, an independent authority will perform certain activities instead of a general purpose government. In the United States, the least encompassing mechanism for delegation is the single or special purpose government, such as a water or school district. The most encompassing are regional authorities such as metropolitan planning organisations and city-county consolidated governments. Regional and consolidated governments are believed to expand capacity to improve service delivery and more effectively address regional issues but can substitute for more self-organising interlocal collaborative efforts (Kwon et al, 2014; Mullin, 2009). Yet, in most cases, consolidation has proven politically infeasible and has been replaced by interlocal agreements and service contracts (Carr and Feiock, 2004). In Europe, special districts typically do not have the power to tax, and municipal corporations, which are usually owned primarily by local governments, are often delegated authority over single issues such as water, energy and transportation. Whereas territorial consolidations have been used successfully in Western Europe, local authority in many Central and Eastern European countries remains fragmented (Tavares and Feiock, 2017).

Imposed authority implies the least autonomy, as higher-level governments maintain the power and legitimacy to control collaboratives and require lower-level governments to work together. Imposed authority is more prevalent in countries which have more centralised provincial and/or national governments. However, the effectiveness and continuity of imposed collaboration is often questioned, as more self-organising mechanisms are thought to enable authorities to maintain autonomy while mitigating ICA dilemmas (Feiock and Scholz, 2010).

Although delegated and imposed authority have received less empirical attention, ICA research in more centralised governments and countries other than the United States is starting to emerge, demonstrating the challenges associated with self-organising mechanisms in such settings. Research on strategic regions in Norway and Sweden finds a general lack of incentives, certainty, visible payoffs and political legitimacy to effectively provide services through newly formed interlocal mechanisms (Andersen and Pierre, 2010; Johansson et al, 2015). Studies from Canada find ILAs are used sparingly and employed mostly for low-risk, short-term arrangements in emergency services (Spicer, 2015; Spicer and Found, 2016). Research on ILAs among small municipalities in Italy also observes low numbers of service agreements, and substantial barriers to voluntary action (Previtali, 2015). Environmental complexity also inhibits self-organising collaboration. In China, authoritative collaborative arrangements are more likely to emerge when participants are economically heterogeneous, greater in number, and national or provincial governments are involved (Yi et al, 2017).

Practical lessons and theoretical propositions

In this section, we translate the findings from our literature survey to actionable prescriptions for governing fragmented governments, and advance theoretical propositions that consider the nuanced tradeoffs and complexities of collaborative strategies. While some of our lessons and propositions can apply to both self-organised and authoritative settings, we emphasise approaches for authorities to reduce collaboration risk and uncertainty and promote more self-organised integration. Table 6.1 (authors' own) summarises these lessons.

Increase face-to-face networking and foster reciprocal relations

Frequent, informal social networking plays an important role in promoting formal collaborative partnerships (Andrew and Carr, 2013; Hawkins et al, 2016; LeRoux et al, 2010). Participation in networks such as regional associations affords more opportunity for frequent, informal, face-to-face dialogue with policymakers who share similar interests and organisational goals. Such activity can strengthen the foundation for shared understanding and increase the likelihood of interlocal cooperation in a more self-organising manner.

Social capital is critical for overcoming ICA dilemmas. Bonding and bridging strategies gain access to structural and relational social capital that can facilitate collective action, although they are believed to do so in different ways. Bridging strategies, or linking to popular, well-connected organisations, appear more useful for low-risk informational exchanges and discovering cooperative opportunities, but these weak-tie networks may be more vulnerable to exogenous shocks (Jung et al, 2017). On the other hand, bonding strategies, or developing close-knit, reciprocal relations with partners, appear more useful for fostering trust and lowering risk in dyadic relations (Berardo and Scholz, 2010). Policymakers should employ these networking strategies for different aims depending on their organisational needs, the size of the collaborative, and their vulnerability to external circumstances.

While Berardo and Scholz conclude the value of bridging strategies may diminish in favour of bonding strategies as networks mature and begin to take on riskier, larger-scale cooperation problems, bridging strategies may be as equally if not more important as networks become established. This is because the need for monitoring shifts to the need for information as networks become more defined and closed. Burt (1992) contends dense networks are valueless as a monitoring device because each actor knows what other actors know, and they return less diverse information than sparse networks; therefore, more value is created by adding new contacts to dense networks. This implies that as the level of authority increases in scale and networks become more stabilised with defined rules, roles and expectations, the value of bridging strategies may increase vis-à-vis

Table 6.1: Practical recommendations for reducing collaboration risk and uncertainty

Increase face-to-face networking and foster reciprocal relations
• Build stronger foundations for collaboration by networking informally, frequently, and face-to-face in regional associations
• Increase access to information and opportunities by networking with well-connected or heterogeneous organisations
• Strengthen collaborative relationships through reciprocal exchange and shared memberships and activities
• Tailor networking strategies in a complementary fashion to meet organisational needs and environmental demands
Craft collaborative strategies around service characteristics
• Create network closure with multilateral partnerships when it is difficult to monitor and measure service outputs and outcomes
• Link to well-connected organisations to access information when specialised investments are required to produce services
• Employ adaptive or restrictive arrangements depending on the level of collaboration risk, environmental uncertainty and problem complexity
• Utilise short-term agreements in shared services to achieve cost savings, but longer-term agreements for improved service delivery and regional coordination
Exploit commonalities with partners
• Identify similarities in policy preferences, values and problems with neighbouring governments through regional networking
• Collaborate with homogeneous authorities to speed up collaborative processes, but network with heterogeneous authorities to access new information and opportunities
Increase transparency, accountability and equity through inclusiveness
• Include citizens from diverse backgrounds in collaborative decision making
• Encourage citizen participation in meetings, planning, budgeting and oversight
Develop collaborative capacity through incrementalism
• Resolve lower-level coordination problems before addressing higher-level cooperation problems
• Learn by doing and develop collaborative management competencies by achieving 'smalls wins' on intermediate goals
• Increase resources and learning opportunities by working with higher-level governments and lead network agencies

bonding strategies as actors look for ways to innovate and have less need to monitor. However, more stabilised arrangements, particularly in larger-scale cooperation, can still benefit from bonding strategies, since agreements are typically 'incomplete' or underspecified as parties cannot predict the future and there is no guarantee that actors will behave in good faith (Williamson, 1979).

Ultimately, the relation between network structure and effectiveness is not one- size-fits-all (Bodin and Crona, 2009). Policymakers should utilise differentiated combinations of bonding and bridging strategies tailored to specific organisational needs – establishing dense relations that reduce collaboration risk through reciprocity and network closure, but also obtaining diverse information from new contacts that can lead to opportunities and innovation. Moreover, policymakers should practice reciprocity and face-to-face interaction regardless of their relational strategy. Bonding and bridging strategies are complementary and interrelated since lower-level informational exchanges can lead to stronger collaboration over time (Ingold, 2017).

Proposition 1a: More frequent, informal, face-to-face networking among policymakers will reduce collaboration risk and uncertainty and increase the likelihood of adopting more self-organised mechanisms for resolving ICA dilemmas (Figure 6.2).

Proposition 1b: Bonding and bridging network strategies are complementary in developing social capital and mitigating collaboration risk and uncertainty, which increases the likelihood of resolving ICA dilemmas through more self-organised mechanisms (Figure 6.2).

Craft collaborative strategies around service characteristics

Policymakers can craft effective strategies that minimise collaboration risk and uncertainty by considering service characteristics. Preferred collaborative arrangements will vary by service area because service characteristics differ in terms of measurability and asset specificity. Consider public safety service contracts. When the outputs of a service are more difficult to measure, such as in crime or fire prevention, bonding social capital approaches that establish MLAs between three or more parties create network closure and defend against opportunism (Andrew and Hawkins, 2013). By creating network closure whereby participants know everyone else in the network, organisations reduce information and monitoring uncertainties that inhibit self- organising collaboration. However, for highly specific services, such as investigative or medical services, bridging strategies can be more advantageous since they can more easily tap into a larger market of specialised contractors and provide greater information (Andrew, 2009).

Utilising adaptive arrangements can also be advantageous when services have riskier features and policymakers face greater environmental turbulence and ambiguity (Andrew and Hawkins, 2013). Adaptive arrangements, such as mutual aid agreements between local governments in emergency management, allow policymakers to leave agreements open for adjustment and fill in the details later, in order not to burden individual organisations or hamper interorganisational efforts in the future.

When facing high collaboration risk, restrictive arrangements can also help mitigate uncertainty and risk. Policymakers can specify restrictive rules that ensure partners abide by agreements. Such restrictions can help ensure partners comply with contractual obligations. Examples of restrictive arrangements include requiring participants to pay annual fees, incorporating a financial reporting system, making financial records reviewable by a third party, or setting performance targets. While these rules appear to be applied more in vertical interlocal relations, they also have applications to horizontal agreements, particularly when collaboration risk is high and policymakers seek greater predictability (Andrew et al, 2015).

Restrictive arrangements, however, increase other uncertainties such as negotiation and agency costs, which hinder self-organising collaboration. Restrictions designed to reduce defection risks may have drawbacks of signalling distrust and losing momentum in cultivating norms of reciprocity and trust. Performance restrictions may also impede self-organised collaborative partnerships designed to solve complex and unpredictable problems, where 'softer' governmental steering in the form of providing funding and expertise could be more helpful (Martin and Guarneros-Meza, 2013).

Finally, collaborative strategies should also reflect the objectives of shared-service agreements. While short-term contracts can achieve cost savings in shared services, authorities aiming for improved regional coordination and service delivery outcomes will be likely to need longer-term agreements to achieve these broader public values (Aldag and Warner, 2017).

In sum, collaborative strategy making is complex and entails tensions between flexible and formalised arrangements at different stages of collaboration (Ansell, 2015). Policymakers should therefore consider the historical foundation upon which collaborative relations exist and the degree of collaboration risk they face before entering any adaptive or restrictive arrangement, and modify these arrangements as circumstances change.

Proposition 2: Bonding and bridging network strategies will reduce collaboration risk and uncertainty by better reflecting service characteristics, problem complexity, and policy objectives, which increases the likelihood of resolving ICA dilemmas through more self-organised mechanisms (Figure 6.2).

Exploit commonalities with partners

Partner similarities lower collaboration risk and uncertainty, which increases the likelihood of adopting more self-organised integrative mechanisms. Jurisdictions which are politically, socioeconomically, and geographically similar have lower barriers to collaboration and therefore a higher likelihood of partnering (Gerber et al, 2013; Lee, 2016; Song et al, 2017). Authorities can exploit similarities with other authorities to begin cultivating shared norms and common ground that can lead to self-organising collaboratives. Informal networking in regional associations or with neighbouring jurisdictions, for example, allows policymakers to identify other organisations with commonalities in policy preferences, values and problems. Similar authorities may also be able to work together in a more informal, self-governing style and move faster through or bypass lower-risk coordination problems and begin tackling higher-risk cooperation problems, because a foundation for shared understanding is established. Conversely, in cases where more heterogeneous organisations are required to collaborate, more formalised and authoritative mechanisms may be needed to overcome ICA dilemmas (Yi et al, 2017).

An important caveat to the homophily strategy, however, is that similar organisations may have similar networks, which limits the ability to acquire diverse information that can lead to new opportunities and innovation. Homophily could also breed regional inequality over time, particularly if munificent governments collaborate more with each other and leave disadvantaged governments to work out problems on their own. Thus, policymakers can facilitate collaborative processes by working with similar organisations, but they should network with heterogeneous organisations to access new information and reduce disparate outcomes.

Proposition 3a: Homophily will increase the likelihood of adopting more self- organised mechanisms for resolving ICA dilemmas (Figure 6.2).

Proposition 3b: Heterogeneity will increase the likelihood of adopting more authoritative mechanisms for resolving ICA dilemmas (Figure 6.2).

Proposition 3c: Heterogeneous networks will afford greater equity in joint gains over time, and the most effective collaboratives will complement homogeneous with heterogeneous networks.

Increase transparency, accountability, and equity through inclusiveness

Increased transparency, accountability and equity can also reduce risk and uncertainty in collaborative governance. Governments may be able to address all three considerations by enhancing inclusivity in decision making. Inclusiveness in collaborative governance refers to processes which place 'few formal restrictions on participation' (Leach, 2006, 101). Inclusivity provides diverse viewpoints and sensitivities to fairness and equity issues, which could lower uncertainty over whether public officials represent their citizen principals and enhance public understanding of collaborative objectives and challenges.

Citizen involvement in rule-making processes builds legitimacy and accountability for collaborative governance. The lines of accountability, which can be obscured in the process of building collaborative arrangements, can be clarified through citizen participation, which helps ensure that collaborative aims address issues important to citizens. This mitigates the 'democratic deficit' problem which often arises in cases where authority is delegated to entities which are only indirectly accountable to citizens (Andersen and Pierre, 2010). Policymakers can increase inclusiveness in collaboratives by encouraging citizen participation in meetings, planning, budgeting and oversight. Collaborative planning and agreements should be accessible to the public so that citizens have a sense of which services are being provided through collaboration and at what cost (Spicer and Found, 2016). Participatory budgeting can also be used to obtain citizen input into budget allocation and priority setting for collaborative arrangements (Gollagher and Hartz-Karp, 2013). Policymakers might also consider including citizens in the direct oversight of collaborations, which can further enhance transparency and accountability for collaboration (Dollery et al, 2016). Greater inclusivity encourages policymakers to consider equity issues and diverging policy impacts of collaboration on different groups. Equitable distribution of joint benefits is important for governments with limited experience in voluntary collaboration. While negative perceptions of power imbalance or unequal division of gains can hinder collective action, several precedents of mutually-benefiting activity can begin to change such perceptions (Boschet and Rambonilaza, 2017). When citizens have a voice in collaborative processes, they feel more confident that public negotiation is genuine (Ansell and Gash, 2008). While there can be inefficiencies with over-inclusiveness, which could amplify heterogeneity and create greater need for more authoritative mechanisms, policymakers should strive to meaningfully engage citizens from diverse backgrounds in collaborative processes to cultivate public trust.

Proposition 4a: Greater inclusivity will lead to more transparency, accountability and equity in collaboratives, which increases the likelihood of resolving ICA dilemmas through more self-organised mechanisms (Figure 6.2).

However,

Proposition 4b: At some point, greater inclusivity will result in more inefficiencies and heterogeneity, which increases the likelihood of adopting more authoritative mechanisms (Figure 6.2).

Develop collaborative capacity through incrementalism

Professional competencies and resources facilitate collaboration. Since collaboration typically requires intensive financial, human and technical resource commitments (Ansell and Gash, 2008), it is more likely to emerge and work effectively in resource- munificent environments (Emerson et al, 2012; Turrini et al, 2010). To obtain more resources, governments often need to collaborate but may lack the ability to do so, especially when they have little or no history of collaboration. Although collaborative capacity may develop prior to collaboration as common ground and bridging ties emerge between actors involved in separate but similar projects (Spekkink and Boons, 2015), authorities can further develop such capacity incrementally by resolving first- order coordination problems before addressing second-order cooperation problems (Feiock and Scholz, 2010).

The incremental or 'small wins' approach (Ansell and Gash, 2008; Huxham and Vangen, 2005) suggests that before organisations take on larger, more ambitious cooperation problems, they start with smaller, simpler coordination problems of information exchange and gradually escalate the scope of collaboration as they achieve intermediate goals or 'small wins'. For example, if the objective were to restore a watershed ecosystem shared by multiple jurisdictions with little history of collaboration, then these authorities should first share information and coordinate on smaller projects, such as joint fact finding and planning, before making larger resource commitments to collective watershed restoration.

While incrementalism may not be suitable in all situations and could accelerate collaborative inertia in some cases, this strategy may be more advantageous for governments with limited experience in voluntary collaboration (Previtali, 2015; Spicer, 2015). However, small wins may be applicable even in cases where authorities have some collaborative experience. Since few policy problems can be precisely defined at the problem-realisation stage, collaborative arrangements should be refined and fine-tuned through a process of learning and mutual adjustment over time (Pressman and Wildavsky, 1973). Small wins and continued modification could nurture collaborative capacity and increase the likelihood that actors will comply with second-order cooperative agreements.

Managerial competencies and learned attributes are also a key part of collaborative capacity. Research suggests effective collaborative managers possess certain individual attributes (such as open-mindedness and emotional intelligence), interpersonal skills (such as communication and listening) and managerial skills (such as negotiation and problem solving) (O'Leary et al, 2012; Williams, 2002). Although training programmes can develop these competencies, managers often learn by doing. Learning by doing enables organisations to build 'mutual knowledge' with partners, which promotes collaborative development and joint problem solving (Martinez- Moyano, 2006). Incrementalism allows policymakers to gain hands-on experience with coordination problems and gradually develop the capacity to deal with riskier cooperation problems with less authoritative interventions.

Higher-level authorities and lead network agencies can also help cultivate collaborative capacity. Collaborating with higher-level governments addressing similar policy issues provides access to resources and expertise that smaller, lower-level governments often lack (Mullin and Daley, 2009). Working with a trusted, well- resourced lead agency can also enhance collaborative capacity in that lead agencies can reconcile divergent interests, enhance stakeholder engagement and dialogue, and develop informal processes that support policy learning (Conrad, 2015).

Proposition 5a: Resolving first-order coordination problems, learning by doing, and working with higher-level authorities and/or lead agencies will incrementally develop the capacity for resolving second-order cooperation problems through more self-organised mechanisms (Figure 6.2).

However,

Proposition 5b: For institutions with considerable collaborative capacity, incrementalism is more likely to frustrate actors and accelerate inertia, thus increasing the likelihood of adopting more authoritative mechanisms as collaborations fail (Figure 6.2).

Conclusion

Fragmentation of authority is ubiquitous and presents key challenges for policymakers. Authorities often need to collaborate to achieve policy objectives but can be reluctant to do so because of the risk and uncertainty associated with the commitment and competency of their partners. ICA dilemmas manifest at every scale of governance: from interlocal service agreements to combat homelessness across a metropolitan area to ongoing multi-jurisdictional efforts to restore estuary ecosystems to the exiting of countries from international agreements. In all such cases, better understanding ICA dilemmas and strategies for mitigating collaboration risk and uncertainty can help policymakers design self-organising arrangements that expand autonomy and reduce the transactions costs of collaboration. However, authorities will choose different integrative mechanisms depending on their history of collaboration, institutions for regional governance and cultural context (Tavares and Feiock, 2017).

This chapter has contributed to the broader study of collaborative governance by teasing out practical lessons for promoting self-organising collaboration and advancing theoretical propositions based on a systematic review of the ICA literature. ICA is a promising institutional approach to understanding interorganisational collaboration, but it is not the only perspective on collaborative governance. Although our prescriptions tend to align with findings from other collaborative governance frameworks (Ansell and Gash, 2008; Emerson et al, 2012; Sørensen and Torfing, 2009), our suggestions are only the tip of the iceberg for actionable advice for policymakers looking to mitigate collaboration risk and uncertainty and foster self-organising integration. Future research should further explore the overlap and distinctions between ICA, collaborative public management and policy network studies.

Our suggestions are limited in that most ICA research has focused on how authorities deal with horizontal fragmentation through interlocal collaboration. Fewer ICA studies have investigated how authorities overcome vertical fragmentation issues through delegation to special districts and regional authorities, and even fewer analyses consider how policymakers confront problems related to functional fragmentation. Future research in such directions holds much promise for extracting practical and theoretical insights.

Previous scholarship has also yet to systematically compare the effectiveness of integrative mechanisms for resolving ICA dilemmas, and the assumed relationships between such mechanisms and uncertainty and risk mitigation are not yet fully investigated. Moreover, while the emergence of some integrative mechanisms has been widely examined, to what extent these mechanisms improve policy outcomes remains largely uncharted empirical territory. Such an endeavour calls for comparing alternative mechanisms over time through in-depth case analysis and larger N studies. Finally, although applications of ICA in diverse institutional and political contexts are on the rise, many more practical lessons and theoretical insights could be gleaned from considering the fit between ICA and countries other than the United States. Examining how governments collaborate under more authoritative and/or centralised systems, or cases where there is little history of voluntary collaboration, is especially needed.

Acknowledgement

We would like to thank three anonymous reviewers and the 'Practical Lessons for Policy Theories' workshop participants for their helpful comments on earlier drafts of this chapter.

References

Aldag, AM, Warner, M, 2017, Cooperation, not cost savings: Explaining duration of shared service agreements, *Local Government Studies*, doi:10.1080/03003930.201 7.1411810

Andersen, OJ, Pierre, J, 2010, Exploring the strategic region: Rationality, context, and institutional collective action, *Urban Affairs Review* 46, 2, 218–40

Andrew, SA, 2009, Regional integration through contracting networks: An empirical analysis of institutional collection action framework, *Urban Affairs Review* 44, 3, 378–402

Andrew, SA, Carr, JB, 2013, Mitigating uncertainty and risk in planning for regional preparedness: The role of bonding and bridging relationships, *Urban Studies* 50, 4, 709–24

Andrew, SA, Hawkins, CV, 2013, Regional cooperation and multilateral agreements in the provision of public safety, *American Review of Public Administration* 43, 4, 460–75

Andrew, SA, Short, JE, Jung, K, Arlikatti, S, 2015, Intergovernmental cooperation in the provision of public safety: Monitoring mechanisms embedded in interlocal agreements, *Public Administration Review* 75, 3, 401–10

Ansell, C, 2015, When collaborative governance scales up: Lessons from global public health about compound collaboration, *Policy & Politics* 43, 3, 391–406

Ansell, C, Gash, A, 2008, Collaborative governance in theory and practice, *Journal of Public Administration Research and Theory* 18, 4, 543–71

Axelrod, R, 1984, *The evolution of cooperation*, New York: Basic Books

Berardo, R, Scholz, JT, 2010, Self-organizing policy networks: Risk, partner selection, and cooperation in estuaries, *American Journal of Political Science* 54, 3, 632–49

Bodin, Ö, Crona, BI, 2009, The role of social networks in natural resource governance: What relational patterns make a difference?, *Global Environmental Change* 9, 366–74

Boschet, C, Rambonilaza, T, 2017 Collaborative environmental governance and transaction costs in partnerships: Evidence from a social network approach to water management in France, *Journal of Environmental Planning and Management* 1, 1–9

Brown, TL, Potoski, M, 2005, Transaction costs and contracting: The practitioner perspective, *Public Performance & Management Review* 28, 3, 326–51

Buchanan, JM, Tullock, G, 1962, *The calculus of consent*, Ann Arbor, MI: University of Michigan Press

Burt, RS, 1992, *Structural holes: The social structure of competition*, Cambridge, MA: Harvard University Press

Calanni, JC, Siddiki, SN, Weible, CM, Leach, WD, 2015, Explaining coordination in collaborative partnerships and clarifying the scope of the belief homophily hypothesis, *Journal of Public Administration Research and Theory* 25, 3, 901–27

Carr, JB, Feiock, RC (eds), 2004, *City-county consolidation and its alternatives: Reshaping the local government landscape*, Armonk, NY: ME Sharpe

Carr, JB, LeRoux, K, Shrestha, M, 2009, Institutional ties, transaction costs, and external service production, *Urban Affairs Review* 44, 3, 403–27

Carr, JB, Hawkins, CV, Westberg, DE, 2017, An exploration of collaboration risk in joint ventures: Perceptions of risk by local economic development officials, *Economic Development Quarterly* 31, 3, 210–27

Coleman JS, 1988, Social capital in the creation of human capital, *American Journal of Sociology* 94, S95–120

Conrad, E, 2015, Bridging the hierarchical and collaborative divide: The role of network managers in scaling up a network approach to water governance in California, *Policy & Politics* 43, 3, 349–66

Dollery, B, Kortt, MA, Drew, J, 2016, Fostering shared services in local government: A common service model, *Australasian Journal of Regional Studies* 22, 2, 225–42

Emerson, K, Nabatchi, T, Balogh, S, 2012, An integrative framework for collaborative governance, *Journal of Public Administration Research and Theory* 22, 1, 1–29

Feiock, RC, 2007, Rational choice and regional governance, *Journal of Urban Affairs* 29, 1, 47–63

Feiock, RC, 2013, The institutional collective action framework, *Policy Studies Journal* 41, 3, 397–425

Feiock, RC, Scholz, JT (eds), 2010, *Self-organizing federalism: Collaborative mechanisms to mitigate institutional collective action dilemmas*, New York: Cambridge University Press

Feiock, RC, Steinacker, A, Park, HJ, 2009, Institutional collective action and economic development joint ventures, *Public Administration Review* 69, 2, 256–70

Feiock, RC, Lubell, M, Lee, IW, 2014, *The political market framework and policy change*, Tallahassee, FL: Local Governance Research Lab, Florida State University

Feiock, RC, Krause, RM, Hawkins, CV, 2017, The impact of administrative structure on the ability of city governments to overcome functional collective action dilemmas: A climate and energy perspective, *Journal of Public Administration Research and Theory* 27, 4, 615–28

Gerber, ER, Henry, AD, Lubell, M, 2013, Political homophily and collaboration in regional planning networks, *American Journal of Political Science* 57, 3, 598–610

Gollagher, M, Hartz-Karp, J, 2013, The role of deliberative collaborative governance in achieving sustainable cities, *Sustainability* 5, 6, 2343–66

Hawkins, CV, Hu, Q, Feiock, RC, 2016, Self-organizing governance of local economic development: Informal policy networks and regional institutions, *Journal of Urban Affairs* 38, 5, 643–60

Head, BW, Alford, J, 2015, Wicked problems: Implications for public policy and management, *Administration & Society* 47, 6, 711–39

Huxham, C, Vangen, S, 2005. *Managing to collaborate: The theory and practice of collaborative advantage*, New York: Routledge

Ingold, K, 2017, How to create and preserve social capital in climate adaptation policies: A network approach, *Ecological Economics* 131, 414–24

Jimenez, BS, 2016, Externalities in the fragmented metropolis: Local institutional choices and the efficiency–equity trade-off, *American Review of Public Administration* 46, 3, 314–36

Johansson, J, Niklasson, L, Persson, B, 2015, The role of municipalities in the bottom- up formation of a meta-region in Sweden: Drivers and barriers, *Scandinavian Journal of Public Administration* 19, 4, 71–88

Jung, K, Song, M, Feiock, R, 2017, Isolated and broken bridges from interorganizational emergency management networks: An institutional collective action perspective, *Urban Affairs Review*, doi:10.1177/1078087417690257

Koppenjan, JFM, Klijn, EH, 2004, *Managing uncertainties in networks: A network approach to problem solving and decision making*, London: Routledge

Kwon, SW, Feiock, RC, 2010, Overcoming the barriers to cooperation: Intergovernmental service agreements, *Public Administration Review* 70, 6, 876–84

Kwon, SW, Feiock, RC, Bae, J, 2014, The roles of regional organizations for interlocal resource exchange: Complement or Substitute?, *American Review of Public Administration* 44, 3, 339–57

Leach, WD, 2006, Collaborative public management and democracy: Evidence from western watershed partnerships, *Public Administration Review* 66, 1, 100–10

Lee, Y, 2016, From competition to collaboration: Intergovernmental economic development policy networks, *Local Government Studies* 42, 2, 171–88

LeRoux, K, Brandenburger, PW, Pandey, SK, 2010, Interlocal service cooperation in US cities: A social network explanation, *Public Administration Review* 70, 2, 268–78

Lyons, WE, Lowery, D, 1989, Governmental fragmentation versus consolidation: Five public-choice myths about how to create informed, involved, and happy citizens, *Public Administration Review* 49, 6, 533–43

McGinnis, MD (ed), 1999, *Polycentricity and local public economies: Readings from the workshop in political theory and policy analysis*, Ann Arbor, MI: University of Michigan Press

Martin, S, Guarneros-Meza, V, 2013, Governing local partnerships: Does external steering help local agencies address wicked problems?, *Policy & Politics* 41, 4, 585–603

Martinez-Moyano, IJ, 2006, Exploring the dynamics of collaboration in interorganizational settings, in S Schuman (ed) *Creating a culture of collaboration*, pp 69–85, San Francisco, CA: Jossey-Bass

Maser, SM, 1998, Constitutions as relational contracts: Explaining procedural safeguards in municipal charters, *Journal of Public Administration Research and Theory* 8, 4, 527–64

Mullin, M, 2009, *Governing the tap: Special district governance and the new local politics of water*, Cambridge, MA: MIT Press

Mullin, M, Daley, DM, 2009, Working with the state: Exploring interagency collaboration within a federalist system, *Journal of Public Administration Research and Theory* 20, 4, 757–78

O'Leary, R, Choi, Y, and Gerard, CM, 2012, The skill set of the successful collaborator, *Public Administration Review* 72, s1, S70–S83

Oakerson, RJ, Parks, RB, 2011, The study of local public economies: Multi-organizational, multi-level institutional analysis and development, *Policy Studies Journal* 39, 1, 147–67

Olson, M, 1965, *The logic of collective action: Public goods and the theory of groups*, Cambridge, MA: Harvard University Press

Ostrom, E, 1990, *Governing the commons: The evolution of institutions for collective action*, New York: Cambridge University Press

Ostrom, E, 2005, *Understanding institutional diversity*, Princeton, NJ: Princeton University Press

Ostrom, V, Tiebout, CM, Warren, R, 1961, The organization of government in metropolitan areas: A theoretical inquiry, *American Political Science Review* 55, 4, 831–42

Park, HJ, Feiock, RC, 2006, Institutional collective action, social capital and regional development partnership, *International Review of Public Administration* 11, 2, 57–69

Pressman, JL, Wildavsky, AB, 1973, *Implementation*, Berkeley, CA: University of California Press

Previtali, P, 2015,The Italian administrative reform of small municipalities: State-of- the-art and perspectives, *Public Administration Quarterly* 39, 4, 548–68

Putnam, R, 1993, *Making democracy work*, Princeton, NJ: Princeton University Press

Salamon, L, 2002, *The tools of government: A guide to the new governance*, Oxford: Oxford University Press

Song, M, Park, HJ, Jung, K, 2017, Do political similarities facilitate interlocal collaboration?, *Public Administration Review*, doi:10.1111/puar.12887

Sørensen, E, Torfing, J, 2009, Making governance networks effective and democratic through metagovernance, *Public Administration* 87, 2, 234–58

Spekkink, WA, Boons, FA, 2015, The emergence of collaborations, *Journal of Public Administration Research and Theory* 26, 4, 613–30

Spicer, Z, 2015, Regionalism, municipal organization, and interlocal cooperation in Canada, *Canadian Public Policy* 41, 2, 137–50

Spicer, Z, Found, A, 2016, *Thinking regionally: How to improve service delivery in Canada's cities*, Toronto: The CD Howe Institute

Tavares, AF, Feiock, RC, 2017, Applying an institutional collective action framework to investigate intermunicipal cooperation in Europe, *Perspectives on Public Management and Governance*, doi:10.1093/ppmgov/gvx014

Turrini, A, Cristofoli, D, Frosini, F, Nasi, G, 2010, Networking literature about determinants of network effectiveness, *Public Administration* 88, 2, 528–50

Uzzi, B, 1997, Social structure and competition in interfirm networks: The paradox of embeddedness, *Administrative Science Quarterly* 42, 35–67

Williams, P, 2002, The competent boundary spanner, *Public Administration* 80, 1, 103–24

Williamson, OE, 1979, Transaction-cost economics: The governance of contractual relations, *Journal of Law and Economics* 22, 2, 233–61

Williamson, OE, 1981, The economics of organization: The transaction cost approach, *American Journal of Sociology* 87, 3, 548–77

Yi, H, Suo, L, Shen, R, Zhang, J, Ramaswami, A, Feiock, RC, 2017, Regional governance and institutional collective action for environmental sustainability, *Public Administration Review*, doi:10.1111/puar.12799

CHAPTER SEVEN

Drawing practical lessons from punctuated equilibrium theory

Chris Koski and Samuel Workman

Introduction

Promoting informed decision-making is a recurring theme in improving the efficacy and responsiveness of government. Consistent with this theme is the assumption that decision-makers face an information deficit – that if decision-makers simply had access to the right knowledge that they would make better decisions. There exists an overarching normative consensus that more information in the policy process is generally good, but there are limits to how much decision-makers can process. Scholars of public policy, and particularly agenda setting, have tended to find that the central problem of policymaking is not a deficit of information, but instead, an oversupply of information. Very often, then, the central problem confronting decision-making is prioritising among this information. Information-processing, specifically attention, is seen as the driver of policy change in theories of agenda-setting such as multiple streams (see Cairney, this issue) and particularly so in punctuated equilibrium theory (PET). PET scholars have long understood that policy and institutional design are critical to information-processing (Baumgartner and Jones, 1993). This chapter represents a guide for scholars wishing to bridge the divide between PET theory and the practice of institutional design.

The engine of information processing in policy systems are subgovernments. Subgovernments are defined collections of policy actors in government, and around government, who develop and make policy within substantively specific issues. Usually, these subgovernments will contain an authoritative body (for example, a city council or congressional committee), an administrative unit for implementing policy (for example, the ministry of transportation or the police department), and supportive constellations of those interested in the policy issue (for example, Greenpeace or the Chamber of Commerce). Finally, subgovernments may also operate within specific policy areas (for example, energy policy), but be delineated along functionally differentiated lines (for example, regulate energy or subsidise the industry).

It is commonly understood that more information in the policy process is generally a good thing, but building the capacity to process that information creates classic challenges of delegation, coordination, accountability and organisation. Subgovernments have their own information processing limitations, irrespective of how narrow their focus. Information processing limitations and oversight challenges lead to inadequate problem redress even on the parts of subgovernments. For governments, centralisation of decision-making is a natural impulse to contend with the daunting twin challenges of corralling myriad subgovernments coupled with still suboptimal outcomes. Where it concerns the process of problem definition, or how we come to define and understand particular policy problems, the centralisation impulse is wrong and often counterproductive. In particular, it leaves policy systems vulnerable to leaving out important dimensions of problems, dimensions that left unattended, will lead to policy failures and volatility in governance outcomes (Jones and Baumgartner, 2005).

The trade-offs between organisational impulses to delegate or to centralise are widely discussed in public administration and public policy circles (May et al, 2008; Ostrom, 2008; Selznick, 1949). Governments understand that there is not one strategy of delegation that solves decision-making dilemmas; further, public officials know that such dilemmas are rarely, if ever, solved. However, we argue that thinking of these organisational choices in the context of broader theories of information processing can help to not only structure a better decision-making apparatus in government – but also to work with the structures that currently exist. The centralisation–decentralisation argument is fantastical in terms of many of the solutions it offers for policymaking: restructuring government is hard and, like any policy choice, may produce more problems than it solves.

If PET shows that government efficacy and efficiency is hindered by information processing challenges, then the unstated practical contribution of PET and other information-processing scholarship is to make governments better at generating appropriate information for problem solving and managing the flow of information. Our work offers information processing scholars, particularly PET scholars, five ways of thinking about matching future policy research with solutions to underlying problems that this literature has identified as impediments to policymaking. We caution that (1) centralisation does not solve problems of information search, instead, centralisation creates bottlenecks, and (2) multiple venues offer more representation and opportunities for citizen influence, but suffer from attention limitations. Given these cautions, we suggest that (3) institutions be explicitly designed to be information- seeking, (4) issue bundling can prompt more holistic information searches, and (5) that governments consider the correlation of information from subgovernments as policy information.

Information processing in public policy research

The classic economics of information views it as a good held private, necessitating rents (Stigler, 1961). Previous understandings of government decision-making have assumed an information-poor environment in which decision-makers' tasks were focused on information-gathering, or building incentives to reveal information. In the competitive political environments, information is provided freely in an effort to steer the course of policy (Workman, 2015). Conceptualisations of governmental, non-governmental, firm and individual decision-making rested on a now softened conceptualisation of choice that assumed information flows to governance units were controllable through some kind of intentional search.

Here we leverage Baumgartner and Jones' (1993) widely applied PET to characterise the information processing environment of governments, non-governmental organisations, and other groups that are charged with solving problems via policy. PET profoundly challenges the convention that governments cannot make good decisions because they don't have enough information. It contends that governments have too much information, that they are cognitive misers, and that subgovernments

- entities to which decision-making is delegated – replicate similar static patterns of policymaking. This leads to governments ignoring problems and then overcorrecting for them. Broadly, we now understand that the real governance problem is not an inability to find information, but instead, to prioritise and synthesise information.

In the sections that follow, we outline the major features of PET. As scholars who are part of the PET research community, we are struck by two features: 1) the fact that most of the policy process community beyond PET scholars is aware of the theory and 2) the simple parts of the metaphor give way to vague understandings of the inner workings of the informational processing theory that underlie the actual theoretical mechanisms that give rise to a predicted pattern of change. Our experience is that many scholars think of PET as a theory that attempts to explain major change that results from exogenous shocks. While PET can help explain large changes, some of which emerge from exogenous shocks, such a limited understanding is, well, wrong.

A unified theory of information processing and policy change

From a methodological perspective, PET is a unified theory of information processing and policy change. This is to say that PET incorporates a model of decision-making that is intended to be broadly applied to a variety of policy venues and integrates individual and organisational decision-making. For PET scholars, shifting attention is the causal driver of choice. Limited attention is key to understanding human cognition (Jones, 2017), and the strategies that human beings use to deal with an information- rich environment (for example, Thomas (2017) on cue-taking). Under the strain of policy failures, focusing events, or salient issues and the increased cognitive load they bring, focusing attention is even more difficult for individuals (Shaffer, 2017). Organisations can be seen as one way to address the attention limits of individuals (Jones, 2001), and the delegation of attention defines institutional organisation (Workman, 2015). Institutional capacity renders more stable policymaking, even in the face of a complex stream of information that might otherwise produce volatility in attention (Epp and Baumgartner, 2017).

To this end, PET is a distributional theory of policy change in that it intends to understand a wide range of outcomes from policy venues, and the processes that underlie these. Among policy scholars, the importance of incrementalism in explaining policy punctuations is a never-ending source of irony and confusion. Charles Lindblom (1959) is 'alive and well' in PET (Howlett and Migone, 2011). Plainly, the theory seeks to explain long periods of stability, short periods of rapid change, *and* the lack of much in between – moderate change. It is here where the concept of policy punctuations is perhaps the most intuitively interesting part of the theory to most casual consumers of policy process research, but, is simply one component of understanding policy change for scholars that apply PET.

Policymaking venues must prioritise issues and information about them. Policy venues have much information that they could use for decision-making, but ultimately use a systematically biased subset, potentially in the face of dramatically changing problem and political conditions. The path by which policy venues, policymaking systems, or governing institutions seek or sort information is a function of the relative strength of subgovernments to allow for alternative problem definitions. Subgovernments attend to issues as a function of their preferences and capacity, but occasionally are overwhelmed by macro-political forces that focus the attention of the broader institutions in which they are situated.

As a theory that explains information processing, PET relies on a mixture of empirical assessments of policy venue outputs and assumptions regarding causal mechanisms. The vast majority of PET research asserts the mechanisms (described in the sections that follow) that create conditions for institutionally-induced stability and change. We characterise the major assumptions of PET in the next section.

Decision-making and attention in punctuated equilibrium theory

We begin with a discussion of two key underlying assumptions of PET: an understanding of how individuals and institutions make decisions and the role of attention in decision-making. The basic theoretical understanding of decision-making is found in Jones' early works on decision-making (1994; 2001) in which the rational model of the individual is challenged. Based in works of cognitive psychology and behavioural economics, PET envisions individuals who are limited in their capacity to seek and make sense of information. This makes individuals 'cognitive misers' in the face of multiple decisions. While political behaviourists (Rugeley and Gerlach, 2012) and other theorists of the policy process are concerned with the formation and change of beliefs (see also Weible and Ingold this issue), PET assumes preferences are relatively fixed – or at least fixed enough that shifts in choice are not the result of changes in beliefs or preferences.

Practically, this means that there is a fixed range of issues to which individuals can attend coupled with a cognitive limitation regarding how much time individuals can attend to those issues. Individuals largely rely on heuristics to make choices rather than engage in a full information search in order to address choices with which they are faced. Individuals are consistently attuned to certain issues (May, 1991), but occasionally are forced to make choices on issues they do not regularly attend. Choices individuals make on these issues are a function of the preferences they currently hold rather than preferences that are developed in problem solving the issue over time. In other words, attention activates preferences, and is the precursor of choice – a necessary, but not sufficient condition for action.

Organisations are designed to alleviate the limits of attention in individuals (Jones, 2001). The concept of 'institutions' can take on a variety of meanings in the study of politics and policy, even within the narrow field of public policy process research. Here, we understand institutions to mean the rules, norms and units along which lines of delegation, accountability and authority operate. Institutions help alleviate individual decision-making limitations in two ways. First, institutions contain numerous individuals, extending the information processing capacity of individuals. Second, institutions are designed to attend to a finite set of issues; that is, they are designed to allocate attention (Hammond, 1986).

As the rational model of the individual is challenged by the foundational assumptions of PET, so is the foundation of the rational model of institutions. At some level of aggregation, institutions ultimately face the same limits of attention and information processing as individuals. Institutions face severe problems when forced to allocate attention to issues for which they are not designed, or did not anticipate. Furthermore, institutions are often populated by either the same individuals or the same interests over long time periods. Thus, institutions privilege certain types of information over time, engage in constrained patterns of information search, and have similar agendas. Institutions often are nested within other institutions, which is the result of a macro- institution attempting to delegate attention to a smaller subunit (Workman, 2015; Workman et al, 2009). The resulting delegation of attention can be thought of as an analogue to organisational mission, jurisdiction, or turf.

Subgovernment politics

Subgovernments represent a more restricted and institutionalised form of subsystems in policymaking. While subsystems may include multiple policymaking bodies, jurisdictions and levels of government; subgovernments are subordinate units of government within policymaking institutions. Subgovernments emerge because of the delegation of attention (Baumgartner et al, 2014). Institutions that intentionally delegate authority to smaller groups in order to both create agenda space and focus attention on specific problems do not have the capacity to monitor the activities they have delegated with great frequency. Thus, the institutions created to attend to specific problems often do so with great independence (Workman et al, 2009). Delegation, not control, is the norm in policymaking.

Generally speaking, as governments cede authority to subgovernments, a number of actors in positions of power seek to control the outputs that emerge from the policy venue. These outputs are ultimately dependent upon the macro-institution for passage and legitimacy, but the government has, by design, created a subgovernment for which little attention is required. Insofar as the subgovernment does not attract outside interest, conditions exist for actors within the institution to leverage their position to control what Baumgartner and Jones (1993) refer to as the 'policy image' (Pralle, 2003; Vaughan and Arsneault, 2008).

Empirical examples of subgovernment politics are found in the foundation of the PET literature. An enduring story from Baumgartner and Jones' (1993) original work is the story of problem definition and pesticides. Following the Second World War, pesticide development in the United States and across the world was viewed as a positive step toward food production. In the US, the federal government largely delegated attention to issues related to pesticides to agricultural committees within Congress. Agricultural committees sought and prioritised problems associated with pesticides through the lens of production rather than human or environmental health. As such, for decades following the Second World War, pesticide policy was largely quiet and limited to a few players who maintained a status quo of pesticide promotion. The policymaking environment associated with pesticide policy in the United States resonates with the information processing pathologies of any organisation. All organisations face limited capacity for attention and information processing; at some point they become overwhelmed in processing information for a particular problem. Organisations can simply produce suboptimal outcomes, or choose to create alternative information processing structures and processes. In addition to creating expertise in information processing, this new sub-organisation is delegated attention.

Parallel and serial information processing

PET envisions information processing similar to a circuit. Given the attention dynamics of PET that we previously describe, the delegation of authority from a government to a subgovernment creates policy monopolies processing information largely in parallel with one another. However, each policy venue – subgovernments and governments – processes information serially (Jones, 1994; 2001). This is particularly important for macro-organisations that ultimately have the final decision-making authority over programmatic changes. In general, governments attend little to the inner-workings, information-processing and outputs of subgovernments – a process that buttresses favoured policy images over time.

In Baumgartner and Jones' (1993) case of pesticides, concerned groups began to attempt to frame pesticide problems as human or environmental harms. In addition to agricultural committees, health and welfare committees began seeking and sorting information related to pesticides. Agricultural production is not the priority of health advocates – rather these committees focus on issues related to toxicity and exposure rates. Thus, alternative problem definitions emerged for the same problem across two delegated subgovernments. As these definitions clashed, the policy monopoly of agriculture began to weaken and policy caught up with shifting opinion.

Rapid policy change need not be the fate for all policy change. Complex problems of modern government often demand that authoritative and deliberative organisations synthesise information from multiple substantive issues in order to make policy. The challenge of modern public institutions is to arrive at integrative problem definitions derived from a synthesis of potentially relevant streams of information across substantive and functional dimensions (Jones and Baumgartner, 2015). If policy responses end up falling along one of these substantive dimensions, it should be because of the choice or collective will of the decision-making organisation, and the process is designed to amplify only one among many streams of information.

Issue expansion and feedback

What follows from changes in macro-attention to issues within the purview of the policy subsystem is a function largely of features specific to the policy monopoly itself. In other words, whether 'external perturbations' (Cashore and Howlett, 2007; Howlett and Cashore, 2009) influence otherwise stable policymaking arrangements is counterintuitively a result of endogenous features. Most recent scholarship in punctuated equilibrium is less concerned with causes of shifts in attention and more concerned with how policymakers and policymaking institutions respond. A robust literature on policy entrepreneurs beginning with Kingdon (1995) and expanding across multiple studies describe mechanisms by which politically motivated individuals or groups can act as attention focusers and policy fixers (Mintrom and Norman, 2009). Issue expansion can occur whether generated by specific policy entrepreneurs, political circumstances, events that are impossible to ignore, or all the above.

The extent to which a subgovernment's maintenance of a policy image is robust to macro-political attention is a function of two interrelated features. First, the relative unity of preferences within a subgovernment can create a powerful counterforce against any new information brought into the policy discourse. We will refer to this as the 'strong subgovernment' scenario. Second, the extent to which the subgovernment has considered an expanded agenda of information over previous iterations of policymaking lays the groundwork for an adaptive policy system. We refer to this as the 'weak subgovernment' scenario. Each set of circumstances presents different outputs of policy change. In the first scenario, it is possible that the endogenous strength of the monopoly can fend off challenges, which will maintain stability even in time of new information. In the second scenario, the subgovernment is more open to changes to the policy image by macro-political forces; but it may have already changed sufficiently over time, such that change or reform, even with new attention, is stunted.

The two features of these policy monopolies describe the precursors to different distributions of policy change over time. PET expects policy change to exhibit 'punctuations' under the strong policy monopoly scenario, primarily through the mechanisms of negative and positive feedback. As issues expand, macro-political attention brings in new actors and institutions which have competing definitions of the policy image. Issue expansion is more likely to occur as a function of the distance between the policy monopoly's conceptualisation of the policy image versus actual problem characteristics at the time of macro-attentional focus. As subgovernments are unresponsive to real world changes in the nature of the problem, this structurally- induced stability will itself lead to dramatic policy change as the policy system is increasingly ill-fitted and maladapted to the real problem and the subgovernment succumbs to the disconnect between policy and reality. For practitioners, one of the central lessons of PET is that 'locking-in' policies or governing arrangements, particularly such that they are maladaptive as the problem changes, guarantees policy volatility and disjointedness at some point in the future.

Thus, in general, two types of systems characterise these dynamics of policy change. The first is a system of error correction, in which policymaking is approximal. As the system responds to information, policy is adjusted in response to the information. This adjustment, however, never quite meets the demands of the information at hand. Thus, most policy systems are characterised by disproportionate information processing – that is, the policy system never responds quite in proportion to the new information about a problem. There is both over- and under-response. The second type of system is one of error accumulation. In this system, policy is increasingly out of step with the current stream of information about a problem – representing the real-world status of the issue. Usually this will be owing to unresponsive institutions, which are loathe to move from the current status quo policy – either because of preferences for the status quo, or because of high decision-making costs within the institution or decision-making body. In the latter instance, pressure builds to respond to an ever-divergent stream of information until a drastic policy change is needed. For pesticides, the creation of a new regulatory agency in the Environmental Protection Agency (EPA) in 1970 and resulting committees within Congress provided competing subgovernments which eventually supplanted the agricultural production framing of pesticide problems. This laid the foundation for major agenda and policy change. In some cases, problems span the boundaries of previously defined subgovernments (Workman and Shafran, 2015), which leads to dynamic interactions between groups that previously worked in parallel. Critically, as the expanded issue is addressed, macro-institutional attention eventually recedes leaving in place the new entrants – often in the form of institutions or constellations of actors – to maintain attention on the policy area. Depending on institutional structure, these actors will begin to mould the policy image in the scope of their own preferences, through a process of negative feedback and the approximal policymaking described above. This is the classic punctuated equilibrium scenario.

A less punctuated distribution can occur, however, for policy monopolies whose attention is broader or that serve a variety of competing rather than cooperating interests, or, alternatively in policies for which there are no discernable set of actors or publics (May, 1991). A weak monopoly may be more volatile in its policy outputs, but will have made marginal adjustments over time that maintain a small distance between the 'actual' problem definition and that favoured by the policy image of the monopoly. In this scenario, it is possible for large swings in attention associated with an issue, but with a policy monopoly to maintain its policy image. Empirical studies find that all policy systems are subject to these dynamics of attention and resultant policy change, but some less than others. However, institutional design can mitigate policy volatility by structuring information processing to be adaptive (we come to this point later).

Drawing practical lessons from information processing scholarship: two cautions and three suggestions

In this chapter we have presented an account of PET to motivate future scholars to structure research around practical applications of policy process theories from an information processing approach. We show that theoretical and empirical applications of PET suggest that political systems of policymaking typically are punctuated. However, the degree to which political systems are punctuated is a function of institutional design. Thus, we offer five axioms for scholars engaging in research related to the two audiences that must contend with policy problems that are troubled to process the inherently complex array of problems and solutions that face policymaking systems. The first audience is comprised of entrepreneurs or other political actors who seek strategies to gain precious agenda space. The second audience includes policymakers who hope to devise institutions that have increased information processing capacity – both in terms of information search and attention – to avoid imperfect policymaking that accompanies the large episodic shifts in attention over time.

The practical lessons to be gleaned from information processing perspectives on governance and policymaking are increasingly relevant due to the nature of changing institutional arrangements, the onslaught of globalisation, and the emergence of complex, boundary-spanning problems (Nicholson and Orr, 2016). Given the difficulties of reaching consensus at the federal level, or apex, of modern democracies, actors at other levels of government face increasing pressure to meet modern problems that stretch their capacity. One needs look no further for relevance than the polarisation and gridlock characterising the dysfunctional US Congress (Lewallen et al, 2016). Additionally, the politics of democratic electorates suggests increasing divergence between rural and urban governance reflected in elections in the US and between old and young in the UK (Brexit). This divergence, division and recalcitrance is occurring in an era of policymaking where globalisation is increasingly relevant, and where problems span substantive and jurisdictional boundaries – taxing the limits of divergent institutions to address them. In these contexts, the processes leading to disjointed policy change are potent forces for instability in governing arrangements and for volatility in policy responses.

Our suggestions take the form of two cautions and three suggestions. Many reading this chapter might infer from the structural analysis we present that constantly churning government structure is the only way to ensure governments that maintain a broad focus. We state early on in this chapter that restructuring governments is a natural impulse when things are not going well, but that restructuring is hard and may create more problems than it solves. Our cautions address classic problems of centralisation and delegation using the lens of information processing. We suggest the design of explicitly information-seeking institutions to contend with new problems, for governments to yoke the disparate flows of information from subgovernments through issue bundling and consider the value of convergence of policy signals from subgovernments as policy evidence itself.

Caution 1: Centralised institutions create information processing bottlenecks

Given that venue shopping is identified as a mechanism by which issue expansion and, therefore, policy punctuations occur, designers of political institutions would do well to assume that entrepreneurs will seek venues receptive to their problem definitions. One implication from findings on venue shopping might be to simply create fewer venues; therefore, centralising decision-making into fewer venues offers fewer opportunities for policy entrepreneurs to seek policy change. However, findings from the venue-shopping literature suggest that centralisation is no universal solution to issues related to punctuated policymaking and, indeed, can exacerbate information and attention bottlenecks that lead to intermittent, and punctuated, policymaking. Centralisation of decision-making is shown in the literature to lead to distributions of policy change that are more volatile rather than less.

Centralisation of authority is typically not accompanied by a concomitant expansion of information processing or seeking capacity. In other words, the same challenges that befall processing in serial affect centralised authority wherein attention is limited to a few items at a time while the remainder of issues under the umbrella of an organisation go largely unchecked. The Federal Emergency Management Agency's (FEMA) transition to an 'all-hazards' approach to disaster management provides a useful example. May et al (2008) show that the centralisation of disaster management under the top levels of the Department of Homeland Security destabilised attention to natural hazards. Instead, the all-hazards approach was synonymous with man-made disaster – terrorism, with dire consequences for the people of New Orleans at the arrival of Hurricane Katrina. This study highlights the consequences of attention shifting and centralisation within organisations. Attention is limited and attending to terrorism necessarily meant the traditional disaster management agenda was destabilised (May et al, 2009).

Observers might argue that centralisation allows for responses that demand urgency and speed of action, and that it forces the policy system to focus. This is indeed true, but the urgency and speed of action that centralisation enables is also at the root of maladaptive responses and policy failures when the system fails to incorporate relevant streams of information (for example, natural disasters). Long ago, Heclo (1974) noted that politics is about 'powering and puzzling'. The vast majority of lessons to be drawn from the study of public policy, both in political science and economics, pertain to Heclo's 'powering' – arriving at a decision. With this chapter, we aim to refocus attention on his 'puzzling' which is far less understood, at least in the context of lessons one might draw from policy scholarship.

This research offers a critical lesson for organisations as they attempt to manage their agendas. In general, organisations economise on the scarcity of attention plaguing individual decision-makers. By choosing centralised designs, the attention capacity of organisations is reduced to that of one or a few individuals or offices. While this focus often allows for coordinated and timely action, it should be understood that it will necessarily lead to the loss of attention for other items. Centralised organisations are also stripped of delegation. In the context of a complex, diversified agenda, this means that the organisation is also stripped of much of its analytical capacity. To assume otherwise, is to assume that those who are the beneficiaries of centralisation are experts on the problem, or set of problems, at hand. Under circumstances where this amounts to a 'heroic assumption', organisations not only will have difficulty maintaining attention to other important items, but the solutions developed to address problems will likely reflect less expertise than they would under a delegated arrangement.

Social organisations, of which political and policymaking institutions are a variant, face a fundamental tension that no institutional design, in fact no system of government, can alleviate. Centralised organisations trade off expertise and capacity to address more problems, in return for urgency and coordination. Delegated organisations tend towards expertise and increased agenda capacity at the expense of urgency and coordinated responses. This trade-off is key to understanding how organisations process information and how these designs map onto agenda and policy change. As a design feature, it is perhaps the most important element of understanding the likely consequences of organisational information processing.

There is some evidence from the literature on state budgeting (Breunig and Koski, 2009) that suggests that certain kinds of centralisation of authority can produce more adaptive policymaking structures, however, this is inherently a relativistic impression. In comparison to other institutions – such as citizen legislatures – stronger centralised decision-making (for example, strong governors) may contain a greater capacity to address policy problems. Baumgartner et al's (2017) study of authoritarian regimes and budgeting is suggestive of the more general trend that we argue. Thus, when considering centralisation of decision-making in institutional design, which is often a temptation for many political actors frustrated with intransigence associated with diffuse policymaking, there are caveats.

Caution 2: Fragmented institutions create coordination problems

Policy practitioners rarely find themselves able to create new institutions to solve problems or that policy problems fit neatly within an existing boundary of policymaking. For many policies, policymakers rely on several existing institutions. In creating partnerships to achieve policy outcomes (Koski, 2011), policy designers would do well to understand the resources and goals of each participant. Organisations with little goal overlap and few slack resources may only intermittently attend to the problems of the partnership (Koski, 2015), making such groups ripe for dramatic shifts in policy image definitions that reverberate throughout the partnership.

Multiple-venues are often viewed as advantages from the perspective of policy entrepreneurs, however, policy designs may explicitly create multiple venues to achieve a variety of policy goals. A multi-venue strategy can be part of a general effort to expand the agenda capacity of an existing institution. Additionally, multi- venue strategies serve to offer greater democratic representation; while perhaps not maximising a policy goal, there are other significant benefits associated with citizens feeling as though they have multiple opportunities to access the policy process. In particular, multiple venues act as a democratic 'pressure valve', assuring that the system can accommodate public demand, while simultaneously slowing reform that may destabilise the system. Additionally, multiple venues may represent specific attempts to reduce the speed with which policy occurs by structuring attention to different details at different levels of salience for similar problems. The policymakers must consider which venues will have authority over their policies in order to predict the types of information that might be brought to bear on policy decisions.

Suggestion 1: Design institutions not just to attend to new problems, but to be intentionally information-seeking

Crucial to understanding how institutions process information is the distinction between the problem and solution space of issues (Workman, 2015). Problem solving is comprised of two processes. First, an individual or organisation must develop a problem representation. We label this 'problem definition'. Problem definition involves constructing an understanding of a policy problem that comprises some dimensions of the issue for attention and excludes other dimensions. Problem is important because defining the problem for action is necessary for generating solutions, or policies.

Problem definition also involves a different set of organisational costs than choice or implementation. Traditionally, practitioners and scholars alike have troubled over, and emphasised, the importance of transaction and decision costs in policymaking (Jones et al, 2003). When the job of the institution is to generate solutions and choose among them, these costs do indeed loom large. Both groups, however, overlook the importance of informational and cognitive costs. Informational costs pertain to the generation of information about a problem. Cognitive costs pertain to understanding the problem or processing the supply of information. At the front end of the policy process, where issues are prioritised and problems defined, it is informational and cognitive costs that are the most potent stressors of institutional design.

In combining our understanding of policy entrepreneurs, constituencies and stakeholders with our understanding of the different costs associated with agenda setting and problem definition as opposed to solution generation and choice, a powerful insight for policy system design emerges. As institutions, or their aggregations in policymaking systems, develop issue agendas and craft problem definitions, information search should be inclusive and expansive. The real danger at the agenda setting and problem definition stage consists in missing an important issue deemed irrelevant by limited search, or excluding a dimension of an issue that is important for solution generation. Moreover, the inclusiveness of information sources in the problem definition stage mitigates against the bias of any single actor providing information, because the decision-making body or institution can triangulate this bias (Workman, 2015). Redundancy of information provision enhances its reliability (Bendor, 1985; Landau, 1969).

Inclusive and expansive problem search at the agenda setting and problem definition stage also directly addresses the costs most prominent at this stage. Diverse sources of information, especially if independent, greatly increase the quality and quantity of information available to policymakers. Structuring searches to consider alternative definitions and related issues also reduces the risk that policymakers will be inattentive to potentially important elements of a problem. Examples of this type of search process already exists in federal rulemaking, where diverse institutions and groups provide a flow of information about regulatory problems and policies – no doubt search processes at state and local levels would benefit from similar types of approaches.

Organisationally, the stage of agenda setting and problem definition demands delegation. In piecing together the issues to be addressed on the agenda, or the components of a particular problem, organisations that delegate attention can count on comparative advantage. Organisational units need not address the broader aggregated problem, and instead, focus on producing expertise-laden problem definitions that are aggregated, or blended (see the discussion of issue bundling below), at the apex of the organisation where coordination is paramount.

As policy systems set an agenda and develop definitions for problems, decision and transaction costs become ever more relevant. In addition, there is a need for coordinated, authoritative decision-making that reaches across organisational units. At the stage where problem definition is settled, organisational strategies that constrain participation will move proposed solutions to implementation in an expeditious manner. Constraining participation and choice at this stage presumes, of course, that relevant information has not been excluded during problem definition and agenda setting. It is here that centralisation shines. Given a diverse set of solutions generated from an expansive understanding of the problem, centralised organisations are better situated to coordinate action and act with urgency. Two related processes ensure that coordination and authoritative action at this broader level is both responsive and effective (see, for instance, Gerring et al, 2009).

Suggestion 2: Customising information flows through issue bundling

In his study of federal regulations, Workman (2015, 116–23) finds that Congress is able to shape the contours of information flows generated by bureaucracies through agenda setting, in particular, by considering issues in bundles. At the stage of agenda setting and problem definition, policy entrepreneurs, stakeholders, citizens and bureaucracies all want to steer problem definitions in a way that favours their preferred policies. As policymakers consider issues in bundles instead of separately, these actors are forced to adjust the information they supply in an effort remain relevant in the defining of the problem. This is a key function of upper level organisational units, with the ability to shape information supply such that policymaking is amenable to problems such as boundary- and jurisdiction-spanning issues.

Consider the problem of climate change. Understood only as an environmental problem, the definition of climate change limits the range of solutions that may be developed. Now, imagine that policymakers understand climate change to be composed of environmental, agricultural, energy and transportation elements. By considering these in a bundle labelled climate change, three things happen. First, policymakers are privy to information generated in each of these streams, meaning crucial elements are less likely to be overlooked. Second, authoritative decision- makers in the policy system are free to combine and customise these elements into a holistic approach to the problem, if desirable. Third, issue bundles foster competition among bureaucracies, policy entrepreneurs, interest groups and citizens to be the most prominent provider of information about the problem. This competition encourages an information supply that is responsive to important, but otherwise ignored, elements of the problem. A prime example is the EPA and the Department of Agriculture (USDA) aligning on many of the proposed solutions to climate change from 2006 through to 2013.

In practice, issue bundling occurs through agenda setting and delegation and has two virtues. First, any deliberative body, be it a city council or congressional committee, is able to alter the flow of information from actors in an issue area by simply changing the substantive issues considered in a discussion of policy change. Why? Arriving at this conclusion requires only the assumptions that the deliberative body has some policymaking authority, and that the actors in the process beneath those with authority want to influence policy. The second virtue of issue bundling is that it does not require the passage of a policy directive, legislation, ordinance or bill. It occurs through the process of agenda setting, such that the direction of the deliberative body is innate to the process. Put simply, to change the stream of information, the deliberative body only needs to change the way it discusses an issue. Actors in the process will respond with information addressing the current understanding of the problem, most simply, because they want to steer the problem definition, and hence, solutions generated.

By bundling issues on the agenda, policymakers are able to shape the overall supply of information about policy problems without choking off the expertise at lower levels of the organisation. In such a process, the expertise and delegation at the problem definition and agenda setting stage works in lockstep with the coordination and urgency elements of centralised units in the system. By bringing actors in the policy system into competition with one another, policymakers also increase the value of signalling and what might be learned from information about a policy problem.

Suggestion 3: Taking signals seriously and learning from the messengers

By fostering problem search that is expansive and inclusive, policymakers retain two sources of information. The first of these is the information generated and provided by actors in the system. The second is the more subtle information gleaned from the messengers themselves. In constructing problem search such that diverse flows of information are generated about problems and how they are to be understood, policymakers are able to triangulate among various definitions of the problem. That is to say, policymakers at the upper reaches of the system can blend various problem definitions to address boundary-spanning, complex problems. They are able to triangulate among definitions imbued with expertise to arrive at an understanding that incorporates important elements.

The more subtle form of information conveyed by search processes constructed in this way pertains to the messengers themselves. When suppliers of information about problems have diverse and divergent preferences and problem definitions, their convergence on a problem definition or a set of solutions is a powerful signal to policymakers at the top of organisations or policy systems. For example, the EPA and USDA's convergence on tax incentives for reforestation offer a powerful signal about a policy that is likely not only deemed effective, but also politically feasible. This is, however, not how we normally contemplate organisations or policymaking systems. Especially at state and local levels, where resources and power are more unequal, great effort is taken to constrain participation and dampen competition. This inclination robs the system, and especially those at the top, of powerful signals about the likely benefits and feasibility of various ways of thinking about problems, or solutions to them. This inclination is rampant at all levels of government, but is particularly virulent in local governance systems and within organisations. It severely undermines institutional information processing in these settings.

Concluding thoughts

Finally, we would note that the dimensions of problem solving and decision- making in government cannot be maximised simultaneously. The organisational ramifications of limited attention and institutional information processing represent a tension in governance structures, indeed in all social organisations, that can never be optimised. The balance in any decision context should be reflective of the cautions and suggestions we put forth here. Far from the definitive words on this subject, we fully intend for future scholars to investigate, corroborate and challenge the practical lessons we draw here.

References

Baumgartner, FR, Jones, BD, 1993, *Agendas and Instability in American Politics*, Chicago, IL: University of Chicago

Baumgartner, FR, Jones, BD, Mortensen, PB, 2014, Punctuated equilibrium theory: Explaining stability and change in public policymaking, *Theories of the Policy Process*, 59–103

Baumgartner, FR, Carammia, M, Epp, DA, Noble, B, Rey, B, Yildirim, TM, 2017, Budgetary change in authoritarian and democratic regimes, *Journal of European Public Policy* 24, 6, 1–17

Bendor, J, 1985, *Parallel systems in government*, Berkeley, CA: University of California Press

Breunig, C, Koski, C, 2009, Punctuated budgets and governors' institutional powers, *American Politics Research* 37, 6, 1116–38

Cashore, B, Howlett, M, 2007, Punctuating which equilibrium? Understanding thermostatic policy dynamics in Pacific Northwest forestry, *American Journal of Political Science* 51, 3, 532–51

Epp, DA, Baumgartner, FR, 2017, Complexity, capacity, and budget punctuations, *Policy Studies Journal* 45, 2, 247–64

Gerring, J, Thacker, SC, Moreno, C, 2009, Are parliamentary systems better? *Comparative Political Studies* 42, 3, 327–59

Hammond, TH, 1986, Agenda control, organizational structure, and bureaucratic politics, *American Journal of Political Science* 30, 2, 379–420

Heclo, H, 1974, *Modern social politics in Britain and Sweden: From relief to income maintenance*, New Haven, CT: Yale University Press

Thomas, HF, 2017, Modeling contagion in policy subsystems, *Cognitive Systems Research*, 44, 74–88, August

Howlett, M, Cashore, B, 2009, The dependent variable problem in the study of policy change: Understanding policy change as a methodological problem, *Journal of Comparative Policy Analysis: Research and Practice* 11, 1, 33–46

Howlett, M, Migone, A, 2011, Charles Lindblom is alive and well and living in punctuated equilibrium land, *Policy and Society* 30, 1, 53–62

Jones, BD, 1994, *Reconceiving decision-making in democratic politics: Attention, choice, and public policy*, Chicago, IL: University of Chicago Press

Jones, BD, 2001, *Politics and the architecture of choice: Bounded rationality and governance*, Chicago, IL: University of Chicago Press

Jones, BD, Baumgartner, FR, 2005, *The politics of attention: How government prioritizes problems*, Chicago, IL: University of Chicago Press

Jones, BD, Baumgartner, FR, 2015, *The politics of information: Problem definition and the course of public policy in America*, Chicago, IL: University of Chicago Press

Jones, BD, 2017, Behavioral rationality as a foundation for public policy studies *Cognitive Systems Research*, 43, 63–75, June

Jones, BD, Sulkin, T, Larsen, HA, 2003, Punctuations in political institutions, *American Political Science Review* 97, 1, 1–23

Kingdon, JW, 1995, *Agendas, alternatives, and public policies*, New York: Harper Collins

Koski, C, 2011, Committed to protection? Partnerships in critical infrastructure protection, *Journal of Homeland Security and Emergency Management* 8, 1

Koski, C, 2015, Does a partnership need partners? Assessing partnerships for critical infrastructure protection, *The American Review of Public Administration* 45, 3, 327–42

Landau, M, 1969, Redundancy, rationality, and the problem of duplication and overlap, *Public Administration Review* 29, 4, 346–58

Lewallen, Jo, Theriault, SM, Jones, BD, 2016, Congressional dysfunction: An information processing perspective, *Regulation & Governance* 10, 2, 179–90

Lindblom, C, 1959, The science of muddling through, *Public Administration Review* 19, 2, 79–88

May, PJ, 1991, Reconsidering policy design: Policies and publics, *Journal of Public Policy* 11, 2, 187–206

May, PJ, Workman, S, Jones, BD, 2008, Organizing attention: Responses of the bureaucracy to agenda disruption, *Journal of Public Administration Research and Theory* 18, 4, 517–41

May, P, Sapotichne, J, Workman, S, 2009, Widespread policy disruption: Terrorism, public risks, and homeland security, *Policy Studies Journal* 37, 2, 171–94

Mintrom, M, Norman, P, 2009, Policy entrepreneurship and policy change, *Policy Studies Journal* 37, 4, 649–67

Nicholson, J, Orr, K, 2016, Local government partnership working: A space odyssey. Or, journeys through the dilemmas of public and private sector boundary-spanning actors, *Policy & Politics* 44, 2, 269–87

Ostrom, V, 2008, *The intellectual crisis in American public administration*, 3rd edn, Tuscaloosa, AL: University of Alabama Press

Pralle, SB, 2003, Venue shopping, political strategy, and policy change: The internationalization of Canadian forest advocacy, *Journal of Public Policy* 23, 3, 233–60

Rugeley, CR, Gerlach, JD, 2012, Understanding environmental public opinion by dimension: How heuristic processing mitigates high information costs on complex issues, *Politics & Policy* 40, 3, 444–70

Shaffer, R, 2017, Cognitive load and issue engagement in congressional discourse, *Cognitive Systems Research* 44, 89–99, August

Selznick, P, 1949, *TVA and the grass roots: A study of politics and organization*, Berkeley, CA: University of California Press

Stigler, GJ, 1961, The economics of information, *Journal of Political Economy* 69, 3, 213–25

Vaughan, SK, Arsneault, S, 2008, Not-for-profit advocacy: Challenging policy images and pursuing policy change, *Review of Policy Research* 25, 5, 411–28

Workman, S, 2015, *The dynamics of bureaucracy in the US government: How Congress and federal agencies process information and solve problems*, New York: Cambridge University Press

Workman, S, Shafran, JS, 2015, Communications frameworks and the supply of information in policy subsystems, in M Howlett, J Hogan (eds) *Policy Paradigms in Theory and Practice: Discourses, Ideas, and Anomalies in Public Policy Dynamics*, New York: Palgrave MacMillan

Workman, S, Jones, BD, Jochim, AE, 2009, Information processing and policy dynamics, *Policy Studies Journal* 37, 1, 75–92

CHAPTER EIGHT

Policy design and the added-value of the institutional analysis development framework

Tanya Heikkila and Krister Andersson

Introduction

Public policies are institutional arrangements that set the official rules of the game for society as we work together to provide public goods and solve complex social dilemmas, such as maintaining orderly and healthy communities, educating the public, protecting vulnerable populations, and sustaining natural resources. Designing policies to manage these complex social problems can be challenging. In part, this is because the institutional arrangements that comprise policies can be complex and may affect a diverse set of actors and issues in ways that may be uncertain or difficult to predict. Scholarship on institutional analysis, particularly from the research that employs the Institutional Analysis and Development (IAD) framework, can offer useful tools to help understand and assess this complexity. Previous assessments and descriptions of the IAD framework, however, have not clearly explained how insights from the IAD can enhance the practical relevance of scholarly research on policy design.

As its name suggests, institutions are at the heart of the IAD framework. Institutions are the rules, norms, and shared strategies that structure human behaviour and choices, and are collectively created, adapted, monitored, and enforced (Ostrom, 2005). Thus, by 'institutional arrangements', we are not referring to bricks-and- mortar buildings or political venues. While institutions can be formalised, as written into policy documents, they often are defined by what people have agreed with one another about what they may, must or must not do in relation to other people or to their environment.

How and why people design institutions to solve shared problems, and what makes institutions work, has been the focus of much of the institutional analysis associated with IAD research. As Schlager and Cox (2018, 217) note, the 'IAD Framework has a problem solving orientation'. However, the intellectual history of this framework and its complexity can make it difficult for scholars and policy analysts who are not trained deeply in the application of the IAD to understand and appreciate this problem-solving orientation. For those who are trained in the IAD approach to policy analysis, the jargon and tacit knowledge associated with this community of scholars also makes it difficult to step back and communicate its core message. This chapter therefore extracts new practical insights and research strategies from IAD scholarship framework.

Before discussing these insights, we provide a brief background of the IAD's foundational concepts and the framework's theoretical and empirical underpinnings. Given that several in-depth discussions exist on the inner workings of the IAD, and on state of the art in theorising and empirical research, we avoid duplicating the excellent work of our colleagues (for example, see Ostrom, 2005; Andersson, 2006; Poteet et al, 2010; Ostrom, 2011; Ostrom et al, 2014; Schlager and Cox, 2018). Instead, we develop a novel synthesis of strands of IAD research to help translate the somewhat opaque language of the IAD and offer lessons for scholars who wish to enhance the practical lessons of policy design research. We close with some words of caution in terms of the boundaries of these lessons and recommendations.

The state of the IAD art and science

Research within the IAD framework is extensive and has emerged over several decades as part of a larger research programme, often associated with the work of Vincent and Elinor Ostrom and that of their colleagues and students. Within this research programme, seeds of the IAD framework largely began with Vincent Ostrom's analyses of the organisation of metropolitan governance in the 1950s and 1960s. This research was followed by Vincent Ostrom's political philosophy work on public administration in the 1970s and empirical research by the Ostroms and colleagues in the early 1970s on the organisation of public services such as policing and groundwater governance (for example, see Ostrom et al, 1973). The formalisation of the IAD framework in the academic literature started in the early 1980s (see Kiser and Ostrom, 1982; Ostrom, 1983; 1986), and empirical and theoretical development of research questions under the framework began in earnest in the late 1980s and 1990s, as Elinor Ostrom and colleagues' research on the management 'common pool' resources (for example, water, fisheries, forests) took off. In 2009, Elinor Ostrom was recognised for her extensive contributions to the study of the commons and institutions when she received the Nobel Prize in Economics. Recent research has focused on testing key questions around common-pool resources and has extended the IAD framework to develop a more interdisciplinary framework (the social-ecological systems framework).

In summarising the state of the art with IAD-related research, we focus on three general themes: 1) the IAD's lessons on self-governance, 2) the core concepts and features of the IAD framework, and 3) how IAD studies have produced contextually- specific insights on institutional design. Understanding these three themes are essential for scholars unfamiliar with the IAD who want to begin to apply it. These three focal areas also set the stage for the lessons that scholars can communicate to students and practitioners, which we offer in the following section.

Self-governance as a way to solve collective action problems

A fundamental tenant of the IAD is that individuals, under certain circumstances, are capable of solving shared problems from the bottom-up or through self-governance. Moreover, the IAD assumes that people are fallible problem-solvers; that is, they are capable of learning and adapting institutions when problems or issues change. The shared problems of interest within the IAD are typically referred to as collective action problems. Collective action problems are those dilemmas that arise when individual contributions to a collective good can be costly and when no single individual can control the outcome. In the context of public policy, collective action problems often surround the production of a public good or service (for example, public education, healthcare, roads and water infrastructure) or management of a shared resource (for example, fisheries, grasslands, irrigation systems). They also emerge around the challenges associated with coming to agreement around a set of rules that could benefit a group, but where those rules might impose some costs on particular actors who must comply with or enforce those rules (for example, rules to reduce pollution from industries).

From the IAD perspective, individuals, local communities, governments, or any group of actors or organisations working together can solve collective action problems as they design and adapt institutions. Vincent Ostrom's research earlier in his career, which argued strongly against centralised models of policy and administration (Ostrom, 1974), and promoted the value of contestation and deliberation when designing institutions (Ostrom, 1997), represents some of the core philosophical foundations of IAD-related research. The research questions that have ensued since his earlier work have continued to examine how and under what conditions people can address collective action problems, and how the design of the institutions that citizens themselves create can shape the success of these problem-solving efforts.[1]

The framework as an analytical lens

The goal of the framework within the IAD research programme has been to guide researchers and analysts who want to diagnose the motivation for individuals to devise or change institutions, including public policies and how those institutions perform. As such, the framework offers a roadmap or diagnostic approach to analyse various aspects of policy processes where institutional choices are made or implemented. The IAD framework itself does not offer any direct answers to questions that its users might have about a collective action problem or a policy design that might solve it. Rather, the framework raises questions for the researcher to consider as he or she seeks to develop a deeper understanding of both the problem under study and potential solutions. These questions are based on a long tradition of empirical research about the key groups of variables that often influence individuals' ability to solve collective action problems.

The IAD framework recognises the complexity that can shape or surround institutional choice processes, but like any framework (which is akin to a map or camera lens), it focuses analysts' attention to particular features of the policy process in guiding research, while paying less attention to others. It also provides a rigorous conceptualisation of the institutions that structure and are produced within policy processes, clarifies the characteristics of actors (for example, their information, resources and beliefs) that underlie their choices, and lays out a set of contextual variables that condition the interactions and outcomes of actors. It pays limited attention to other features of the policy process that scholars recognise as potentially important in understanding outcomes, such as crises or how policy subsystems are structured (Cairney and Heikkila, 2014). As it focuses largely on questions related to collective action problems, its applications may be less useful for other types of policy problems, such as how policy actors solve distributional conflicts or what drives learning among individual policy actors.

The starting point of any application of the IAD framework is the identification of an action situation. An action situation involves multiple individuals who engage in a set of actions that together lead to outcomes (Ostrom, 2005). The actions, interactions and outcomes of an action situation are structured by the set of existing institutions, or rules, that determine who, what, or how collective actions are undertaken. A biophysical context and community context also shape the action situation. The participants or actors in an action situation possess different types of information, values and information processing strategies, which all influence an individual's decision to contribute (or not) to the collective efforts to address a shared problem. In addition, the IAD framework recognises that institutional choice in action situations can occur at multiple levels, including constitutional, collective choice, operational levels. In a policy setting, these levels are akin to policy choices about who can engage in policy choice, when and how (constitutional); choices about what rules or strategies should govern a particular issue (collective choice); and choices about how to implement the collective choice decisions (operational). Any one action situation can also be influenced by rules within these three levels, but most action situations are primarily situated within one of these levels. Thus, the concept of an action situation allows IAD analysts to delve into a diversity of policy processes, venues or types policy choices; it is not restricted to a specific type of policy activity in a particular type of policy venue. Hence, this approach allows researchers to study how decision-making processes at different levels of governance influence decisions and actions in a specific situation of interest.

The emphasis of the IAD on problem solving or addressing collective action dilemmas further raises questions about how policy actors coordinate and compete or engage in conflict (Schlager and Cox, 2018). As such, it is open to different forms of interactions and different stages of policymaking, ranging from rule-making or policy choice to implementation, monitoring and evaluation. Finally, the IAD Framework recognises that analysts can employ different evaluative criteria to assess the outcomes of action situations. These can embrace questions around equity, efficiency, adaptability and robustness of particular action situations.

Although the framework is applicable to a wide range of action situations, or types of policy and institutional choice settings, applying it can require an investment in learning the deeper terminology and concepts associated with the framework. To understand the depths of the framework, analysts need to understand the precise definitions of concepts related to institutional design that are built into the IAD (McGinnis, 2011a). For instance, the IAD has a typology of seven types of 'rules', which are one type of institution (along with norms and shared strategies) that structure how people interact in an action situation (Ostrom, 2005). Additionally, IAD research has identified grammatical components of rules, norms and shared strategies – or institutions (Crawford and Ostrom, 1995; Ostrom, 2005). It further acknowledges underlying differences between types of goods such as common-pool resources and public goods. (Ostrom and Ostrom, 1977; Ostrom, 2005) and its research has drawn a clear distinction between the production and provision of public goods (Oakerson, 1999). These examples are just the tip of the IAD's conceptual iceberg.[2]

Conceptual development in the IAD framework is not a purely theoretical exercise, or meant to confuse the potential IAD consumer or new user. Instead, it provides clarity for scholars when they attempt to observe empirically the vague and difficult concepts we often seek to measure in policy design. At the same time, it helps provide the 'meat' to the 'bones' of the framework, which then opens up avenues for new questions. For example, research that has used the rule typology and grammar of institutions (Crawford and Ostrom, 1995) has begun to develop theories about how institutional designs can be validly measured, and theoretically assessed across different types of formal policy documents (for example, Siddiki et al, 2011; Carter et al, 2016). While all of these conceptual distinctions in the IAD framework are valuable for advancing the science of institutions, they also create barriers to understanding the implications of the framework in practical terms. Table 8.1 provides definitions of some of the key terms associated with the IAD framework and its related research.

IAD applications: learning about how institutions work in context

The framework itself is just a starting point for IAD research. It provides a lens to break down complexity and focus on key features that help us understand institutional or policy design. However, the framework does not, on its own, lay out specific guidance about what makes institutions work and under what contexts. This is because particular types of institutional settings can vary widely and institutions that work in one context may not work in another. Therefore, IAD scholarship explicitly uses the framework to guide research, but seeks out more specific theories to explain how key concepts are related and what outcomes they produce in a given institutional setting (Ostrom, 2011). Additionally, IAD scholars embrace the use of models to test theoretical expectations under more constrained conditions, which can further illuminate the contexts under which particular theories hold (Ostrom, 2011). Empirically, a wide variety of research methods – that is, comparative field research, lab experiments, field experiments, game theory and agent-based modelling have been employed to test and build the empirical foundation for IAD research (Poteete et al, 2010).

Much of the early research that spawned the IAD centred on questions about how public goods and services could be delivered to achieve efficiency and accountability (Ostrom et al, 1961; Ostrom and Ostrom, 1971). One of the broad lessons from this earlier work was the importance of institutional diversity and multiple, overlapping centres of decision-authority for enhancing public service delivery. Within this line of research, clarifying how institutions structure individual motivations and behaviours was foundational to interpreting empirical research. For instance, the

Table 8.1: Key terms within the IAD framework

Institutions	The rules, norms, and strategies that structure interactions between individuals so that there is less uncertainty in these interactions.
Institutional analysis	The study of how people create rules, norms, and strategies and how they affect people's ability to solve collective-action problems
Self-governance	The process of people devising institutions collectively, without force or interference of a central or higher-level authority.
Institutional choice	The process of making decisions to create, adapt, or refine institutions
Rules Rules-in-use Rules-in-form	The things that you may, may not, or must do, or else... The rules that are actually followed and respected by people The rules that have been formalized and written down, but may or may not be respected by people
Action situation	A setting where actors interact on a particular issue or topic and produce a shared outcome. The action situation is structured by institutions/rules and biophysical and community contexts.
Collective action	Working together to achieve things that no one can achieve individually
Levels of choice/action Constitutional Collective choice Operational	A nested view of institutional choices, about: Who can engage in policy choice, when, and how What rules or strategies should govern a particular issue How to implement collective choice decisions
Common pool resource	A resource system (e.g. an irrigation system or fishery), whose size or characteristics makes it costly (but not impossible) to exclude potential beneficiaries from accessing the resource. Once accessed, the resource faces problems of congestion or overuse because it is subtractable, which means that if I extract one unit of the resource, it will no longer be available for other people's use.
Public goods	Like CPRs, it is costly to exclude potential beneficiaries to public goods. Examples include free-to-air television, air, or national defence.
Rule typology	Seven different types of rules that comprise institutional designs, including scope, boundary, authority, choice, information, enforcement and payoff rules.
Evaluative criteria	The standards by which IAD analysts explicitly assess the outcomes of institutional design

literature offered insights on why public entrepreneurs within jurisdictions would work with each other to provide public goods, what motivates citizens to live in particular jurisdictions that matched their personal preferences, and how these preferences incentivise government actors to ensure that the types of goods and services produced by governments meet citizen's needs (Ostrom et al, 1973; Ostrom, 1975; Oakerson, 1999; Oakerson and Parks, 2011).

Among the many applications of the IAD, a substantial proportion has focused on understanding institutions for managing common-pool resources. These include questions about why people create institutions to manage common-pool resources and what makes the institutions enduring or robust. For example, empirical research on common-pool resources, both in the field and in the laboratory, has explored and tested ideas about how individual communication and information influences how people would work together to create institutions to manage resources – or engage in collective action (Ostrom, 2005; Poteete et al, 2010; Wright et al, 2016). This research has highlighted empirically the importance of face-to-face communication and dialogue needed for building robust institutions for managing common-pool resources (Ostrom et al, 1994; Ostrom, 1999; 2005; Andersson, 2004). Other policy areas, such as international development aid, the digital commons, non-profit management, and collaboration among public agencies have also expanded our understanding of the different contexts within which people can devise institutions and what factors might make them successful (Ostrom et al, 2014).

Development of contextually-specific theories and models has worked hand-in- hand with the more general IAD framework. For example, for the work that led to Elinor Ostrom's Nobel Prize, the framework informed the diagnosis of the cases of common-pool resources, but the research on the commons also helped illuminate some of the variables that were critical to explore in the IAD framework. Through the framework's broad insights on different types of rules, scholars have been able to highlight the institutional design features that were specific to successful versus unsuccessful cases of common-pool resource governance.

Key insights for policy analysis and design

Given the 'problem-solving' orientation of IAD related research, its insights should not rest in academic books and articles. It is also important for scholars to be able to communicate what IAD research can offer students and analysts of public policy. Several popular press articles and think-tank reports have already translated lessons from Elinor Ostrom's research on the commons following her 2009 Nobel Prize, including lessons for governance that extend beyond natural resources (for example, see Bollier, 2009; Economist, 2012; Harford, 2013; Wall, 2014; Hastings, 2017). These lessons have generally focused on the argument that, under the right conditions, solutions to natural resource management problems can be addressed at the local level, outside of central government interventions. They have also described how the 'design principles' associated with long-enduring common-pool resource institutions (see Ostrom, 1990; Ostrom et al, 1994; Schlager, 2004) offer strategies for communities and policymakers alike. These lessons include recognising the need for participatory and adaptive rule-making by people who are closely tied to the policy issue, and ensuring that policies have effective monitoring, conflict resolution mechanisms, and meaningful linkages to related institutions across scales of decision-making.

While we do not disagree with these insights, we argue that there are additional lessons from IAD-inspired research that extend beyond those that emerged following Ostrom's Nobel Prize. Both IAD novices and experts can use these lessons, we argue, to enhance the practical value of research on policy design, potentially beyond some of the narrower empirical domains that have been the focus of IAD-related research. We summarise these three key insights below.

Self-governance is possible, under certain conditions, across a diversity of policy venues

The deeper philosophy of the IAD framework, based on the recognition of the capacity of humans to collectively solve problems (with and without the support of government), can be taken to an extreme. That is, a naïve reader of IAD literature might assume that IAD scholarship promotes self-governance as 'the' institutional solution. A closer read of the literature, however, underscores that although people are capable of bottom-up or shared problem solving, certain conditions make it more or less feasible. Additionally, the insights about when self-governance is possible can be just as valuable outside local or small communities. In particular, we argue that in many formal policy settings or government venues, decision-makers face serious collective action problems and disincentives to work together to find common policy solutions to shared problems. This is evident by the deep political divide that seems to be growing within many democracies, making it even more challenging for decision-makers to find common ground on issues that need urgent public attention: healthcare; immigration; climate change; gun control; free-trade; education; and tax reform, to name but a few.

We recognise that new language and theoretical insights from IAD research, as currently applied, may needed to grapple with some of the policy issues that are emerging in government venues. For example, the IAD has not effectively diagnosed how political 'agents', or those people in operational choice situations, relate to the 'principals' they are representing (for example, often people in collective choice or constitutional choice situations). However, the lessons from IAD research on self-governance still have important parallels for government venues. For example, within the IAD literature, scholars have theorised and empirically shown that several conditions can increase the likelihood that individuals are able to design institutional arrangements that can solve contentious collective action problems related to the governance of the commons (Ostrom, 1990; Ostrom et al., 1994; Ostrom, 1999; Schlager, 2004; Lejano et al, 2014). In short, these conditions include: trust, norms of reciprocity built among actors, actors who have a common understanding of common-pool resource (aka the policy issue), the majority of the actors having dependency on the resource and a long-term view of the resource benefits (or policy issue benefits), prior organisational experience and leadership and autonomy to organise.

In examining these conditions, several strategies can be gleaned for designing institutions related to various policy issues. One of the more difficult, but critical strategies for policy actors involves building social capital and experience working together on a shared issue. As Ostrom (1990, 184) found, when individuals 'have developed shared norms and patterns of reciprocity, they possess social capital with which they can build institutional arrangements for resolving dilemmas'. The second condition – dependency or a long-term view – may be less likely to emerge outside or local communities or resource settings. Therefore, translating this lesson to other settings, such as healthcare or immigration, may require re-conceptualising the theoretical constructs associated with successful institutions. For example, where policymakers recognise a collective dependency and the long-term value of these issues for society as a whole, they may be more likely to devise policies that can sustain shared benefits.

We know from Ostrom's research and others that as the number of decision-makers or people in a group increases, or with frequent turnover or substantial heterogeneity among the actors, building shared norms is more difficult. A particular type of group heterogeneity that makes the development of norms of trust and reciprocity between people challenging is economic inequality (Rothstein and Uslaner, 2005; Bjørnskov, 2007; Algan and Cahuc, 2014). For example, forest user-groups with relatively high levels of economic inequality have a harder time in managing their shared forest resources (Andersson and Agrawal, 2011). There are institutional factors, however, which can help overcome these challenges. As suggested by the IAD research, identifying skilled leaders who have experience on an issue and who have experience working with people from different backgrounds and convictions can be critical. Having adequate information on the nature of the problem and feasible solutions to the problem is also valuable for enhancing group norms. As information and data become more contested in modern politics, IAD research further implies that having localised information (that is, from actors who are engaged in implementing a policy issue) and trusted information can increase capacity for successful institutional design. By identifying these conditions that can support self-governance in a diversity of policy settings, researchers can develop testable propositions to help compare policy successes and failures, while practitioners may be able to use these insights as strategies to enhance governance processes.

Use the framework as a diagnostic approach for public policy

The IAD framework can help diagnose the key elements of a policy process that analysts need to consider when trying to design new policies or analyse existing policies. First, at a basic level, the institutional analysis approach directs analysts to clarify what is the action situation of interest. To do this, the analyst can use the IAD as a systematic checklist of the components of the action situation. This includes:

- identifying who are the relevant actors that an existing or new policy (as a type of institution) would target, and what are the actors' resources, information, experience, social norms and knowledge;
- understanding what rules (including rules in-form) can constrain or enable particular actions of these actors. These rules, as discussed further below, can be categorised according different types and can interact with one another;
- assessing how the characteristics of the biophysical setting and characteristics of the broader community within which the action situation occurs might affect how people interact and respond to institutions. The biophysical setting may focus on different types of contexts. A public goods context, for example, differs from a common-pool resource context. These differences matter when determining what rules will effectively address problems associated with managing or providing these goods.

Analysts can then use the IAD framework to ask a set of disciplined questions when delving into a particular policy context (Ostrom, 2005). In thinking prospectively about a new policy, for example, one might start with questions such as: What are the characteristics (for example, values, resources, norms) of the actors? What is the nature of the problem (for example, the physical characteristics) that they are encountering? What is the nature of the good or service they are trying to produce, distribute, consume, or maintain? Then one can ask: How might different types of rules change the interactions or behaviours of the specific types of actors involved in the specific context of this action situation? In analysing an existing policy, one could also ask: How would a new set of rules interact with the broader contextual factors or with the types of actors involved? It is also important to consider whether the rules that are 'in-use' within an existing action situation might conflict with or be compatible with formal or proposed rules.

The IAD 'rule typology' can help take this approach to policy analysis to an even deeper level. Ostrom (2005), in fact, view rules 'as tools' that can be employed to help change behaviour. Keep in mind that rules are those subsets of institutions that are designed to be enforceable. At the same time, many different types of rules can be relevant to a policy analyst – that is, scope rules, authority rules, information rules, enforcement rules, payoff rules and others. Breaking up a policy to dissect these types of rules highlights how institutions – both formal and informal – could potentially influence who has access to policy venues, what authorities are granted to different actors, what constrains or enables how particular actors engage and share information, and who benefits (or loses) when rules are followed (or ignored). It can also help open up questions such as: Which actors can enter or exit this situation (boundary rules)? What are actors allowed to do or not do (authority rules)? Who must provide information to whom (information rules)? How do actors reach agreement on decisions (aggregation rules)? Furthermore, if we consider the interactive nature of these rules, one may need to ask how changing one rule could affect actions with respect to the other rules.

In other words, the IAD framework can provide a set of diagnostic questions for parsing out the key features of an institutional context that may affect policy outcomes. This can be particularly helpful for scholars and practitioners interested in exploring multifaceted institutional designs. For example, policy analysts often aim to observe if a policy as a whole is working. Yet, asking if a complex policy such as the US Affordable Care Act (ACA) works is too simplistic a question and will not allow for a robust assessment of the policy. Public policies usually comprise many types of rules that target a diversity of types of action situations. For example, the US ACA has rules that apply to various action situations (for example, individual healthcare markets, determinations of Medicaid eligibility within states and the provision of federal subsidies for insurance companies that insure low-income individuals). Moreover, any one of these action situations could be highly complex. One implication of this is that the IAD might be best suited to studying subsets of larger policy systems, rather than the system as a whole.

Finally, the IAD pushes analysts to be explicit about the criteria we use to evaluate the outcomes of these interactions and how the rules structure these interactions (Ostrom, 2005). Is efficiency, equity or effectiveness the primary criterion? Or, is adaptability of the system important? While we recognise that the field of policy analysis is extensive and has many analytical tools and criteria for evaluation that are already in use, the approach of the IAD may bring new insights to institutional diagnoses by dissecting the design of institutions and linking them to the actions of targeted actors within a specified policy context.

We recognise that the IAD, on its own or in its current form, may not provide all of the answers needed for understanding and assessing complex policy designs and processes. Clement (2010), for instance, has recommended bringing 'power' into the IAD, which may more accurately depict many institutional action situations. Alternatively, incorporating theories, such as principal–agent theory, into the language of the framework can help illuminate some of the complex relationships among actors in government policymaking contexts, which may be lacking from the IAD.

Stop looking for panaceas: identify, and experiment with contextually appropriate policies

The third lesson from IAD research is to consider the institutional incentives that different policy interventions produce in particular contexts for a variety of actors, including citizens, law enforcement, policymakers and administrators. This lesson recognises that the framework cannot provide simple answers and the policy tools or institutional arrangements that may appear appropriate in one context can fail in another. This lesson also embraces one of Elinor Ostrom's mantras, which is that there are no panaceas, or one-sized-fits all policy solutions (Ostrom, 2007). A thorough understanding of how particular institutions produce different behavioural incentives can help policy makers and administrators ensure that the proposed policy intervention produces the desired outcomes. The IAD framework can help policy analysts map out how a given policy intervention is likely to affect the incentives of a variety of different groups in society.

For example, Gibson et al (2005) use the IAD framework to examine how international aid interventions affect the incentives of aid recipients in developing countries to promote sustainable development activities locally. They find that many well-intended aid interventions produce weak incentives for local ownership, learning about development outcomes and programme adaptation in donor countries. More importantly, perhaps, the authors lay out a diagnostic tool, based on the IAD framework, which can help development workers identify potential incentive incompatibility issues ex ante. Doing so helps develop an institutional design of the intervention that can address incompatibility issues and hence reduce the risk of failed interventions and unintended consequences.

On a practical-level, understanding how interventions affect incentives can help prevent policy interventions from backfiring. Work in behavioural science has pointed out risks associated with common policy intervention approaches, such as using cash incentives and fines as well as top-down regulation to induce local collective action (Frey and Oberholtzer-Gee, 1997; Gneezy and Rustichini, 2000; Cardenas et al, 2000). Most public policies explicitly target local people's incentives to try to sway their behaviour in a predetermined direction. If someone runs a red light and hits a pedestrian, she will have to pay a fine and may even have her driver's licence temporarily suspended. If she buys a fuel-efficient car, her government may give her a tax credit. These interventions often work quite well to produce incentives that effectively induce desired group behaviour. However, mounting evidence suggests that these conventional policy instruments that rely on top-down solutions and cash payments can be problematic in the sense that they may – under some specific contextual conditions – end up weakening the incentives to act collectively (see Matson et al, 2016, for a review). In essence, what this research is discovering is that to predict what specific incentives will be produced by a given policy intervention, it is necessary to consider how the prescribed rules interact with the local context. In other words, the effectiveness of using extrinsic incentives – such as fines or cash awards – often depend on individuals' social norms, beliefs and values. This research also suggests that interventions are more likely to succeed when they acknowledge the autonomy and problem-solving capabilities of people whose behaviour the interventions are trying to change.

Boundaries of the IAD's practical insights and final reflections

For scholars, students, or practitioners who lack deep training in the IAD approach, it can be difficult to apply this framework, and its related theories and models, to analyse and understand policy designs. This chapter has brought together diverse strands of IAD literature in novel ways that help communicate its lessons about policy design, which can further enhance the practical value of policy research. Integrating previously disconnected lessons from the IAD about policy analysis and design can aid in making the IAD more accessible to new scholars, and more useful to a wider diversity of policy researchers. A growing segment of the academic community, arguably, is interested in improving the usability of knowledge for decision-makers (Clark et al, 2016). These scholars recommend that for information to be usable, it not only needs to be credible, but also digestible and implementable. Therefore, to reach a broader audience, including those students interested in applied policy analysis or policymaking, below we summarise three simple lessons related from this paper.

1. Recognise that people are capable of solving problems from the bottom-up, both outside and within government settings, but they need to develop norms of reciprocity, trust, experience and adequate information to make it happen. For scholars, this means studying the conditions that can build self-governance capacity in diverse domains or venues, not just legislatures or central public agencies. For practitioners, this means embracing existing local institutions and/ or empowering local citizens and communities to become policy designers.
2. Embrace the value of the IAD framework as a systematic approach for examining the key factors that researchers or policymakers should consider when analysing policies or trying to devise new policies.These factors include: the actors devising and implementing policy and their information, knowledge motivations, and interactions; the rules in use among the actors; the biophysical and community context surrounding the actors; and the evaluative criteria appropriate for assessing the policy in question.
3. Policy incentives need to be contextually-appropriate.A key proposition from the IAD is that policy designs are more likely to be successful when they acknowledge the autonomy and problem-solving capabilities of people whose behaviour the interventions are trying to change. Therefore, scholars, analysts and practitioners should scrutinise the design elements of policies (for example, the types of rules embedded in policies), how they interact with the incentives and information that different actors use in devising or implementing a policy, and the factors that can structure their choices in light of the local context where policies are used.

Of course, there are important boundaries to the IAD framework that users and consumers of public policy research should understand. First, the theoretical and empirical lessons of IAD research has focused heavily on collective action and community-based policy processes. Therefore, some caution should be afforded when translating lessons on institutional design to more formalised or national-level government processes, such as legislative decisions or bureaucratic rule-making. Second, lessons on self-governance and collective action may not be applicable for certain types of policy contexts. For instance, highly redistributive policy issues may impose very different incentives for collective action than cases where collective benefits are more widely distributed.

Another boundary condition to consider when applying the IAD framework is that the complexity of some policy contexts, or those that extend to subsystems, may be difficult to situate within an action situation. Other policy process theories, such as the Advocacy Coalition Framework, Multiple Streams, or Punctuated Equilibrium Frameworks, may be more appropriate for such contexts. We note, however, that efforts to identify 'linked' action situations may help in approaching policy contexts that extend beyond a single action situation (McGinnis, 2011b). At the same time, the IAD framework may not be the best fit for all institutional design questions. Understanding institutional path dependency, for instance, might be more appropriately addressed by theories or frameworks that use a historical institutional lens (see Pierson and Skocpol, 2002; Hall, 2010). Finally, many questions that are central to policy processes, such as how politics or conflicts arise or how the framing by political interests shapes public opinion and policy choices, are not particularly well suited for studying through an institutional framework.

Fortunately, other theories and frameworks of the policy process examined in this special issue can more easily shed light on these types of questions. While the IAD does not offer specific theoretical insights on these other questions, incorporating some of the methodological insights from the IAD around institutional design could complement such theories. As one example, scholars have long recognised that politics and policy design are closely related (Lowi, 1972; Schneider and Ingram, 1993; Howlett, 2011; Weible and Heikkila, 2017). The IAD framework arguably offers tools for measuring the component parts of policy designs (Siddiki et al, 2011), which could help provide a reliable approach for understanding the connection between policy design features and political outcomes.

Perhaps one of the most important lessons from decades of IAD research is that there are no silver bullets to policy designs (Ostrom, 2005). Both institutional analysis and institutional design requires deep, contextualised understanding of the situations that structure institutional choices and outcomes. Yet, just as humans are quite capable of creating complex institutions, we are also capable of diagnosing and evaluating those institutions if we are patient and take advantage of the tools and frameworks that have been tried and tested. In other words, we need to embrace the complexity of institutions and the hard work needed for effective institutional analysis and design. We hope that this chapter offers some useful starting points in that direction.

Notes

1. For a deeper examination of the philosophical underpinnings of the IAD Framework and the work of the Ostroms, see Aligica and Boetkke (2011) and Aligica (2014).
2. Read Ostrom (2005) for a more complete accounting and explanation of the concepts that comprise the IAD Framework.

References

Aligica, PD, Boettke, PJ, 2011, The two social philosophies of Ostroms' institutionalism, *Policy Studies Journal* 39, 1, 29–49

Aligica, PD, Tarko, V, 2012, Polycentricity: From Polanyi to Ostrom, and beyond, *Governance* 25, 2, 237–62

Algan, Y, Cahuc, P, 2014, Trust, growth, and well-being: New evidence and policy implications, in P Aghion, S Durlauf (eds) *Handbook of economic growth*, vol 2, Amsterdam: Elsevier, pp 49–120

Aligica, PD 2014, *Institutional diversity and political economy: The Ostroms and beyond*, Oxford: Oxford University Press

Andersson, K, 2004, Who talks with whom? The role of repeated interactions in decentralized forest governance, *World Development* 32, 2, 233–49

Andersson, K, 2006, Understanding decentralized forest governance: An application of the Institutional Analysis and Development framework, *Sustainability: Science, Practice, & Policy* 2, 1, 25–35

Andersson, K, Agrawal, A, 2011, Inequalities, institutions, and forest commons, *Global Environmental Change* 21, 3, 866–75

Bjørnskov, C, 2007, Determinants of generalized trust: A cross-country comparison, *Public Choice* 130, 1–2, 1–21

Bollier, D, 2009, Elinor Ostrom and the digital commons, *Forbes*, 13 October, www.forbes.com/2009/10/13/open-source-net-neutrality-elinor-ostrom-nobel-opinions-contributors-david-bollier.html

Bushouse, B, Never, B, Christensen, R, 2016, Elinor Ostrom's contribution to nonprofit and voluntary action studies, *Non-Profit and Voluntary Sector Quarterly* 45, 7S–174S

Cairney, P, Heikkila, T, 2014, A comparison of theories of the policy process, in PA Sabatier, CM Weible (eds) *Theories of the policy process*, Third Edition, Boulder, CO: Westview Press, pp 363–89

Cardenas, JC, Stranlund, J, Willis, C, 2000, Local environmental control and institutional crowding-out. *World Development* 28, 10, 1719–33

Carter, DP, Weible, CM, Siddiki, SN, Basurto, X, 2016, Integrating core concepts from the Institutional Analysis and Development framework for the systematic analysis of policy designs: An illustration from the US National Organic Program regulation, *Journal of Theoretical Politics* 28, 1, 159–85

Clark, WC, van Kerkhoff, L, Lebel, L, Gallopin, GC, 2016, Crafting usable knowledge for sustainable development, *Proceedings of the National Academy of Sciences* 113, 17, 4570–78

Clement, F, 2010, Analysing decentralised natural resource governance: proposition for a 'politicised' institutional analysis and development framework, *Policy Sciences* 43, 2, 129–56

Crawford, SES, Ostrom, E, 1995, A grammar of institutions, *American Political Science Review* 89, 3, 582–600

Economist, 2012, Elinor Ostrom, www.economist.com/node/21557717

Frey, BS, Oberholzer-Gee, F, 1997, The cost of price incentives: An empirical analysis of motivation crowding-out, *The American Economic Review*, 746–55

Gibson, C, Andersson, K, Ostrom, E, Shivakumar, S, 2005, *The Samaritans' dilemma: The political economy of development aid*, Oxford: Oxford University Press

Gneezy, U, Rustichini, A, 2000, Pay enough or don't pay at all, *Quarterly Journal of Economics* 115, 3, 791–810

Hall, PA, 2010, Historical institutionalism in rationalist and sociological perspective, in J Mahoney, K Thelen (eds) *Explaining institutional change: Ambiguity, agency, and power*, Cambridge: Cambridge University Press, pp 204–24

Harford, T, 2013, Do you believe in sharing? *The Financial Times*, 30 August, www. ft.com/content/afc5377e-1026-11e3-a258-00144feabdc0

Hastings, H, 2017, Lessons from the tragedy of the commons, *Inside Higher Education*, 16 January, www.insidehighered.com/views/2017/01/16/ reversing-decline-state- support-public-universities-essay

Howlett, M, 2011, *Designing public policy*, New York, NY: Routledge

Kiser, LL, Ostrom, E, 1982, The three worlds of action: A metatheoretical synthesis of institutional approaches, in E Ostrom (ed) *Strategies of political inquiry*, pp 179–222, Beverly Hills, CA: Sage.

Lejano, R, Araral, E, Araral, D, 2014, Interrogating the commons., *Environmental Science & Policy* 36, 1–92

Lowi, TJ, 1972, Four systems of policy, politics, and choice, *Public Administration Review* 32, 4, 298–310

Matson, P, Clark, W, Andersson, K, 2016, *Pursuing sustainability: A guide to the science and practice*, Princeton, NJ: Princeton University Press

McGinnis, M, 2011a, An introduction to IAD and the language of the Ostrom workshop: A simple guide to a complex framework, *Policy Studies Journal* 39, 1, 163–77

McGinnis, M, 2011b, Networks of adjacent action situations in polycentric governance, *Policy Studies Journal* 39, 1, 51–78

McGinnis, M, Ostrom E, 2011, Reflections on Vincent Ostrom, public administration, and polycentricity, *Public Administration Review* 72, 1, 15–25

Oakerson, R, 1999, *Governing local public economies: Creating the civic metropolis*, Oakland, CA: ICS Press

Oakerson, R, Parks, R, 2011, The study of local public economies: Multi-organizational, multi-level institutional analysis and development, *Policy Studies Journal* 39, 1,147–67

Ostrom, E, 1975, The design of institutional arrangements and the responsiveness of the police, in LN Rieselbach (ed) *People vs. Government: The Responsiveness of American* Institutions, pp 274–364, Bloomington, IN: Indiana University Press

Ostrom, E, 1983, The elements of an action situation, *Working Paper* W83–23, Bloomington, IN: Indiana University Workshop in Political Theory and Policy Analysis

Ostrom, E, 1986, An agenda for the study of institutions, *Public Choice*, 48, 1, 3–25

Ostrom, E, 1990, *Governing the commons: The evolution of institutions for collective action*, New York: Cambridge University Press

Ostrom, E, 1999, Coping with tragedies of the commons, *Annual Review of Political Science* 2, 493–535

Ostrom, E, 2005, *Understanding institutional diversity*, Princeton, NJ: Princeton University Press

Ostrom, E, 2007, A diagnostic approach for going beyond panaceas, *Proceedings of the National Academy of Sciences* 104, 15181–7

Ostrom, E, 2011, Background on the institutional analysis and development framework, *Policy Studies Journal*, 39, 1, 7–27

Ostrom, E, Whitaker, G, Parks, R, 1973, Do we really want to consolidate urban police forces? A reappraisal of some old assumptions, *Public Administration Review* 33, September/October, 423–33

Ostrom, E, Gardner, R, Walker, J, 1994, *Rules, games, and common-pool resources*, Ann Arbor. MI: University of Michigan Press

Ostrom, E, Cox, M, Schlager, E, 2014, An assessment of the Institutional Analysis and Development framework and introduction of the social–ecological systems framework, in C Weible, P Sabatier (eds) *Theories of the Policy Process*, pp 267–306, Boulder, CO: Westview Press

Ostrom, V, 1974, *The intellectual crisis in public administration*, Tuscaloosa, AL: University of Alabama Press

Ostrom, V, 1997, *The meaning of democracy and the vulnerability of democracies: A response to Tocqueville's challenge*, Ann Arbor, MI: University of Michigan Press

Ostrom, V, Ostrom, E, 1971, Public choice: A different approach to the study of public administration, *Public Administration Review* 13, 203–16

Ostrom, V, Ostrom, E, 1977, Public goods and public choices, in ES Savas (ed) *Alternatives for delivering public services: Toward improved performance*, pp 7–49, Boulder, CO: Westview Press

Ostrom, V, Tiebout, CM, Warren, R, 1961, The organization of government in metropolitan areas: A theoretical inquiry, *American Political Science Review* 55, 4, 831–42

Pierson, P, Skocpol, R, 2002, Historical institutionalism in contemporary political science, *Political Science: The State of the Discipline 3*, 693–721

Poteete, A, Janssen, M, Ostrom, E, 2010, *Working together: Collective action, the commons, and multiple methods in practice*, Princeton, NJ: Princeton University Press

Rothstein, B, Uslaner, EM, 2005, All for all: Equality, corruption, and social trust, *World Politics* 58, 1, 41–72

Schlager, E, 2004, Local governance of common pool resources, in R Durant, D Fiorino, R O'Leary (eds) *Environmental governance reconsidered: Challenges, choices, and opportunities*, pp 145–75, Cambridge, MA: MIT Press

Schlager, E, Cox, M, 2018, The IAD framework and the SES framework: An introduction and assessment of the Ostrom workshop frameworks, in M Weible, PA Sabatier (eds) *Theories of the Policy Process*, 4th edn, pp 215–252, New York: Westview Press

Schneider, A, Ingram, H, 1993, Social construction of target populations: Implications for politics and policy, *American Political Science Review* 87, 2, 334–47

Siddiki, S, Basurto, X, Weible, C, Calanni, J, 2011, Dissecting policy designs: An application of the institutional grammar tool, *Policy Studies Journal* 39, 1, 79–103

Wall, D, 2014, What Elinor Ostrom taught: Democratic control is not only possible, it's normal, *Open Democracy*, www.opendemocracy.net/ourkingdom/derek-wall/what- elinor-ostrom-taught-democratic-control-is-not-only-possible-it%27s-normal

Weible, CM, Heikkila, T, 2017, Policy conflict framework, *Policy Sciences* 50, 1, 23–40

Wright, GD, Andersson, KP, Gibson, CC, Evans, T, 2016, Decentralization may reduce deforestation when user groups engage with local government, *Proceedings of the National Academy of Sciences* 113, 52, 14958–63

CHAPTER NINE

Why advocacy coalitions matter and practical insights about them

Christopher M Weible and Karin Ingold

Introduction

People can influence government in a number of ways. For some, elections serve as the principal conduit, whereas for others political party affiliation serves this purpose. People might join an interest group, while others might participate in a social movement. All of these paths have been studied in the varied corpuses of academic literature and have been translated into numerous hands-on textbooks and 'how- to' articles that offer recommendations for people wanting to impact decisions and policies (della Porta and Diani, 2006; Cigler and Loomis, 1995). The purpose of this chapter is to focus on another way that people can influence government: 'advocacy coalitions'; and draw lessons about why they matter and what practical advice can be gleaned from the scholarship about them.

Advocacy coalitions is a term that refers to a type of alliance involving people aligned around a shared policy goal. People associated with the same advocacy coalition have similar ideologies and worldviews and, therefore, wish to change a given policy (concerning health, environmental, or many other issues) in the same direction. The coalition that these people form is an informal network of allies that usually operate against an opposing coalition consisting of other people who advocate for different policy directions. As one coalition tries to outmanoeuvre the other coalition in influencing government, the result is an ongoing game of political one-upmanship of making and unmaking public policies that can last years to decades.

One of the deeper literatures on advocacy coalitions falls under the Advocacy Coalition Framework (ACF), which has supported over 30 years of research and more than 400 publications spanning the globe (Jenkins-Smith et al, 2017). This chapter relies heavily on the ACF literature in drawing lessons about coalitions, but also derives lessons from parallel literatures on policy networks, social movements, political participation and others (Amenta et al, 2010; Knoke et al, 1996; Wright, 1996).

This chapter provides scholars with a different way to think about theory and how to draw practical lessons from it. Along with scholars, audiences for this chapter may also include people actively engaged in politics involving public policy issues or undergraduate or graduate students, who through their courses and readings are learning about various theories of public policy and politics and wondering how – if at all – these theories might matter in a career outside the craft and science of academic theoreticians.

Knowing more about advocacy coalitions might be important or at least helpful for researchers for several reasons. Public policies are not shaped by single individuals. More often, they are the result of complex interactions among different actors and organisations, such as political parties, think tanks, grassroot citizen groups, interest groups and many others. The term 'actor' is used instead of individuals to denote the idea that people fill positions or roles in organisations and policy subsystems, and that they have agency (that is, choice) in the decisions they make when filling those positions. To disentangle this complex network of interactions, the concept of advocacy coalitions can be very useful: it structures the political decision-making and implementation process, and more concretely the people participating in it, along with ideological dimensions. Following the proverb that 'birds of a feather flock together', political participants tend to join forces, exchange knowledge, and share resources with those who are ideologically their kin. Based on these shared beliefs, they tend to coordinate action, engage in joint strategies, and share efforts in impacting political decision-making. Thus, knowing what participants are in the same coalition helps practitioners, students and researchers identify the political pressures that shape public policies and their outcomes.

In attempting to offer some utility from theoretically-focused research, this chapter joins ongoing efforts by scholars who ask the simple 'so-what' question about scholarship in policy, management and politics literatures (Cairney, 2016; Weible et al, 2012; Minoque, 1983). These efforts to draw lessons from theories tend to avoid prescriptions with regards to specific policy dilemmas (for example, should Colorado pass a regulation to limit its oil and gas development) and instead draw general tactical or strategic recommendations for people involved in politics of policy issues. In this respect, the chapter offers scholars an argument that builds from the various ways of thinking about political relations in the form of advocacy coalitions and then how people can effectively deal with them without becoming so particularised that the arguments herein lack any generalisations.

Background

Concepts are the building blocks of theory and knowledge in academia. The purpose of this background section is to provide clear, understandable, and relatable definitions of concepts that are related to advocacy coalitions.

Advocacy coalitions and other forms of political associations

Advocacy coalitions are groups of people, and usually their organisational affiliation, who form informal alliances on policy issues. The glue binding these coalitions together are beliefs and ideological viewpoints on how the world should be structured and policies should be shaped. People in coalitions coordinate their political behaviours, such as planning a social media campaign, organising protests, or lobbying government officials.

Advocacy coalitions are often confused with other forms of political associations. To help clarify their contribution to the study of policy and politics, a comparison is provided in Table 9.1. For example, advocacy coalitions are similar yet somewhat distinct, with *interest groups*. Scholars offer a variety of definitions of interest groups (Baumgartner and Leech, 1998). In general, they are groups with formal membership led by an organisation that seeks to influence specific or general policy issues (Wright, 1996). Interest groups may also join so-called interest group coalitions, involving one or more interest groups (Mahoney, 2007). They do so to develop a strategic 'coalition portfolio' (Heaney and Lorenz, 2013, 253) and thereby increase their policy influence (Box-Steffensmeier et al, 2013). Interest group scholars use the term 'coalitions', but do so as formal phenomena with a clear portfolio, a quasi-organisational structure and institutionalised membership. They also assume that people can identify coalitions by name (Mahoney, 2007). Varone et al (2017) demonstrate that such coalitions are often active in political decision-making, but can appear also in the legislative, judicial, direct-democratic, or even administrative arenas. Advocacy coalitions refers to a more encompassing concept than interest group coalitions by involving any type of politically engaged individual or organisation. For example, advocacy coalitions have been shown to involve elected, appointed and administrative government officials, scientists and consultants, private and nonprofit organisational representatives, and the news media. In this regard, coalitions are broader than interest groups and refer to general and often informal relational forms.

Social movements is a term that can be defined as 'Actors and organizations seeking to alter power deficits and to effect social transformations through the state by mobilising regular citizens for sustained political action' (Amenta et al, 2010, 288). Per this definition, social movements usually refer to mobilisation of people towards political action, which is usually in the short term. Social movements operate until their cause becomes institutionalised into public policies. An alliance of social movements is akin to the advocacy coalition concept. However, the advocacy coalition concept is also applicable, and is almost always applied to more established policy issues; that is, those policy issues arising after their institutionalisation is established. As a result, advocacy coalitions are mostly comprised of policy actors (those individuals with government or non-government affiliations seeking to influence public policy) whereas social movements are comprised of both policy actors and the general public. Furthermore, a core characteristic of advocacy coalitions is their stability over time, especially in democratised forms of government. By contrast, social movements are often more ephemeral (that is, transient) and disappear once new policies have been adopted or defeated.

Another form of alliance is an epistemic community, which refers to groups of experts joined by a common foundation of knowledge (Baumgartner, 2013). Also, the ACF assumes that coalition associates will share knowledge, but knowledge is usually just one of a number of different resources and coordination patterns that coalition associates share. For example, Weible and Moore (2010) find that knowledge of policy issues is secondary to beliefs in shaping alliances and oppositions within and across advocacy coalitions. Epistemic communities can be related to advocacy coalitions in a number of ways. One such way, for example, is imagining an epistemic community as a subset of an advocacy coalition, particularly by reference to the various decision-making habitats occupied by scientific experts under the auspices of one or more coalitions.

Advocacy coalitions are also different to political parties. Political parties tend to operate around broad ideological platforms that span policy issues. These platforms serve to simplify choice and direct attention among the general public. Political parties are also formal in their structure and membership. In the study of political parties, coalition formation is also a prominent strategy used by political parties in parliaments of multi-party systems in order to pass legislation or form a government (Müller and Strom, 2003). The literature on legislative decision-making focuses on the formation of governmental coalitions and the voting behaviour of legislators in parliament. Alternately, political parties have also been argued to form under a grand coalition, operating at the society level, the concern of which is winning elections and advocating for a set of general policy positions; for these grand coalitions, political parties are a vehicle of change (Baun et al, 2012). Even though advocacy coalitions

Table 9.1: Comparing advocacy coalitions to other forms of political associations

		Attributes of political association			
		Formal or informal membership	**Type of actors involved**	**Glue binding network together**	**Stability**
Type of political association	**Advocacy coalition**	Informal	Any 'policy actor' or individual or organisation seeking to influence public policy	Common beliefs or values about a policy issue	Usually stable
	Coalition of convenience	Informal	Any policy actor	Common beliefs or values about a policy issue	Ephemeral, usually around a specific policy decision
	Epistemic community	Informal	Experts, usually scientific, seeking to influence public policy	Common knowledge about a policy issue	Stable or ephemeral
	Social movement	Informal	Citizens and policy actors	Common beliefs or values about a policy issue, usually at the societal scale	Ephemeral
	Political party	Formal	Citizens and policy actors	General and specific policy issues and strong focus on electoral campaigns	Stable
	Interest group & Interest group coalition	Usually formal	Led by policy actors affiliated with the association with citizen membership	Policy issues related to the organisation	Stable or ephemeral

and political parties are conceptually distinct, political party members can be part of advocacy coalitions.

Another difference exists regarding coalitions of convenience or advocacy communities. Coalitions of convenience only form around a given policy project over a short time period to steer a policy idea toward adoption in a particular venue, such as a legislature (Kreps, 2011). They might, at a later, more mature stage in the policy process, turn into advocacy coalitions. When passing from a coalition of convenience to an advocacy coalition, ideological and coordinative congruence becomes stronger, more visible, and more elaborate (Ingold et al, 2016). Therefore, when comparing the different types of alliances in policy processes as outlined in Table 9.1, coalitions of convenience are probably conceptually closest to advocacy coalitions compared to the other forms of alliances.

The context of coalitions via policy subsystems and political systems

Advocacy coalitions emerge, operate, and sometimes stabilise or disperse in policy subsystems. A policy subsystem is a term used to describe the area or space within a country where policy issues are governed, such as the processes of formulating and adopting public policies and implementing and enforcing them. Policy subsystems thus have a topical or substantive focus related to these public policies and a geographic scope. This geographical component of a policy subsystem might be local, sub-national, or national. In this respect, policy subsystems can be nested in other policy subsystems. For example, a subnational water management policy subsystem could be nested within a nation-wide water management policy subsystem.

Policy subsystems are embedded in the larger political system of a country, hence the 'subsystem' name. A political system refers to the broad rules or institutions, such as a written constitution, that structure the general operation of politics and policymaking. A political system also conditions the rules of the game of policy subsystems. For example, the rules of a political system might determine the allocation of the decision-making authority among one or more positions for making policies (for example, between an executive and a legislature). This, in turn, might shape political strategies, such as who to lobby or the degree of consensus needed for adopting a public policy.

Political systems require the presence of a degree of democratisation, such as a degree of openness in the political system, the range of civil liberties and rights, the nature of elections and representation, and other factors (Dahl, 1998). The institutional component of political systems also shapes the overall structure of government, for example, federal vs

Table 9.2: A comparison of political systems and policy subsystems

	Political system	**Policy subsystem**
Territory	Whole country and can include a subset of a country in a federal system of government	Subset of the country or the whole country
Substantive/topical focus	Not required	Required
Formal jurisdictional boundaries	Yes	No
Nestedness in a political system or another subsystem	Yes, in federal systems of government, but no in unitary systems of government	Yes

unitary systems, which alters the organisation and degree of freedom of sub-national entities and jurisdictions (Lijphart, 1999). All of these variables can affect the operation of subsystems, particularly political behaviour, policymaking processes, and the handling of conflict (for example, the consensus, collaborative or pluralistic style of decision-making). See Table 9.2 for a summary that compares and contrasts political systems and policy subsystems.

Policy subsystems can emerge in several ways. Typically, it happens when a new issue, such as hydraulic fracturing, aquatic micro-pollutants or new evidence about global climate change, arrives on the political agenda (Ingold et al, 2016). It can be absorbed by an existing subsystem and tackled by the introduction of legal guidelines and regulation, it can lead to the elaboration of new pieces of regulation, or even to the creation of a nascent subsystem (Weible et al, 2016). In the latter situation, the new subsystem can evolve as a 'spin-off' and constitute a new topical entity spanning a specific geographical scope, and can include its own set of actors and issues (Nohrstedt and Olofsson, 2016).

Typology of actors in advocacy coalitions

Given the varied types of actors involved in politics and policy processes, the concept of coalitions offers a way to cluster them into opposing factions or teams. There are various ways to understand the actors that comprise coalitions. Advocacy coalitions are not only open to elected officials and government collaborators, but to a large variety and number of actors. Although sometimes individuals participate in a policy subsystem as unaffiliated private parties, more often they participate via their affiliation with an organisation. Their organisational affiliation might be formal, as the organisation could be their source of income as the employee of a private or nonprofit entity. Other times their affiliation with an organisation is without financial compensation, as might happen when an individual volunteers for a nonprofit or has been elected to a city council. Thus, some individuals participate in a policy subsystem wearing multiple hats; that is, they might be employed as a business owner and serve on a city council or they may hold office with a political party, help govern a trade union, and be paid as an executive director of a nonprofit. The reason that organisational affiliation matters is because organisations help individuals to overcome resource and time constraints.

Given the importance of organisational affiliation in helping to equip individuals with political resources, the ACF offers a typology of resources. This includes: access to legal authority; support from the public; the ability to mobilise supporters; financial resources; information; and leadership (Jenkins-Smith et al, 2017). Per their organisational affiliation, individuals also deploy a variety of strategies. For instance, non-government affiliated individuals might lobby a government official or stage a protest. Such typologies and listings are useful in helping to understand the behaviour of advocacy coalitions; mainly because resources and strategies, depending on the context, might be as important drivers for political decisions as belief systems. For example, support from the public might be extremely relevant in national-level policy subsystems on salient issues (for example, such as a national subsystem on health care) and less important for some local policy subsystems (for example, disaster preparedness). Furthermore, people are responsive to the effective use of political strategies and resources and will counter and adapt accordingly over time; so the use of a particular set of strategies or resources might be effective at one point in time, but less effective at a different point in time, because coalitions can learn and adapt to each other. Thus, it is unfeasible to specify that sets of specific strategies or resources are more important than others because political behaviour in policy subsystems evolve over time.

Organisational affiliation, resources, strategies and the context of the policy subsystem can interact in complex ways. For example, Heikkila and Weible (2016) studied coalitions in oil and gas development using hydraulic fracturing in three USA states: Texas, Colorado and New York. Echoing the federal structure of government and pluralists political traditions in the USA, they show that these individuals organise in advocacy coalitions in accordance with their organisational affiliation, for example, oil and gas groups, governments, academic institutes or environmental organisations. A sizeable proportion of organisational type in the coalitions found by Heikkila and Weible (2016) were interest groups. Different insights can be found in Nohrstedt and Olofsson (2016) study of a hydraulic fracturing policy subsystem in Sweden. Whereas the federal structure of the USA provides opportunities for coalitions to form at the sub-national level, Sweden's unitary structure led to the formation of national-level coalitions. Similar to the USA, the coalitions in Sweden include a diversity of organisational affiliations. However, coalitions in Sweden consist of more political parties, more international organisations (the European Union), and fewer interest groups. The differences between coalitions in Sweden and the USA likely reflect a range of differences between the countries, including the size, the federal vs unitary structure of government, different political traditions, and the nature of the issue under dispute. Yet, this brief comparison underscores the point that coalitions can exist across countries but with characteristics that can vary based on a range of contextual factors.

Depending on their organisational affiliation and the contextual characteristics of a policy subsystem, actors might play different roles in their coalitions. They can be very central and principal actors, or instead can act as auxiliaries. For example, some coalitions have been shown to be anchored by principal affiliates associated with government administrative units and a small number of interest groups over time, but with several auxiliary affiliates whose participation varies over time. For example, an auxiliary affiliate of a coalition might be 'one-shot' participants, entering the debate for a very short period of time, possibly influencing processes and products of public policy, and then exiting soon after. Table 9.3 summaries five main types of categories of actors engaged in advocacy coalitions.

Policy brokers can be motivated to find compromise and negotiated solutions between coalitions in policy subsystems. These policy brokers are typically actors with connections to the individuals of competing advocacy coalitions (Ingold, 2011). Those actors seek stability in the subsystem and try to avoid stalemates. For them to be accepted as policy brokers, and mediate agreements between two or more conflictive coalitions, it is necessary that they avoid becoming ideologically isolated in one of the coalitions (Ingold and Varone, 2012). The intervention of policy brokers can be crucial, particularly in subsystems where, in the presence of coalitions, clear decision- making by state officials is not always possible without the intervention of mediating actors (Ingold, 2011). In such situations, policy brokers might seek stability, facilitate policy compromise and prevent political stalemates. Kingiri (2014), in her study about biosafety policy in Kenya, convincingly shows that it is not just any actor that is able to play such brokerage roles: ideologically neutral actors might, typically (but not always) administrative agencies, play this role. Administrative agencies are most often not directly involved in the political negotiations, but provide crucial case knowledge and contacts

Table 9.3: Categories of actors and their attributes related to advocacy coalitions

	Description	Centrality in an advocacy coalition network	Constancy of association with coalition
Principal coalition actors	Individuals or organisations who are steady in their coalition affiliation	Central	Most likely a constant affiliate of a coalition over time
Auxiliary coalition actors	Individuals or organisations who are not steady in their coalition affiliation but share some of the general coalition goals	Periphery	Most likely a sporadic affiliate, per episode of conflict
Policy brokers	One or more individuals or organisations whose primary goal is consensus and the mitigation of conflict	Central between coalitions or peripheral to one coalition	Most likely a constant affiliate in the subsystem
Policy entrepreneurs	One or more individuals or organisation whose primary goal is championing a particular policy idea	Central	Can be both, constant or sporadic affiliate of a coalition
General citizens	People interested in and/or affected by subsystem affairs but not regularly participating in politics or policy issue	Not members of coalitions but better viewed as a resource or a support/foundation for coalitions	Mobilised occasionally for conventional and unconventional forms of political action

to different kinds of actors that are associates of the conflicting coalitions. Identifying policy brokers, or even acquiring brokerage characteristics, might be important tools to understand or shape public policies and their design decisively.

A different position to policy brokers in a policy subsystem is that of policy entrepreneurs. Policy entrepreneurs are the champions of ideas (that is, policy solutions) and are strategic in mobilising support for their ideas. As leaders, they connect and coordinate with others to translate their policy solution into final policy outputs (Mintrom and Norman, 2009). Policy entrepreneurs are often the leaders of coalitions in their willingness to bear the transaction costs of finding information, building networks and strengthening coalitional ties, making agreements, and sometimes monitoring and enforcing those agreements.

We conclude, at this stage, that individuals can play very different roles and engage to different degrees in subsystem politics. Very often, these are not fixed attributes of actors, but are rather roles actors play at a given point in time (Christopoulos and Ingold, 2015). Thus, roles might change (for example, an auxiliary becoming a principle), overlap (for example, a principal taking the role of an entrepreneur), depend upon the organisational affiliation, and may vary due to the salience, interest or degree of conflict in the current policy discussion.

Beliefs and coordination

Coalition associates are informally affiliated in that they do not necessarily sign a formal document to participate. What holds coalition associates together are similar beliefs, worldviews and ideologies. Actors of the same coalition usually agree upon problem attributes, policy solutions or policy instruments, and whether there should be government intervention. Where two or more advocacy coalitions are in conflict, it often entails a pro-change and an anti-change coalition.

To better understand such ideological divergences, the ACF distinguishes between a three-tiered belief system. Policy beliefs serve as the primary perceptual filter for actors in a policy subsystem to determine interaction. The deep core of the actors' belief system consists of fundamental normative and ontological axioms. These worldviews, including the role the state should take in policymaking, the importance of nature and nature conservation to an actor, or the degree of freedom given to certain individuals or firms, are difficult to change. They influence the second belief level, namely the policy core beliefs. Policy core beliefs are expressed within one specific policy subsystem. If one actor is in favour of complete state intervention, this actor might also favour regulative policy intervention of the state when it comes to protecting the nature from human intervention. Finally, the last level of beliefs are so-called secondary aspects comprising a multitude of instrumental decisions necessary to implement the policy core beliefs.

An advocacy coalition is defined by both shared beliefs and coordination (Henry, 2011). Coordination can come in many forms. Two major categories are strong coordination, defined as planned and acknowledged political behaviour, and weak coordination, which complements the behaviour of coalition associates without conscious planning (Kriesi and Jegen, 2001). Table 9.4 summarises the belief systems and coordination attributes of coalitions.

Practical lessons

This section is divided into two subsections. The first is what we know and how to think about coalition formation and maintenance. The

Table 9.4: Belief system and coordination as two defining features of advocacy coalitions

		Definition	Examples
Three-tiered belief system	**Deep core beliefs**	Fundamental normative orientations	• Political ideologies • Normative values (e.g. religious beliefs) • Identities • Cultural orientations • Basic priorities (e.g. freedom vs security) • Views of human nature
	Policy core beliefs	Normative and empirical beliefs concerning policy subsystems	• General goals for a policy subsystem • Positions on general policy solutions and policy instruments • Problem severity and cause • Role of government in subsystem affairs (e.g. vs markets)
	Secondary beliefs	Instrumental beliefs or beliefs about a subset of a policy subsystem	• Instrumental means for achieving policy-core ends (or goals) • Relative weight of various causal mechanisms of problems • Solutions and problems associated with part of a policy subsystem
Two forms of coordination	**Strong coordination**	Activities agreed upon and acknowledged by coalition actors	• Formulation and implementation of a common plan • Sharing resources
	Weak coordination	Activities that are in sync toward achieving a common goal but are not jointly agreed upon	• Monitoring the use of resources and deployment of strategies and altering behaviour accordingly • Understanding the positions and niches of allies and behaving in a complementary manner

Source: Adapted from Sabatier and Jenkins-Smith, 1999, pp 133 and 140.

second summarises lessons for scholars who are studying and/or working with coalitions.

How should we think about the formation and maintenance of advocacy coalitions?

There is no single way to think about how coalitions form and maintain themselves. The conditions vary across policy subsystems and political systems and by substantive topic. One of the driving forces underlying the formation and maintenance of coalitions is a perceived threat by coalition associates. We categorise these threats into four categories that we expect to overlap and sometimes work in tandem (see Table 9.5). The categories vary in their temporality (for example, chronic, acute, sporadic) and in their likely affect (for example, coalition formation and/or maintenance). One category of threat is from an event or shock to the policy subsystem; this usually points to problems that harmed or could have harmed the interests of one of the coalition. The result is a shift in resources and a mobilisation of one or both coalitions. The second category is chronic threats: these are threats motivated by the different normative orientations of opponents, which tend to be stable over time. These chronic threats are one of the reasons that coalitions have been found to be stable over time. The third category is spillover from problems and solutions. Coalitions often emerge or new alliances form when externalities from one policy subsystem spill over into another. A longitudinal study of nuclear power politics in the US found that an anti-nuclear coalition emerged to rival a pro-nuclear coalition when they perceived effects from the industry on environmental and public health (Duffy, 1997). In California, Weible (2007) found that a policy solution to create marine protected areas affected the policy subsystem governing the commercial fishing industry and the recreational fishing industries, resulting in a clash of management approaches of marine ecosystems.

Finally, in the fourth category, coalitions often form because of changing societal values. Different to the other categories, this has less to do with changes with the problem or solution attributes of a policy subsystem. The meta-analysis by Jang et al (2016) of more than 60 applications of the ACF in South Korea showed that changing societal values in that country happened, at least partly, in response to rapid changes in economic conditions and democratisation (for example, see Kwon, 2003). These societal changes fuelled the formation of advocacy coalitions on a range of social and environmental policy issues.

Table 9.5: Four major categories spurring coalition formation or driving coalition maintenance

		Description	Temporality	Maintenance or formation	Examples from literature
Threat categories	**Events (shocks)**	Encompass varied phenomena marked by sudden change with potential harms	Sudden	Coalition formation and maintenance	Olson et al (1999) identi- fied the formation of a coalition after an earthquake Nohrstedt (2008) related a crisis to coalition attrib- utes on Swedish national security policies
	Chronic threats	Constant threats from policy positions in a policy subsystem, particularly around normative orientations of coalition rivals	Enduring	Coalition maintenance	Jenkins-Smith et al (1991) studied coalitions over time as spurred by con- flicting beliefs in offshore oil and gas development in the US
	Spillover of problems or solutions between policy subsystems	Negative externalities of problems and solutions associated with a policy issue that affects another policy subsystem or people previously not mobilised within the territory of a policy subsystem	Short-term	Coalition formation and maintenance	Weible (2007) studied marine protected areas and the counter-mobi- lisation of commercial and recreational fishing industries Duffy (1997) analysed nuclear power and the formation of anti-nuclear coalition after perceived public and environmental health risk
	Changes in societal value orientations	Shifts in societal values accompanying changes in socio- economic–cultural conditions	Long-term sporadic	Coalition formation	Jang et al (2016) conducted a meta-analysis of coali- tions in South Korea find- ing that rapid develop- ment and changing social values over a 20-year period was a major source of coalition formation and policy change Albright (2011) studied a pro-environmental coali- tion in water manage- ment over time in Poland

How to form and maintain coalitions?

This section summarises how scholars might identify coalitions and, more practically, how coalitions can be formed and maintained and how actors might shape coalition formation and maintenance.

Coalitions emerge from forces that are beyond the control of any single individual. Additionally, coalition formation is an ongoing process resulting from continuous waves of the forces of politics that link to electoral campaigns, policy and problems from other policy subsystems, and the mobilisation of previous immobilised latent populations. Coalitions might also emerge from threats outside or within a specific policy subsystem (see Table 9.5).

Similarly, there are different ways of thinking about coalitions and, more concretely, about how to look for or identify potential coalition partners. Usually, people think that coalitions are something rather small, comprised of individuals that are in regular or direct contact with their own organisation. But advocacy coalitions are different to interest groups or parties (see Table 9.1) and can consist of a broad network of actors, not joining forces through formalised membership, but through ideological similarity. Some individuals might therefore be part of an advocacy coalition (through sharing beliefs with others) without being aware of it. Such individuals are probably auxiliaries, rather than principals, in a coalition (Table 9.3) and are less active or aware of coordination patterns within this coalition.

Scholars have used at least four approaches for identifying coalitions. One prominent way to identify coalition associates, accounting for an inclusive strategy, but also including informal methods of coalition participation, stems from policy network analysis (Knoke et al, 1996). Although policy network analysis is a recognised way of collecting and analysing data in a research study, there are also practical implications for people engaged in the policy process. For instance, actor identification in policy network analysis is based on a four-fold approach. The first three approaches are strongly inspired by early elite studies (French, 1969). The fourth approach focuses on the attributes of the problem (or issue) as is often done in studies of common pool resource problems (Ostrom, 2000), particularly in collaborative or local settings (Berardo and Scholz, 2010) communities or citizens are similarly affected by a particular problem (for example, natural resource degradation or disasters such as floods or droughts).

1. Positional approach: All actors and entities having formal competences in shaping, designing, or even introducing the policies of interest in a subsystem are listed. Not only government representatives are

entered in this first list, but also courts or regulatory agencies that can overrule government decisions can be taken into consideration. These individuals identified in the decision approach are often those who have the authority to support or veto a policy solution.

2. Decisional approach: Not everyone who is influential has the authority to change policy; often, people can influence decisions via other mechanisms. To identify these individuals, an attempt has been made to specify the whole policy process that leads to the political change of interest (or the decided status quo). This could be the most laborious approach because, as well as identifying all the different stages of a policy process, including research projects about the topic, state-induced round tables and hearings and civil societal actions like information campaigns etc., one also has to collect relevant documents setting out which actors and organisations participated during all those different stages.
3. Reputational approach:This third approach emphasises a reputational perspective. That is, it is important to ask which actor is known to be influential in a policy subsystem, as these actors might not be captured via the first two approaches. For example, the two lists from the first two approaches could be merged and shown to people in the field, who could then validate the list and add further actors or organisations. The three approaches are called positional, decisional and reputational approaches, and were applied either completely or partially in various ACF applications (Ingold, 2011).
4. Latent-actor approach: In some policy subsystems not everyone is mobilised, especially marginalised populations or in newly formed (or nascent) policy subsystems. To identify these latent individuals, the following questions can be asked (Gerber et al, 2009): who is particularly threatened by the policy problem at stake? Who depends directly or indirectly on the resource under study (for example, drinking water, specific land use)? And, who might be the direct or indirect target group of policy and state intervention?

These four approaches are an encapsulation of current research techniques used by scholars for identifying coalitions. For practitioners, the four approaches need not be applied for the same reasons or as rigorously as is done by academics. Still, actors engaged in the policy process should look to who holds important positions in a policy subsystem, where the important decisions are made, who makes them, and who is known. Of course, these four approaches are often reinforcing. Sometimes the same names appear across them and sometimes one approach might alter how another approach is conducted.

The four-fold approach above is one way to identify actors in a policy subsystem and coalition associates, but it does not yet identify their positions and coalition membership. To evaluate if those actors might be allies or opponents in the given policy subsystem, three strategies can be combined. First, experiences from previous but similar subsystems can be consulted. For example, the deep core beliefs motivating one set of actors to take a particular policy position in a climate change subsystem during the last ten years might generate a similar position in a subsystem on the future promotion of renewable energies. Second, identifying the ideological position of an individual is often specified in their organisational mission. For example, environmental groups, in contrast to private firms, are often in favour of strong state intervention in relation to issues concerning natural resource protection. Third, positions based on existing relations can be assessed. Political negotiations are shaped by a variety of different interactions among actors: exchange about political strategies; exchange about knowledge and technical information; collaborating on a joint policy draft; sharing ally versus enemy relations; and others (Weible and Sabatier, 2005). Identifying crucial interaction patterns and then listing with whom such patterns are shared might help to identify close coalition peers (for example, with whom an organisation shares strong collaboration and drafts joint positions), coalition auxiliaries (for example, with whom an organisation shares information); or opposing coalition associates (for example, with whom an organisation stays in conflict). To evaluate with whom one maintains stable or less stable relations is also a useful strategy to help allocate more or less effort when seeking to maintain a certain degree of coordination with allies over time.

Applied axioms about advocacy coalitions

To summarise this chapter's arguments, we offer a set of applied axioms. These axioms are knowledge-based principles generally supported by the literature with an applied appeal.

Applied Axiom 1. People relate to their government; and advocacy coalitions are one form of such relations around policy issues

There are many ways in which people can relate to their government. Most political scientists focus on traditional forms of political participation, such as voting, becoming a member of a political party, engaging in a social movement, or becoming a member of an interest group. These are all legitimate forms of engagement, but the images they afford are far from definitive. Another way that people influence a government is through advocacy coalitions, which are policy-focused informal networks of people from any organisational affiliation seeking to steer the course of government. The advantages of adding this concept to the array of choices for political participation is that it emphasises the enduring nature of political debates over normative issues: sharing similar beliefs and worldviews is seen as the 'entry ticket' for coalition participation. This results in the fact that advocacy coalitions are not only accessible by elected officials but, rather, as soon as an individual shares ideologies with the majority of coalition associates, he or she might also be part of it. This is why alongside state officials, members of political parties or interest groups, scientists, journalists, or members of trade unions and non-for-profit organisations can integrate into an advocacy coalition. Furthermore, advocacy coalitions have the ability to span levels of government from local to national and they integrate traditional points of influence in a political system, from electoral politics to regulatory decision-making.

Applied Axiom 2. The context of advocacy coalitions vary and such contexts affect coalition attributes

Another advantage of the advocacy coalition concept is that it serves as a reminder of the importance of the policy subsystem setting or context within which political debates over policy issues occur. This context might include the socio-cultural norms and rules (institutions) that shape what strategies might be affected and the usefulness of political resources. The coalition concept elevates the importance of context from an overlooked set of opportunities and constraints to a set of factors that should be considered as conditioning the political behaviour of both the actor and the target of such behaviour. Typologies of coalition strategies and resources can be developed, but their utility and effectiveness will be contextually driven and will change over time; that is, what works for political influence today might not work in the future.

Applied Axiom 3. People become involved in advocacy coalitions in different ways, as auxiliary, principal, brokers, and entrepreneurs

The advocacy coalition concept acknowledges that people engage in politics differently based on a range of factors, including how important the issue is to them, their available time, skills, and resources, and general motivations. People with less time or knowledge can engage in coalitions as auxiliary participants. In contrast, individuals to whom an issue is of high relevance or those who see their major expertise in a specific subsystem might want to shape coalition politics and strategies decisively and become principal participants. Furthermore, people wanting to mitigate conflict might choose to play a policy broker role, whereas people championing ideas can play the role of policy entrepreneurs. Moreover, general citizens can see themselves playing the role of a political soldier contributing to their cause when called upon by the leaders of any coalition. People can choose to play a number of different roles in a coalition, but making this happen remains challenging. Three established recommendations still apply: build your network, learn deep and broad knowledge on the topic, and stay involved for extended periods of time (Weible et al, 2012).

Applied Axiom 4. Coalitions form and are maintained from threats to beliefs

Underlying the coalition concept is an assumption that people are most responsive to threats to what they care about. Coalitions form because of these threats, including spillover from proposed policy solutions and problems, events or shocks. Motivated by deep normative orientations, the chronic presence of threats from opponents is another reason that coalitions persist over time. That is, people stay mobilised because they know people with whom they disagree may influence societal outcomes if they disengage. Finally, the coalition concept reminds us that societal values are constantly changing and certain issues in society (for example, perceptions of poverty or environmental degradation) rise or fall in importance over extended periods of time.

Applied Axiom 5. Coalitions can be identified through multiple approaches and empirical strategies

There is no single way to identify a coalition, or coalition peers, in a subsystem. The four approaches summarised in this chapter (positional, decisional, reputational and latent-actor) can help identify who is involved in a given policy subsystem. They emphasise both formal competences and informal relations, and the motivations that actors might have to participate in an issue. Advocacy coalitions are not defined through formal membership or jurisdictional boundaries, but by the shared similar views on how to shape policies in a given field or domain. Strategies for ascertaining patterns of coalitional allies and opponents can be deduced from past experiences on the same or different policy issues, from organisational affiliations, or from personal contacts.

Conclusion

All societies comprise of people and their governments. Yet, how people relate to their governments can come in many forms. Traditional ways of thinking of such relations often happens via representation and participation in political parties or by various mechanisms of direct democracy, such as voting. Other forms of relations involve interest groups in pluralist political systems, as found in the United States, or formalised collective groups as found in corporatist systems in many European countries. The purpose of this chapter is to highlight another way to think about how people connect with their government, namely advocacy coalitions.

Advocacy coalitions is a concept that draws attention to individuals and organisations involved in policy issues over an extended period of time. Unlike political parties, the concept emphasises both the political system and the policy subsystem as ways to imagine the bounds of government per policy topic. The advocacy coalition concept offers multiple means of participation, either as general citizens, policy entrepreneurs and brokers, or principal and auxiliary coalition associates. In this regard, people can engage with policy issues that they care about in different ways.

The contributions of this chapter are manifold. First, we have yet to find a paper that offers a focused discussion of coalitions and that explores the more practical meaning of coalitions. Contrasts and comparisons with concepts, such as social movements and political parties, help to link the common ways that we imagine different forms of political relations. We expect such clarity to help the field avoid confusion in these concepts and inspire more effective research agendas. Second, this is the first chapter that offers a set of applied axioms in how to think about and act on coalitions. These axioms are meant as knowledge summations, that is, what we know about coalitions and what practical lessons can be gleaned from them. As a result, these applied axioms are not created as hypotheses to be falsified or to guide original research. Instead, they serve as a type of knowledge bank to be updated and changed as our knowledge continues to accumulate on this topic. Third, this chapter is one of the few efforts to draw practical lessons from policy theories (Cairney, 2016; Weible et al, 2012). Most of the literature on this subject is focused on theoretical development and overlooks lessons about how and why this information matters for scholars, students, activists, and citizens. While we need better theories, we also need to connect these theories to some sort of practical orientation. The reverse is also true. The theoretically-oriented sciences in the study of policy, politics, and management would benefit from continual feedback from the people living the processes depicted in their theories. Feedback from practitioners would help scholars ask the 'right' or relevant questions, and would benefit the methods and empirical approaches in the current stable of theories.

The arguments in this chapter are not as concrete as some people would like. Concrete recommendations, for example, activity X will help person Y achieve their policy goal Z, are constrained to a specific context, country and policy field. Political strategies are not applicable all the time and vary in degree of success and failure based on a gamut of factors. The best we can do is to offer ways of thinking about political engagement, such as through the ideas that are summarised in the five applied axioms and then trust people to assess their current situation, act in effective ways and, ideally, communicate their experiences back to the scholarly community in order to enhance mutual exchange and future learning.

This chapter does not tackle the normative issues about the role of coalitions in any form of government. If we assume some of the principles of democracy as benefiting a political system (Dahl, 1998), coalitions offer a means by which people can affect agendas, alter the rules that shape elections and voting behaviour, and disseminate information to influence perceptions and saliency of issues. However, coalitions can also obscure exercises of power, exclude people from the policy process, and exacerbate the degenerative effects of conflicts. At this point, we have yet to assess coalitions via moral and ethical lenses and how coalitions contribute – or not – to sustainable politics. We can argue that these normative questions elevate the importance of the real choices of people involved in coalitions and the possible effects of those choices in buttressing or destabilising democratic governments. For now, we hope this chapter raises some normative questions about coalitions and urge scholars to explore this issue in their theoretical and empirical work.

Our efforts are not absolute. We encourage other scholars to challenge the usefulness of our axioms. This might be accomplished by refining them, proposing alternates, or posing an argument against their usefulness. Over time, these axioms might be refined and subdivided toward particular contexts. Scholarship is advanced through constant development of evidence and arguments, and further evidence and counter arguments. Perhaps the main contribution of this chapter is the postulation of arguments on the applied lessons of coalitions that will propel further exploration into this very important theme.

References

Albright, EA, 2011, Policy change and learning in response to extreme flood events in Hungary: an advocacy coalition approach, *Policy Studies Journal*, 39, 3, 485–511

Amenta, E, Caren, N, Chiarello, E, Su, Y, 2010, The political consequences of social movements, *Annual Review of Sociology* 36, 287–307

Baumgartner, F, 2013, Ideas and policy change, *Governance* 26, 2, 239–58

Baumgartner, F, Leech, B, 1998 *Basic interests: The importance of groups in politics and in political science,* Princeton, NJ: Princeton University Press

Baun, K, Cohen, M, Karol, D, Masket, S, Noel, H, Zaller, J, 2012, A theory of political parties, policy demands, and nominations in American politics, *Perspectives on Politics* 10, 3, 571–97

Berardo, R, Scholz, J, 2010, Self-organizing policy networks: Risk, partner selection and cooperation in estuaries, *American Journal of Political Science* 54, 632–49

Box-Steffensmeier, J, Christenson, D, Hitt, M, 2013, Quality over quantity: Amici influence and judicial decision making, *American Political Science Review* 107, 3, 446–60

Cairney, P, 2016, *The politics of evidence-based policy making,* Basingstoke: Palgrave Macmillan

Christopoulos, D, Ingold, K, 2015, Exceptional or just well connected? Political entrepreneurs and brokers in policy making, *European Political Science Review* 7, 3, 475–98

Cigler, A, Loomis, B, 1995, *Interest group politics*, 4th edn, Washington, DC: CQP

Dahl, R, 1998, *On democracy*, New Haven, CT: Yale University Press

Duffy, RJ, 1997, *Nuclear politics in America: A history and theory of government regulation*, Lawrence, KS: University Press of Kansas

French, RM, 1969, Effectiveness of the various techniques employed in the study of community power, *The Journal of Politics* 31, 3, 818–20

Gerber, JD, Knoepfel, P, Nahrath, P, Varone, F, 2009, Institutional resource regimes: Towards sustainability through the combination of property-rights theory and policy analysis, *Ecological Economics* 68, 798–809

Heaney, M, Lorenz, G, 2013, Coalitions portfolios and interest group influence over the policy process, *Interest Groups and Advocacy* 2,3, 251–77

Heikkila, T, Weible, CM, 2016, Contours of coalition politics on hydraulic fracturing within the United States of America, in CM Weible, T Heikkila, K Ingold, M Fischer (eds) *Comparing coalition politics: Policy debates on hydraulic fracturing in North America and Western Europe*, pp 29–52, Basingstoke: Palgrave MacMillan

Henry, A, 2011, Power, ideology, and policy network cohesion in regional planning, *Policy Studies Journal* 39, 3, 361–83

Ingold, K, 2011, Network structures within policy processes: Coalitions, power, and brokerage in Swiss climate policy, *Policy Studies Journal* 39, 3, 435–59

Ingold, K, Varone, F, 2012, Treating policy brokers seriously: Evidence from the climate policy, *Journal of Public Administration Research and Theory* 22, 2, 319–46

Ingold, K, Fischer, M, Cairney, P, 2016, Drivers for policy agreement in nascent subsystems: An application of the Advocacy Coalition Framework to fracking policy in Switzerland and the UK, *Policy Studies Journal* 45, 3, 442–63

Jang, S, Weible, CM, Park, K, 2016, Policy processes in South Korea through the lens of the Advocacy Coalition Framework, *Journal of Asian Public Policy* 9, 3, 274–90

Jenkins-Smith, H, St Clair, G, Woods, B, 1991, Explaining change in policy subsystems: Analysis of coalition stability and defection over time, *American Journal of Political Science* 35, November, 851–72

Jenkins-Smith, H, Nohrstedt, D, Weible CM, Ingold, K, 2017, The Advocacy Coalition Framework: An overview of the research program, in CM Weible, P Sabatier (eds) *Theories of the Policy Process*, 4th edn, Boulder, pp 135–72, CO:Westview Press

Kingiri, A, 2014, Comparative strategic behavior of advocacy coalitions and policy brokers: The case of Kenya's biosafety regulatory policy, *Journal of Comparative Policy Analysis: Research and Practice* 16, 4, 373–95

Knoke, D, Pappi, FU, Broadbent, J, Tsujinaka, Y, 1996, *Comparing policy networks: Labor politics in the US, Germany, and Japan*, Cambridge: Cambridge University Press

Kriesi, H, Jegen, M, 2001, The Swiss energy policy elite: The actor constellation of a policy domain in transition, *European Journal of Political Research* 39, 251–87

Kreps, S, 2011, *Coalitions of convenience: United States military interventions after the cold war*, Oxford: Oxford University Press

Kwon, HJ, 2003, Advocacy coalitions and the politics of welfare in Korea after the economic crisis, *Policy & Politics* 31, 1, 69–83

Lijphart, A, 1999, *Patterns of democracy*, New Haven, CT: Yale University Press

Mahoney, C, 2007, Networking vs allying: The decision of interest groups to join coalitions in the US and the EU, *Journal of European Public Policy* 14, 3, 366–83

Minoque, M, 1983, *Theory and practice in public policy and administration* 11, 1, 63–85

Mintrom, M, Norman, PH, 2009, Policy entrepreneurship and policy change, *Policy Studies Journal* 37, 4, 649–67

Müller, WC, Strom, K, 2003, *Coalition governments in Western Europe*, Oxford: Oxford University Press

Nohrstedt, D, 2008, The politics of crisis policymaking: Chernobyl and Swedish nuclear energy policy, *Policy Studies Journal* 36, 2, 257–78

Nohrstedt, D, Olofsson, K, 2016, Advocacy coalition politics and strategies on hydraulic fracturing in Sweden, in CM Weible, T Heikkila, K Ingold, M Fischer (eds) *Comparing coalition politics: Policy debates on hydraulic fracturing in North America and Western Europe*, pp 147–75, Basingstoke: Palgrave MacMillan

Olson, RS, Gawronski, VT, Olson, RA, 1999, *Some buildings just can't dance: Politics, life safety, and disaster*, Stamford, CT: Jai Press, Inc

Ostrom, E, 2000, Collective action and the evolution of social norms, *Journal of Economic Perspectives* 14, 3, 137–58

della Porta, D, Diani, M, 2006, *Social movements- an introduction*, 2nd edn, Hoboken, NJ:Wiley

Sabatier, PA, Jenkins-Smith, H, 1999 The Advocacy Coalition Framework: An assessment, in P Sabatier and H Jenkins-Smith (eds) *Theories of the policy process*, Boulder, CO: Westview Press, pp 117–68

Varone, F, Ingold, K, Jourdain, Ch, 2017, Defending the status quo across venues and coalitions: evidence from California interest groups, *Journal of Public Policy* 37, 1, 1–26

Weible, CM, 2007, An Advocacy Coalition Framework approach to Stakeholder analysis: Understanding the political context of California marine protected area policy, *Journal of Public Administration Research and Theory*, 17, 95–117

Weible, CM, Moore, RH, 2010, Analytics and beliefs: Competing explanations for defining problems and choosing allies and opponents in collaborative environmental management, *Public Administration Review* 70, 5, 756–66

Weible, CM, Sabatier, PA, 2005, Comparing policy networks: marine protected areas in California, *Policy Studies Journal* 33, 181–201

Weible, CM, Heikkila, T, deLeon, P, Sabatier, PA, 2012, Influencing the policy process, *Policy Sciences* 34, 1–21

Weible, CM, Heikkila, T, Ingold, K, Fischer, M, 2016, *Comparing coalition politics: Policy debates on hydraulic fracturing in North America and Western Europe*, Basingstoke: Palgrave MacMillan

Wright, JR, 1996, *Interest groups and congress: Lobbying, contributions, and influence*, Boston, MA: Allyn and Bacon

CHAPTER TEN

Reflections and resolutions in drawing practical lessons from policy theories

Christopher M Weible and Paul Cairney

Introduction

We began this edited volume by challenging policy scholars to translate their findings to a wider audience and improve communication among academics. This volume tackled this challenge through its eight chapters that sought to draw practical lessons from various theoretical approaches.

No other book or article gathers as many theoretical perspectives with the goal of extracting practical insights, although past efforts have focused on single theoretical approaches (for example, Shipan and Volden, 2012) or synthesized lessons at a high scale of abstraction and generalizability for example, Weible et al, 2012; Cairney, 2015). In doing so, we hope to shift academic focus back towards a bugbear in public policy scholarship: *relevance*. Relevance has long served as a key founding aim of the field (Lasswell, 1951) but has also contributed to acrimonious debates about whether relevance should be an aim and whether the field even comes close to realising it (deLeon, 1997).

Contributions

The challenge today is not whether policy theories should make their work relevant but how it should be done. This edited volume provides a number of different ways to do so. We organise them into three categories for new and experienced policy process scholars interested in translating practical lessons from policy theories.

Contribution 1: Clearer summaries of policy theories

Each chapter summarises the state of the art developments of different theories. They help new students understand the field for the first time *and* experienced scholars seeking to learn what each theory now represents (since many have changed dramatically since their first exposition). This contribution is most evident in the chapters that summarise aspects of relatively complicated and dynamic policy process theories such as Punctuated Equilibrium Theory (Koski and Workman, 2021), the Advocacy Coalition Framework (Weible and Ingold, 2021), and Institutional Analysis and Development Framework (Heikkila and Andersson, 2021). These approaches have become so complicated – partly as a function of their theoretical and empirical expansion – that a single chapter can no longer describe all of their nuances. Rather, each chapter shows how key components of each perspective can be useful to specialist and non-specialist audiences. In other situations, the contributions emphasise relatively new takes on old ideas or ways of thinking, including Swann and Kim's (2021) insights from the Institutional Collective Action Framework or Simmon's (2021) work on Cultural Theory.

Contribution 2: Synthesised lessons from this special issue

The chapters offer practical insights that sometimes overlap in dealing with various themes of the policy process. We synthesise some of these lessons in Tables 10.1–10.3. Table 10.1 focuses on the cognitive aspects of the policy processes by focusing on strategies related to persuasion and learning. Among the lessons are recognising cognitive shortcuts, telling good stories and developing the right opportunities for learning.

Table 10.2 identifies lessons regarding behavioural engagement via political participation and collective action. In most government settings, policy actors build alliances to make or influence policy. Such coalitions can come in many forms that link citizens (including organised groups and associations) and governments, or link governments to governments.

Table 10.3 shows how policy theories can offer lessons on structuring government and designing public policy. Some lessons are procedural, focusing on shaping the behaviour of government, and others are substantive, focusing on shaping non-government entities.

Tables 10.1–10.3 offer insights, which are so foundational, that policy scholars might take them for granted, even though they may be new to a different audience. For example, Crow and Jones (2021) challenge the commonly held assumption that more evidence is key to persuasion, when telling a better story might be a better strategy.

Policy theories also offer a different lens for influencing public policy than commonly found in political science, which often assumes that:

- only elections and political parties matter in influencing government and politicians (instead, most policymaking takes place in many levels and types of government through the influence of coalitions)

Table 10.1: Synthesised lessons for persuasion and learning

Persuasion
1. Know your values and beliefs, yet be cautious of your cognitive and cultural biases 2. Avoid relying too much only on evidence and analyses, instead combine evidence with framing strategies and storytelling 3. Structure your stories into a full narrative that includes setting the stage, establishing a plot, casting characters (heroes, victims, villains), and specify a moral
Learning
1. Recognise policy actors constantly learn about problems and solutions and that learning is relational; it happens between policy actors and experts, through deep social reflection among policy actors, through exchange and bargaining policy actors' relationships, and through hierarchical, top-down settings 2. Recognise that learning opportunities can be serendipitous but can be triggered by both societal and individual factors, such as cultural values that both filter and foster learning 3. policy actors can learn the wrong lessons and might not always signify progress

Table 10.2: Synthesising lessons for political participation and collection action

Political participation linking citizens and governments
1. Self-governing from the bottom-up can be effective in making policies, both outside and within government settings, but it requires norms of reciprocity, trust, experience and adequate information 2. Build and maintain advocacy coalitions to influence public policy 3. Become involved in advocacy coalitions as a regular or intermittent participant, as brokers negotiating agreements between coalitions, or as policy entrepreneurs championing ideas
Collection action linking governments
1. Foster collaboration between governments to solve shared problems by building networks that involve frequent and strong ties and less frequent and weak ties, supported by frequent face-to-face interactions 2. Avoid obstacles to collaboration, including transaction costs, by identifying shared commonalities, creating incentives and using monitoring mechanisms and/or adaptive multilateral agreements 3. Facilitate collaboration through leadership, managerial autonomy and government commitment

- policies are mainly made through top-down decision processes (instead, self-governance via bottom-up approaches are possible), and
- policymaking should and can be 'scientific', focusing on objective facts and what works (instead, stories, beliefs and entrepreneurship matter).

Another common thread through Tables 10.1–10.3 is that policy actors operate in complex environments over which they have limited control (Cairney and Weible, 2017). Although many would like to see a simple

Table 10.3: Synthesising lessons for structuring government and designing public policies

Structuring government
1. Focus on the generation, consumption and use of information when structuring governments and their procedures 2. Increase your capacity to process information by balancing between centralisation and fragmentation of government, and varying the levels of citizen representation. 3. Foster effective information searches through bundling issues to deepen and broaden the scope of the catch
Designing public policies
1. Recognise that all policies are designed in venues with their own rules, values and beliefs, information, knowledge, motivations and network relations. 2. Design contextually-appropriate policy incentives, focusing on the types of rules embedded in the policies, and how those rules interact with the incentives and information that different policy actors use in implementing a policy 3. Design policies by incorporating the autonomy and problem-solving capabilities of policy actors whose behaviour the interventions are designed to change.

process with clear stages to which they can respond, it is more effective to engage with a process that actually exists. The lessons from Tables 10.1–10.3 all work from the assumption that policy actors are subject to bounded rationality, which prompts actors to: develop strategies for persuasion and learning; build and maintain coalitions over the long haul with policy actors whose beliefs they share and who give them more political leverage; and, structure government to facilitate information processing and avoid one-size-fits-all policy designs. Moreover, the recommendations in Tables 10.1–10.3 reach beyond the 'policy cycle', which describes the decision-making procedures of government as taking place in an orderly series of stages. The policy cycle may be a useful conceptual framework for simplifying policy processes, but Tables 10.1–10.3 point to a far more complex environment.

Contribution 3: Learning about the challenges in translating practical lessons from theories

This book shows how theories can offer practical recommendations, ways of thinking, or strategies for influencing the policy process. The collection of theories provide an impressive breadth of findings that span topics of persuasion and learning, political participation, collective action, structuring government and designing public policies. However, it also points to several obstacles in continuing this effort.

First, one chapter cannot cover its literature and one book cannot cover the entire field. For example, a single theory such as the Institutional Analysis and Development Framework offers important insights from one research program but not the entire field of policy design (Howlett, 2019). Multiple streams aid the study of policy entrepreneurs, but is only one of many approaches. Further, other approaches with potential lessons include the Ecology of Games (Lubell, 2013), Social Construction and Policy Design (Schneider and Ingram, 1997), Diffusion of Innovation (Berry and Berry, 2017), and Policy Feedback Theory (Mettler and SoRelle, 2017), as well as a broad range of insights under the label of 'interpretive policy studies' (Durnová and Weible, 2020). Most importantly, we need to learn from approaches that combine theory and practice to engage with current threats to social and political equity, including the overlap between policy theory and critical race theory (Michener, 2019; Doucet, 2019). There is a real opportunity to advance the field further if we pull together a broader selection of theories and draw practical insights from them.

Second, the book underscores the complexity of policy processes and encourages humility when describing the capacity of any single theory or collection of theories to offer practical strategies. Any approach is bound by a complex context that researchers have a difficult time grasping. As a result, we continue to struggle to produce generalisable knowledge applicable across time and space, and localised or particularised knowledge applicable to a specific context. The lesson is simple: the field of policy process has made significant advances but we still have a long way to go in contextualising our findings.

Third, future studies could go further, to consider how a new aim – to produce practical lessons, not solely basic science – should inform research design. For example, there is a growing literature on the role of 'coproduction' or 'engaged scholarship' in which academics work with policy actors to produce new policy or new knowledge (Nutley, 2010; Orr and Bennett, 2012; Van de Ven, 2007). Some obstacles are apparent, including: a lack of clarity on what 'coproduction' actually is, prompting some concerns about its potential to 'pollute' scientific research (Flinders et al, 2017); practical concerns about the investment and new skills required; and, ethical concerns about the loss of critical distance if we cooperate to produce research with the policy actors that we would otherwise study. On the other hand, the payoffs can range from an ability to inform policy as we study it, to the greater ability to explain policy theory insights to – and learn from – actors with a different background and way of thinking but eagerness to share perspectives.

Finally, few theories provide directly applicable normative advice on matters such as accountability. If the policy process is as complex and dynamic as we suggest, containing many different policy actors in many venues at many levels of government, and responding to events and policy conditions often outside of their control, it seems unrealistic to expect policy actors at the 'centre' to control all policy outputs (many actors make and deliver policy), and even more unrealistic for them to determine the effect of those outputs on policy outcomes. Indeed, complexity studies describe the 'emergence' of policy at local levels, while others describe policy as the joint product of the interaction between many actors, which makes it difficult to measure the independent effect of government intervention, separate from the myriad of factors that affect social behaviour (Cairney, 2020a).

Consequently, we need a language that allows us to hold elected and appointed policymakers responsible and to account for their actions without extending that responsibility to all outputs made in their name, or the outcomes over which they only have limited control. The aim is not to let them off the hook, but to enhance scrutiny and accountability by focusing on action and reasonable responsibility for the contribution of that action to policy outcomes. This language is a key part of the practical effect of the study of public policy.

Next steps: addressing three key challenges

Our job is far from over. In posing the challenge and taking it on, we encountered many obstacles in drawing practical lessons from policy theories. We learned, for example, that jargon or lexicon as written in the theoretical approaches remains challenging, despite efforts to clarify and make communication better. There are a lot of concepts to learn and learning requires knowing their constitutive definition and their theoretical interconnections. In other words, learning a concept is not a matter of memorising a definition but putting that concept into action.

The presence of a lexicon that is deep and wide represents an indicator of progress, but creates a paradox. We need a lexicon to mediate between our brains and the world, and the more specialised the lexicon the more diverse and precise our observations and interactions. At the same time, this lexicon serves as a barrier to entry. We strive to clarify the language we use but accept that this field's depth is intertwined with the depth of its lexicon. If we remove the 'jargon' will we lose such depth? Should we accept that learning anything of substance and importance requires time and effort?

This book also raises questions of what it means to 'draw lessons'. One unintended consequence of the push for relevance is the potential to generalise too much and overlook context and nuance. If we simply connect lessons from theories to 'what to do' or how to influence a policy decision or outcomes, it disposes us to overextend our conclusions to contexts where they might not apply, or use mental shortcuts that distort or overlook important aspects of the world. Rather, our aim is to use theoretical approaches to help us promote critical thinking, to help us see the world from different perspectives and with a better understanding of the various dynamics and patterns that might be expected. Such insights are not about a particular decision, but rather an overall image of policy processes, the settings in which the policy and political games are played, and hence how to play those games.

What comes next? Inspired by our experiences editing this volume, we identify four steps to advance the goal of drawing practical lessons from policy theories.

1. Clarifying three audiences of policy process research

We need a clear idea of the audience for 'practical lessons'. For example, most authors primarily had experience of teaching policy theories to **new students** and were searching for a way to introduce a complex field in an accessible way. This task is complicated by the high variation of experiences, including undergraduate students without much professional experience, graduate professional students seeking to apply theoretical insights to their work, and research students at PhD level, as well as a tendency for all students to bring their own country and cultural experiences.

For most students, the first challenge is to translate the jargon and lexicon, help students relate these concepts to their own knowledge, and communicate toward shared understandings. The point is not to provide a world of rigid definitions, but this does not mean that we cannot develop a shared understanding of sometimes ambiguous terms. The second challenge is to tailor lessons to the scale of the educational experience. In a course dedicated to policy process research, time can be dedicated to learning the lexicon and associated theories. It can provide a foundation to develop scenario-based strategies and critical thinking. Alternatively, policy process insights will be one part of a larger module, and the point is to contextualise other studies of government and politics.

The second audience is **experienced scholars** who might have taken a policy process course earlier in their career, been trained in a program that emphasises a related but distinct field such as public administration or public management, or specialise in different silos of policy process research. For example, scholars trained in the Institutional Analysis and Development Framework tradition will not see the world via the same lens as those trained in Punctuated Equilibrium Theory. If so, our aim is cross-fertilisation across the silos to reduce the likelihood of recreating and rediscovering what was already learned elsewhere. Essentially, policy process research is threatened by many little echo chambers of scholars with similar worldviews who do not speak enough to each other. In this case, translation still matters because the same terms can have different meanings and uses in each theory, and may even change over time within those theories.

The third audience is ***practitioners*** who do not learn about this field in the classroom or have the time and inclination to invest in policy theories. They have a short exposure to the field, which means that we need to clarify the meaning and lessons of theories to make that exposure worthwhile.

In each case, clarifying the audience also helps clarify the purpose of policy process insights.

2. Clarifying three purposes of policy process research

It is problematic to seek lessons from academia for 'point decisions', which we define as a deterministic way of thinking where people want theories to tell them what to do in particular points in time and space. This is not how theories operate or why they are useful. Rather, we identify and classify three purposes for policy process research to help us all think about its contributions, make them happen, and recognise them when they do happen.

The first is providing a contextualisation in combination with the conduct of policy analysis. Here, we define policy analysis as client-oriented advice, as might be found and described by Bardach and Patashnik (2015) or Weimer and Vining (2017). The purpose of policy analysis is to evaluate a prior decision or to inform current decisions, particularly its advantages or disadvantages often calculated through benefits and costs. Thus, policy analysis serves to understand past decisions or inform current decisions. One of the challenges and understudied aspects of policy analyses is the absence of context. It falters in understanding the politics and policy processes in which these decisions are evaluated and assessed (Weible, 2007; Cairney and Weible, 2017). The solution is marrying policy analysis with policy processes with the former providing advice on that decision and the latter mapping out the context. Such an idea very much echoes the original vision of the policy sciences where Lasswell (1951) envisioned a new science that combined problem oriented research (akin to policy analysis) and contextualisation (akin to policy processes). This is probably best accomplished in policy analysis courses, where the primary focus is on conducting policy analyses and policy process research plays more of a supplemental role.

Second, we use the wisdom found in policy processes to lay out certain scenarios with advice on how to act in them. For example, advocacy groups may seek to launch a campaign to bring an issue onto the media and government agenda. Here, the Multiple Streams Framework can provide a way to think about this choice and factors to consider. Of course, it cannot tell anyone whether they should or should not launch that campaign but it can help people think more critically about the choice and its timing. We can make similar arguments on how to write the narrative underlying the story as part of the campaign and how to approach building a coalition to support the campaign. This is probably best accomplished in policy process courses, where the primary focus is on developing deep understanding of the theories.

For the third, policy process research offers a new way to see the political world and understand issues related to policymaking. It requires a deep understanding of the theories and the jargon and lexicon therein. Any one theory accentuates different aspects of the world via its own lens, and multiple theories give us many ways to analyse the unknowns and uncertainties that constitute policy processes. For example, in any one situation, we may study the coalitions that may foster policy disputes, the ability of people to self-govern and revise the rules that govern them, *and* the flow of information in any governing system, which can be monitored and improved to make more proportionate policy responses. Each example shows that there are dynamics in the world, which we have both created and discovered in our science, and through their representation, we can view policy processes from different viewpoints to foster critical thinking.

3. Using science to assess policy process research Impacts

On the one hand, the lessons from this book are drawn from empirical data that have accumulated over time and offered by experts who understand the setting in which the theory applies. On the other hand, these lessons and insights are speculative. They represent what the authors consider important insights that might somehow prove valuable for students, practitioners, and other researchers involved in policy processes. The question must be asked: what foundation do we have to make such claims?

In putting on our critical hats, we see a great deal of uncertainty in each chapter's claims. What we need is dual empirical and theoretical foci to assess such claims. This means applying our social science techniques to measure the impacts of our claims and to incorporate lessons and insights from other social science disciplines.

Such research can target the three audiences mentioned above. For students, to what extent do the insights actually help them in policy processes when they begin their careers and continue to help them late in their careers? If so, how and in what ways? If not, why not? For practitioners, how and why do our publications and reports of any kind translate into varied impacts, from learning to policy change? We know from the policy learning literature that a great deal of our science enters the practitioner world via the 'enlightenment function' in contributing to their general understandings of the policy process (Weiss, 1977). This means that our academic publications and technical reports are like rocks and sediment falling into a stream, and rarely is our work of sufficient size and proportion to change the stream's course. For other researchers, to what extent do developing deep and broad understandings in the field affect their research and teaching? Likewise, how might engagement in the policy process feedback into their research and what are the effects?

4. Highlighting dilemmas in theory and practice

Policy theories are often driven by a focus on context, which adds value to agency-centred approaches found in policy analysis (Bardach and Patashnik, 2015; Meltzer and Schwartz, 2019; Mintrom, 2012; Weimer and Vining, 2017; Dunn, 2017) and some approaches to managing the main stages of a policy cycle (Wu et al, 2017). However, reconciling these approaches is more difficult than it looks, and a focus on the comparison aids critical thinking.

For example, consider the role of policy learning described by Dunlop and Radaelli (2021) and examined further by Cairney in relation to policy transfer, in which one government might import lessons from another (Cairney, 2020b). A policy analyst would see learning as essential to a wider analytical process summed up in five steps: define the problem, identify feasible solutions, assign criteria to compare them, predict their outcomes, and make a recommendation to your client. Learning and transfer would form part of a functionalist analysis in which actors identify the steps required for actors to turn comparative analysis into policy (Rose, 2005). Or, it would be part of the toolkit of actors seeking to manage the stages of the policy process (Wu et al, 2017: 9).

In contrast policy process research focuses on explanation: learning and transfer is ambiguous and contingent on context. Actors compete to set the policy agenda, which includes competition to define the manner and source of learning. They form part of a policymaking environment in which institutions and structures constrain and facilitate action. For example, institutions provide rules for gathering, interpreting, and using evidence, while structural factors include the socioeconomic conditions that influence the feasibility of policy change. Learning from experts or policy analysts is one of many possibilities (Dunlop and Radaelli, 2021), and the many different outcomes are only called 'transfer' for the sake of simplicity (Stone, 2012).

A comparison of these approaches raises an interesting dilemma: what if actors seek agent-based policy learning as participants *and* accept the context-based story as researchers? They will not benefit from policy process research unless they can make sense of it in practice. Like policy entrepreneurs, they seek ways to respond effectively to their policymaking environments while recognising the limits to their powers (Cairney, 2021).

In that context, can policy process research, focusing primarily on explaining policy processes, actually guide practice? If actors seek to develop guiding questions to anticipate their context, the answer is yes. Useful questions to learn and inform policy transfer include: what is the evidence for another government's success; do the importing and exporting governments tell the same story about the policy problem and the feasibility of each solution; and how comparable are their political and policymaking systems (Cairney, 2020b)? However, if actors seek explicit and detailed guidance on what to do, the answer could well be no. The ability to use policy theory to explain institutional and structural limits does not necessarily help participants overcome them. Rather, it helps explain how their actions contribute to a much wider set of forces that make a major impact on policy.

Concluding thoughts on advancing policy theory translations

Policy process research is nearing 70 years in its growth and development. Over this time, theories have come and gone and some theories have endured and developed. As theories continue to mature, so does the knowledge embedded in them. Our challenge is how to translate complicated theories into something practical and understandable for existing scholars, new students, and policy actors. This edited volume tackles this challenge by providing clearer translations of some of the major theories of policy processes and identifying practical insights from them.

The policy process is inherently messy and marked by a sticky resistance to change. It is also diverse across contexts and constantly changing over time. Given this complexity, there are no easy solutions. Students and policy actors looking for that simple solution to influence or improve policy processes will be disappointed. Instead, policy process theories offer a way of thinking about policymaking-related phenomena. Policy theories also offer systematic ways to simplify the complexity in policy processes, to move from uncertainty towards theoretically-informed action. In this respect, this volume shows the power of general heuristics to inform decisions. Knowing, for example, that stories matter and that the policy actors should consider the setting, plot, characters, and moral is a way to simplify and organise thinking about designing a message for persuasion and gaining attention in the policy process.

This edited volume is the first of its kind and we hope to see this effort continued. We see several steps to encourage such continuation of this effort. First, embrace the notion that clear translations and practical insights from theories is a good idea. Then, think about how we can improve the practical insights of theories through new research. This new agenda requires a reciprocal exchange of information where theories are used to help shape and inform how policy actors understand and act in policy processes, and, in turn, these same policy actors shape and inform the substance, validity and value of theory-based knowledge. This does not mean that policy scholars must do both applied- and theory-based science but rather encourage and reward those that do.

Second, this edited volume shows the initial value in taking a practical turn and the potential to include more theories. One next step is to repeat this exercise with an expanded cast of theories or to try it on a phenomenon (such as agenda setting, for example) that cuts across the different theories. In the longer term, we hope to see insights from a much more global application of policy theories. Many began in the US, and have become established in studies across Europe, but there remains major uncertainty about their coordinated application in most of the world. As such, when we describe 'practical lessons', we accept that their applications have generally been to a small part of the globe.

Third, changing the direction of the field requires coordination and ongoing dialogue. In this respect, we encourage panel organisers and editors of books and journals to support these efforts. The editorial team of *Policy & Politics* is exemplary in supporting the original publication of this effort (Weible and Cairney, 2018).

Rarely can a single individual or academic study wield any observable influence across different contexts and over time. Any policy actor – as well as policy scholars – should not be too self-critical of their lack of influence. The policy process is too complex to guarantee impact. Yet, unlike the past, policy process research is now more globalised, more diverse with a cornucopia of theories, and more likely to explore the practical implications from scholarship. This is an exciting development that we hope will continue.

References

Bardach, E, Patashnik, EM, 2015, A practical guide for policy analysis: The eightfold path to more effective problem solving (5th edn), Thousand Oaks, CA: Congressional Quarterly Inc

Berry, FS, Berry, WD, 2017, Innovation and diffusion models in policy research, in CM Weible, PA Sabatier (eds) Theories of the policy process (4th edn), Boulder, CO: Westview Press, pp 253–300

Cairney, P, 2015, How can policy theory have an impact on policymaking? The role of theory-led academic–practitioner discussions, *Teaching Public Administration* 33, 1, 22–39.

Cairney, P, 2020a, *Understanding public policy*, 2nd ed, London: Red Globe

Cairney, P, 2020b, The role of structures, institutions, and agents in policymaking: a framework to facilitate and explain policy learning and transfer, paper to 18th Annual JCPA/ICPA-Forum Workshop, Istanbul, Turkey, 10–12 September

Cairney, P, 2021, Three habits of successful policy entrepreneurs, in (eds) Weible, C and Cairney, P (eds) *Practical Lessons from Policy Theories*, Bristol: Bristol University Press

Cairney, P, Weible CM, 2017, The new policy sciences: Combining the cognitive science of choice, multiple theories of context, and basic and applied analysis, *Policy Sciences* 50, 4, 619–27

Crow, D, Jones, M, 2021, A guide to telling good stories that affect policy change, in (eds) Weible, C and Cairney, P (eds) *Practical Lessons from Policy Theories*, Bristol: Bristol University Press

DeLeon, P, 1997, *Democracy and the policy sciences*, Albany, NY: SUNY Press

Doucet, F. (2019) *Centering the Margins: (Re)defining Useful Research Evidence Through Critical Perspectives*, New York: William T. Grant Foundation

Dunlop, C, Radaelli, C, 2021, The lessons of policy learning: Types, triggers, hindrances and pathologies, in (eds) Weible, C and Cairney, P (eds) *Practical Lessons from Policy Theories*, Bristol: Bristol University Press

Dunn, W, 2017, *Public Policy Analysis,* 6th Ed, London: Routledge

Durnová, A, Weible, C, 2020, Tempest in a teapot? Toward new collaborations between mainstream policy process studies and interpretive policy studies, *Policy Sciences*, 53, 571–588

Flinders, M, 2013, The politics of engaged scholarship: Impact, relevance and imagination, *Policy & Politics*, 41, 4, 621–42

Flinders, M, Wood, M, Cunningham, M, 2017, The politics of co-production: Risks, limits, and pollution, *Evidence & Policy* 12, 2, 261–79

Heikkila, T, Andersson, K, 2021, Policy design and the added-value of the Institutional Analysis Development Framework, in (eds) Weible, C and Cairney, P (eds) *Practical Lessons from Policy Theories*, Bristol: Bristol University Press

Howlett, M, 2019, *Designing public policies: Principles and instruments*, 2nd Edition, London: Routledge

Koski, C, Workman, S, 2021, Drawing practical lessons from punctuated equilibrium theory. in (eds) Weible, C and Cairney, P (eds) *Practical Lessons from Policy Theories*, Bristol: Bristol University Press

Lasswell, HD, 1951, The policy orientation, in D Lerner, HD Lasswell (eds) *The policy sciences: Recent developments in scope and methods*, Stanford, CA: Stanford University Press, pp 3–15

Lubell, M, 2013, Governing institutional complexity: The ecology of games framework, *Policy Studies Journal*, 41, 3, 537–59

Meltzer, R, Schwartz, A, 2019, *Policy Analysis as Problem Solving*, London: Routledge

Mettler, S, SoRelle, M, 2017, Policy feedback theory, in CM Weible, PA Sabatier (eds) *Theories of the policy process*, 4th edn, Boulder, CO: Westview Press, pp 103–34

Michener, J. (2019) 'Policy Feedback in a Racialized Polity', *Policy Studies Journal*, 47, 2: 423–450

Mintrom, M, 2012, *Contemporary Policy Analysis*, Oxford: Oxford University Press

Nutley, S, 2010, Debate: Are we all co-producers of research now?, *Public Money & Management*, 30, 5, 263–5

Orr, K, Bennett, M, 2012, Public administration scholarship and the politics of coproducing academic–practitioner research, *Public Administration Review* 72, 4, 487–95

Rose, R, 2005, *Learning From Comparative Public Policy: A Practical Guide*, London: Routledge

Schneider, AL, Ingram, HM, 1997, *Policy Design for Democracy*, Lawrence, KS: University Press of Kansas

Shipan, CR, Volden, C, 2012, Policy diffusion: Seven lessons for scholars and practitioners, *Public Administration Review*, 72, 6, 788–96

Simmons, R, 2021, Using cultural theory to navigate the policy process, in (eds) Weible, C and Cairney, P (eds) *Practical Lessons from Policy Theories*, Bristol: Bristol University Press

Stone, D, 2012, Transfer and translation of policy, *Policy Studies*, 33, 6, 483–99

Swann, W, Kim, S, 2021, Practical prescriptions for governing fragmented governments, in (eds) Weible, C and Cairney, P (eds) *Practical Lessons from Policy Theories*, Bristol: Bristol University Press

Van de Ven, AH, 2007, *Engaged Scholarship: A Guide for Organizational and Social Research*, Oxford: Oxford University Press

Weible, CM, 2007, An advocacy coalition framework approach to stakeholder analysis: Understanding the political context of California marine protected area policy, *Journal of Public Administration Research and Theory*, *17*, 1, 95–117.

Weible, CM, Heikkila, T, deLeon, P, Sabatier, PA, 2012, Understanding and influencing the policy process, Policy Sciences 45, 1, 1–21

Weible, CM, Cairney, P, 2018, Practical lessons from policy theories, *Policy & Politics*, *46*, 2, 183–97

Weible, CM, Ingold K, 2021, Why advocacy coalitions matter and practical insights about them, in (eds) Weible, C and Cairney, P (eds) *Practical Lessons from Policy Theories*, Bristol: Bristol University Press

Weimer, DL, Vining, AR., 2017, *Policy Analysis: Concepts and Practice*, Abingdon: Taylor & Francis

Weiss, C H, 1977, Research for policy's sake: The enlightenment function of social research, *Policy analysis*, 531–45.

Wu, X, Howlett, M, Ramesh, M, Fritzen, S, 2017, *The Public Policy Primer*, 2nd ed, London: Routledge

Index

Note: page numbers in *italic* type refer to Figures; those in **bold** type refer to Tables